TOWARDS

A

BETTER WORLD

D1717609

STEPHANIE CLAIRE

Sydney, 2019

Published by

The
Svengali Press

2, 2-4 Notts Ave
Bondi Beach
NSW 2026
AUSTRALIA

ISBN: 978-0-9946155-5-8

Cover illustration by Salvatore Zofrea

CONTENTS

INTRODUCTION

Theosophy has been described as 'a movement that punches well above its weight' in terms of its contribution to the cultural history of Australia. During the 1920s, in what is regarded as the heyday of Theosophy, some members of my family were involved in the movement and as a child I heard many fascinating stories of Theosophical life in Sydney.

The glamorous, cosmopolitan, constantly-travelling Theosophists seemed to inhabit a different universe from some of the other elements of Sydney during this time. While non-Theosophical accounts would often comment on a certain puritanical 'aridity' in Australian urban life, this did not reflect the experience of Theosophists who lived in Sydney at The Manor, a fifty-four-room mansion in Clifton Gardens, Mosman where a Communal Living Project was underway and the famous Amphitheatre at Balmoral was being built.

In the course of researching *Towards a Better World*, I read a number of accounts of this era – scholarly and informative works but none that I felt captured the heady spirit of a time when new ideas and ways of life were being explored and put into practice.

This story is populated by a cast of characters ranging from real-life historical identities through to semi and totally fictional ones. Theosophical 'giants' such as Annie Besant, Bishop Charles Leadbeater and the young Indian, Jiddu Krishnamurti, who many believed was the 'coming World Teacher', play a prominent role in the events that unfold and are heavily influenced by the writings of Madame Helena Blavatsky, who founded Theosophy in New York in 1875.

Apart from being a forward-looking movement, supporting cremation, vegetarianism, birth-control and abolition of the White Australia policy, Theosophy had to deal with several problematic situations that caused social havoc within its ranks and were gleefully taken up by the press. Chief among these was the rumour of pedophilia involving the clergy of the Liberal Catholic Church. This 'new' church (established in 1916) had strong informal links with the Theosophical Society and made its own rules in some areas, including not requiring celibacy of its priests.

As time went on, there developed the vexed question of Krishnamurti who, although educated extensively to take up his central role within the Society, showed signs of moving in his own direction and taking up innovative and radical positions that considerably discomforted many of those in the inner circle.

Some characters in the story, such as Ed Best and his parents, inhabit a world that is influenced by proximity to 'things Theosophical' and who roughly correspond with my father's family. They came from a scientific, atheistic background but fitted in well with the Theosophists due to their own interest in exploring ideas and hypothses.

Theosophy is still active in many parts of the world today, although it has never regained its popularity of the 1920s, when the Theosophical Society in Australia numbered more members than the Communist Party.

An urban myth persists in some quarters that Krishnamurti was going to walk on water though the Sydney Harbour heads to the Amphitheatre at Balmoral to greet his adoring followers. These days this story is only mentioned by people who know very little about this fascinating movement that engaged so many lively and creative minds down the years.

Noam Chomsky (linguist, philosopher and social critic) has observed that:

INTRODUCTION

'It makes sense to work towards a better world, but it doesn't make any sense to have illusions about what the real world i*s.*'

However, as illusions are the impetus for so much social change, I believe the world would be the poorer without them.

Stephanie Claire, 2019

ACKNOWLEDGEMENTS

I would like to thank the following relatives and friends for their contributions to the creation of this book:

Annette Bouwens & Deborah Conyngham	for permission to use their mothers' schoolday reminiscences
Sandra Darrroch & The Svengali Press	for formatting and publishing my book
Sally Dowling:	for suggestions and encouragement throughout
Marge & Bruce Gregory:	for information on east-coast USA and 1920s cars
Elizabeth Harrower:	for listening and sound advice
Christina Steffen:	for identifying medical anachronisms
Carla Molino	for getting me started on the journey of this book
Salvatore Zofrea	for being a wonderful sounding-board throughout the writing process, and for a great front cover illustration

My special thanks also go to Diane Kyneston and Graham Shannon of the Theosophical Society, Sydney for their help regarding Theosophical matters and access to research material.

For Salvatore

PART 1
1922

CONTENTS

CHAPTER 1

A FRIENDLY SUGGESTION

My name is Edwin Best and this is the story of seven remarkable years in my life, telling how at the age of twenty-two, I fell in with a group of the most far-sighted, energetic and, some would say, deluded people one could ever hope to meet.

I lived at home with my parents and I'd just finished a degree in medicine at Sydney University that included some units of psychology. I was so fascinated by 'psych', as we called it, that I'd decided to study more units and write a dissertation in order to graduate in psychology. In 1922, when this story starts, psychology was widely regarded as a pseudo-science – bogus, and quite possibly dangerous. Even at the comparatively progressive Sydney University, this view was not uncommon.

On the day of the first lecture for the year, as I walked towards the psychology building, I was looking forward to hearing more about the dissertation and what it would involve. I spotted a couple of students I knew outside the lecture hall and together we took our place in one of the middle tiers of seats.

Presently, our lecturer entered and a hush fell over the room. Dr Max Herbst, with his beard, pipe and mass of curling grey hair, was a fairly conspicuous figure on campus. He spoke with a thick German accent and rumour had it that he'd undergone psychoanalysis with Sigmund Freud in Vienna prior to the 1914-18 War.

After a perfunctory nod to acknowledge our presence, Dr Herbst got down to business, seeming to intuit what we all wanted to know.

"The overarching aim of the dissertation," he told us, "is to demonstrate your deep understanding of all I've tried to impart earlier in the course."

We were to become 'social anthropologists' over the next six months – joining an organization or group hitherto unknown to us, observing and analysing its social dynamics and writing up our findings in an appropriately professional way.

"In other words," he explained in his courteous yet slightly sardonic way, "you are to find out how this group functions, psychologically-speaking. You will observe and analyse the interactions of individual members and note how these affect group-level behaviours and, conversely, how the group influences the stances and actions of individual members."

Seeing the bemused faces of many of the students, he said with a hint of acerbity, "Look – all you have to do is find out what makes the group 'tick' and then document it."

At this point a student raised his hand with a question about the dissertation's length.

"Oh, between fifteen and twenty thousand words," Dr Herbst replied. "Frankly, I'm more interested in content than wordage."

Another student had a query: "Excuse me, Dr Herbst, can you tell us what *kind* of group we are talking about here?"

Dr Herbst then explained that in this instance the word 'group' covered any organisation, association, club, circle, union or consortium that could meet four requirements.

"It must comprise at least twenty-five members; have a formal structure with clearly stated aims; been active for the past five years; and, last but not least, be of good repute. We certainly don't want any of you getting mixed up with the 'wrong crowd'." Although he said this with a slightly mocking smile it was clear he found us so immature that this explicit warning was necessary. He went on to say we could either be open with our group about what we were doing, or else be covert researchers and not divulge our motivation for joining. Finally, we were to bring to the next lecture a one-page description of our proposed group for his approval.

"Or not, as the case may be."

As I left the lecture hall, I felt somewhat at a loss. I didn't belong to any formal group at all, apart from my local tennis club, which wasn't 'an entirely new social group' and therefore ineligible. My parents were members of a bridge club, located in our home suburb of Stanmore, Sydney, but I couldn't see myself joining this staid gathering as a 'participant-observer'. Furthermore, the bridge club failed to meet the first two criteria, while over-endowed in the others.

Help came in the form of my good friend Russell Fletcher, who'd gone through school and medicine with me. Russell, too, was fascinated by psychology, but instead of wanting to learn more about human nature for its own sake like me, his interest was purely expedient - to use it to get on in life. Also unlike me, Russell was able to hold down two part-time jobs and still have time for an energetic social life. And although he often gave me a pretty frank appraisal of my character – naïve, socially gauche and so on – you couldn't really want for a better mate.

In my view, Russell's main strength was that he 'knew how to get things done', and even before the end of the lecture, he'd settled on his dissertation topic. He was therefore able to focus on me and, as we walked from the university towards Redfern train station in the early evening, he tossed me a few of his discarded ideas.

Only one of these kindled my interest. I'd vaguely heard of the society he mentioned, and knew it had something to do with god and philosophy. But I also had a vague idea it wasn't totally 'respectable' and wondered if it would meet Dr Herbst's 'good repute' requirement.

"Tell me a bit about this . . . The-o-soph-ical Society," I said, stumbling over the strange word. "And how do you know about it, anyway?"

"Well, young Ed," Russell replied. "You've chosen well, my boy. The Theosophical Society – or as we call it, the TS – would be a real corker!" I should probably mention here that Russell had a habit of addressing me in a patronizing way that to him signified close friendship.

This 'young-Ed' business, however, did have a factual basis. My father, who believed that 'you're never too young to learn', had taught me to read at the age of three. This meant that when I started school I was put into a class with children two years older than me and I'd stayed like this though school and university.

"We? Are you a member of this society?" I asked, curious to know why he spoke of the Theosophical Society with such familiarity. If he was indeed a member, it would come as news to me, even though I didn't know what the society was.

"I don't belong to the TS myself, but my parents have been part of it for years," he explained. "And I can point you in the right direction for your research by taking you along to one of the Tuesday evening talks at the TS and introducing you to a few members. You'll have a great time, I can promise that. In fact," he finished with a smirk, "it could be the making of you!"

During the short train journey to Stanmore, I quizzed Russell on whether the Theosophical Society would meet Dr Herbst's four requirements.

"Does the TS have a formal structure and clearly stated aims?" I asked.

"Absolutely," Russell replied. "It's quite conventional in that respect, with a president, vice-president and various office-holders. Regarding its aims, you'll see them displayed in the meeting room, and to answer your next question before you even ask it, the Sydney Lodge of the TS has around 800 members. It's the largest and most prosperous Theosophical lodge in the world, in fact. And as for your next two questions, I'll save you the trouble of asking them: the Sydney Lodge began in 1891 and is certainly 'of good repute', despite the odd hiccup, of which you will doubtless hear sooner or later. Members include a number of eminent citizens as well as many private individuals, all united by some common beliefs that are stronger than their differences – or at least that's how it is, as we speak . . ."

"Thank you, Russell, most comprehensive," I said, getting to my feet and picking up my briefcase as the train slowed down towards Stanmore Station.

"Meet you after lectures next Tuesday and we'll go to the meeting," he called as I left the carriage.

As I walked towards my home in Ethel St, I realized some fairly rapid background work on the TS was needed. And the best place to start would be a chat with my parents, Isabel and Arthur Best, or 'Mum&Dad'.

That evening over dinner, I asked Dad what he knew about the Theosophical Society. Few questions ever daunted my father, and this was no exception. After clearing his throat, always the prelude to a speech, he explained:

"The word 'Theosophy' comes from the Greek '*theosophia*' meaning 'wisdom about things divine'.[1] While many of the concepts Theosophy explores have been around for centuries, the Theosophical Society itself was founded in New York in 1875 by Madame Helena Blavatsky, Colonel Henry Steel Olcott and other like-minds. The Society aimed to establish a worldwide brotherhood based on the truths shared by all religions and drawing on the latent powers that humans possess. And,

---

[1] Jill Roe, *Beyond Belief: Theosophy in Australia* 1879-1939. (Kensington, NSW: NSW University Press, 1986), 1.

far from being *against* religion, the group sought to *re-invigorate* it, to restore what they saw as religion's eroded authority in modern times."

Dad was a walking encyclopedia. However, once he warmed to a theme, it was well nigh impossible to stop the flow. Off he went again:

"The Theosophical Society has attracted quite a following in Britain, Europe, the USA, parts of Asia and here in Australia. Theosophy appeals to people who find themselves challenging conventional religion and its trappings and Theosophists are an interesting bunch whose sincerity is admirable. However . . ." and here he stopped.

"However *what*?" I asked, sensing a slight reticence in his voice that was confirmed by what came next.

"They can tend to . . . get a little carried away by it all," he replied, choosing his words with care. "Of course, it's admirable to have an open mind about the world we live in, but sometimes this can be taken a bit too far . . ."

"How do you mean?" I cut in. "Isn't an open mind one of the strengths of your own scientific approach to life, and what you've always tried to nurture in me?"

My father looked at me in his usual kindly way then said, "Some of the activities of the Theosophical Society have been a little . . . *outre*, shall we say . . ."

I wasn't quite sure what *outre* meant, although the word itself sounded rather 'outre' in an interesting sort of way.

"Theosophists' exploration of the world around us does not simply focus on the tangible world but encompasses a strong interest in the unseen, the occult," he went on.

"Do you mean like Spiritualism, séances, things like that?" I asked, aware that my psychologist heroes Carl Yung, Sigmund Freud and William James had participated in séances in the course of their researches into the workings of the human psyche. I also knew that my father, whose cast of mind was strongly scientific, would not himself be partial to this type of activity.

Dad took my question in his stride.

"Theosophists regard their interests as far wider than those of the Spiritualists," he told me. "They view Spiritualism as dangerously simplistic, and its practitioners as people playing with fire – manipulating powerful unseen elements whose potency they cannot gauge. However," he continued, "in my view, a real strength of Theosophy is that members do not need to jettison their earlier religious beliefs. And that's one reason it appeals to a wide range of intelligent and cultivated people, including poets and writers like W.B.Yeats and George Bernard Shaw. But tell me, what prompts this sudden interest in Theosophy?"

I quickly explained about my psychology dissertation and Russell Fletcher's suggestion. Dad chuckled. He knew Russell and was very fond of him and his often hare-brained schemes.

"I should've known Russell would be involved somewhere along the line," he remarked as he helped himself to a second slice of Mum's delicious apple pie.

Mum&Dad were of course central to my life at this time, and would play a major part in the events about to unfold. My father worked as an accountant in a firm in the city and my mother, who did not work outside the home, was a force to be reckoned with inside it – an excellent cook, ardent bottler of preserves and general all-round organiser. She even made the yearly soap supply for our household, ably assisted by her two unmarried sisters known as 'The Aunts', who lived nearby and took a percentage of the soap as due payment for their labours.

Given Mum's generous heart and huge energy, she should have had a large brood of children instead of just – me. She was reticent about my lack of siblings, simply telling me she 'couldn't have any more'. Dad was slightly more forthcoming – saying that after I was born Mum had a number of miscarriages and eventually they'd 'stopped trying'.

At one point in my childhood, the thought crossed my mind that I might be adopted. One look in the mirror, however, was enough to end this fantasy. I have inherited Mum's olive skin and black hair (legacy of her Welsh ancestors), and Dad had stamped his paternity on me in the form of an unusual hair-type. Although he is getting bald now, every hair on his head stands straight up as in a hairbrush. He is totally unconcerned about this, but I intensely dislike looking like I've just received a strong electric shock, and I use copious amounts of hair-oil to counteract the problem. From both parents I get my blue eyes and thankfully I'm a lot taller and slimmer than them.

My parents are the most sensible, stable and rational couple you could ever hope to meet. In terms of religion, we are 'non-believers' (of Protestant lineage). Although we've never 'made a thing of it' as Mum would say, we do not participate in any form of religious worship. But in the course of the next few years, religion – or something akin to it – would enter our lives to quite a considerable extent.

Dad was an out-and-out atheist, having arrived at his position via Darwin's theory of evolution. At weekends he enjoyed pottering in the garden carrying out experiments with climbing beans to test the laws of heredity discovered by the scientist Gregor Mendel, the 'father of genetics'. Recently, Dad had branched out a little, acquiring a family of mice who exhibited unusual recessive genes. But my father wasn't simply a dry man of science – he also wrote detective stories and was rather chuffed at having several published in *Smith's Weekly* magazine. I should also throw in here that Dad invariably exhibited an extremely courteous manner – even when sorely tried.

Mum's religious views were not theory-based, and in her forthright way she was quite open about having 'no time at all' for religion and explaining the reason why. Many years earlier her brother Alfred, a clergyman in a NSW country town, was suddenly left a widower with four young children to rear. His wife's unmarried sister came to help the family and in due course she and Alfred found they cared for each other and wished to marry. This, however, was viewed with horror by the Church (something like 'Thou shalt not cohabit with thy dead wife's sister') and when Alfred persevered with the wedding plans he was dismissed from his post. Mum staunchly supported the newly-weds and never set foot in a church again.

Although Mum&Dad would describe themselves as 'fairly open-minded', this would only be in comparison with their much more conservative friends and acquaintances. Regarding psychology, the two of them were not overly keen, so I didn't engage in excessive sharing of the vagaries of human behaviour I was learning about.

For about six months now, I'd been keeping a diary, an idea that had come from Dr Herbst, who'd said, "By recording your thoughts and impressions of the world, you'll build up a coherent record of what's on your mind at various times throughout the year. Total honesty regarding your motivations and reactions is essential, and I have no doubt you'll find it an illuminating experience."

Although I knew Mum&Dad would never dream of reading my diary, for total safe-keeping I always stored it upstairs in my bedroom on the bottom shelf of my bookcase behind the weighty tomes of Freud, Jung and William James. And that night as I wrote up my day's entry before retiring, I realised how useful this daily record would be in my coming exploration of the Sydney Theosophical Society.

CHAPTER 2

AT THE THEOSOPHICAL SOCIETY MEETING

The next week at our psychology lecture we handed in our dissertation proposals for review by Dr Herbst. As he was a man of high academic rigour who despised 'sloppy thinking', most of us had tried to describe our topics as cogently as we could. After some hasty reworking just before the lecture, I felt fairly confident my outline would survive his scrutiny.

After the lecture, Russell and I took a tram into the city. Having time to spare before the TS meeting, we dropped in to a café near Wynyard for a bite to eat and over a cup of tea and a scone, I asked Russell how his family's connection with Theosophy had come about.

"My parents joined the TS when they were living over in Perth, Western Australia, where the Society is very active. Interestingly, a number of the members there had first encountered Theosophy in the Dutch East Indies[2] or else in India. When my family moved over here to the east coast, they joined the Sydney Lodge of the TS and found many kindred spirits, including some they already knew from Perth. I was aged eight at the time and it was wonderful – like having a whole bunch of ready-made relatives." All this was new to me – I'd often been to Russell's house but, apart from lots of people dropping in, his parents seemed no different from my other friends'.

At half past five, Russell glanced at his watch,

---

[2] In 1949, the Dutch East Indies became Indonesia.

saying, "The meeting'll start in half an hour. It's just around the corner in Hunter St, but we'd best get a move on." We picked up our bags, paid the bill and set off, Russell striding along George St confidently with me hurrying beside him. We turned the corner into Hunter St and he stopped outside number sixty-nine, an imposing eight-storeyed building.

"The lecture's in the auditorium on the third floor," he told me. "Which do you want to take – stairs or lift?"

I opted for the stairs and as we headed up to the third floor I observed on the walls of the stairwell a number of paintings and notices of a vaguely religious nature. Pointing to them, I asked Russell if they belonged to the TS. When told they did, I then said, "Well it's very good of the building proprietor to let them overflow into this public space. How do the other tenants feel about it?"

At this, Russell laughed kindly: "The whole building belongs to the TS – all eight storeys of it."

"Very impressive," I commented. "But how does the TS come to be so wealthy?"

By now, we'd reached the third floor. Russell paused for a moment to get his breath, then replied, "One of the TS members was talking about that just the other day. As this old boy put it: 'The fact that money always flows into the Society's coffers, when needed for a specific purpose, is a potent sign of the vitality of our movement.'[3]

"An enviable state of affairs," I observed. Like most students, Russell and I were often short of cash.

Looking around, I saw the third floor consisted of a large foyer with a pale marble floor and fluted columns. At one end, folding wooden doors opened into a high-ceilinged room filled with rows of solid chairs facing a dais. From this room came the sound of conversation and laughter.

"It sounds like a party!" I exclaimed.

---

[3] Roe, Beyond Belief, 223.

"Well, TS folk generally have a good time at these meetings," Russell replied, "except when they get embroiled in a controversy . . ."

Once inside the meeting room, we were spotted by a young man who greeted Russell warmly and showed us to our seats. High on the wall nearby, a large varnished wooden noticeboard proclaimed in olden-style gold lettering:

The Theosophical Society's Objects:

1. *To form a nucleus of the Universal Brotherhood of Humanity without distinction of race, creed, sex, caste or colour.*
2. *To promote the study of comparative religion, philosophy and science.*
3. *To investigate unexplained laws of Nature and the powers latent in the human being.*[4]

Taking my notebook from my briefcase, I copied down the Objects.

'Nothing too *outre* there,' I thought. 'And Freud, Jung and William James would certainly be all for Object No.3.'

By now, the room was filling up rapidly. I was struck by the mixture of people – all age-groups, some well-dressed, others who seemed of lesser means, and quite a

---

[4] Roe, Beyond Belief, 22.

number of foreigners, judging from their appearance and accents. The overall mood seemed one of bonhomie and buoyancy.

"It's like a gathering of old friends," I murmured and Russell nodded.

"And right now, there's a real sense of expectancy in the air."

A young woman handed round neatly printed programs informing the gathering:

Mr Karel van Gelder will speak this evening
on
'Communal Living – a solution for
these times.'

The talk will be followed by a discussion on the arrangements made to date for the Sydney Theosophical Society Convention, which will commence on Friday April 16, 1922 (Good Friday in the Christian calendar).

Venues for Dr Annie Besant's lectures in April and May will be announced, with seat reservations now available.

At the conclusion of the meeting, members and friends are cordially invited to enjoy light refreshments in the annex, with background music provided by the Theosophical Society orchestra.

Apologies: Bishop C.W.Leadbeater regrets his inability to be present this evening, due to a temporary indisposition.

To me, these names – Karel van Gelder, Dr Annie Besant, Bishop Leadbeater – sounded tremendously exotic and, in the few minutes before the proceedings began, I asked Russell about them.

"You'll be hearing a lot more about these personages," he said with a faint chuckle. "And by cripes, I reckon you'll have your eyes opened, my young friend."

I mused for a moment on why it is that so often with a good friend, a certain amount of not-so-good comes with the good.

"Just get on with it, Russell, if you'd be so kind," I said. "Time's running short."

"It'd take me hours to fill you in, but here's a start. First, Mr Karel van Gelder – a very clever man. He's Dutch, spent most of his life in Java in the sugar industry. He and his wife were very active in the TS over there and now also here in Sydney. You'll probably meet their daughter, Dora, later on tonight . . .

"Dr Annie Besant – writer, thinker, activist – where to start! Dr Besant has been a Theosophist since 1890 and is now President of the TS worldwide. And as well as working tirelessly for Theosophy, she has another cause very close to her heart: Self-rule for India. Dr Besant is regarded by some as the greatest living orator in the English language and when she comes to Sydney shortly, you'll be able to judge that for yourself. She is very close to CWL, although they differ on a number of important matters."

"CWL?" I queried.

"Bishop Charles Webster Leadbeater," Russell intoned, "of whom I can say without a doubt: once seen never forgotten."

"Bishop?" I queried, surprised that the TS was allied with a church.

"Long story – tell you later," he answered, as a hush came over the room.

A middle-aged, soberly-dressed man carrying a sheaf of papers strode purposefully to the dais and an aide stepped forward. All conversation ebbed away and all eyes and ears were on the aide as he announced: "This evening, our guest speaker is Mr Karel van Gelder, who hardly needs any introduction. Mr van Gelder will address the gathering on a subject very close to his heart, that of Communal Living."

A smattering of applause greeted this, then Mr van Gelder took the floor.

"Good evening everyone," he began. "I'd like to welcome all our friends, new and old, to this meeting and enjoin you to enter into the discussion at any point. I hope my Dutch accent won't make it too difficult to follow me."

After putting on a pair of horn-rimmed spectacles and adjusting his papers on the lectern, Mr van Gelder proceeded to speak of his longstanding interest in how economic issues impact on the way people manage their lives. He felt that today, in these years following the Great War, things were particularly difficult, especially for young people.

"The old order is gone, irrevocably, so now we must find new ways of living that meet our present-day needs and constraints," he explained. "After exploring a number of approaches, I have concluded that Communal Living offers us the greatest number of important advantages. These are discussed in my treatise, *The Ideal Community: a Rational Solution to Economic Problems*, to be published later this year."

The audience responded with great interest to Mr van Gelder's talk, and it was obvious that many people present were only too familiar with the problems he described. When all questions from the floor were answered, he said:

"And now, I'd like to take the topic of communal living out of the purely theoretical and place it into everyday life. Our very energetic Communal Living

Committee has spent the past months scouring Sydney for a suitable venue in which to put our ideas into practice."

A round of applause greeted this statement and when it subsided he continued,

"We believe that we have found an ideal site – a large, and I really *do* mean large, house located in Mosman overlooking Sydney Harbour."

At this point a voice cut in: "Excuse me, Sir, but exactly *how* large is this building?"

Mr van Gelder smiled. "Would fifty-four rooms be large enough?" he asked. "And we have already five families as foundation members as well as a number of single people wanting to join in."

A tall, well-dressed woman rose to her feet. "The building you refer to wouldn't be 'Bakewell's Folly', by any chance?" she asked. "It's in Clifton Gardens, which is part of Mosman, and it's an enormous and very imposing edifice."

Mr van Gelder looked pleased. "Yes," he replied. "That is indeed the building in question. Architecturally, it's most unusual. The locals call it 'Bakewell's Folly' because the owner and builder, Mr Bakewell, went bankrupt over it. His dream was to have all his children and their families living together under the same roof. But when it was finished, it transpired they did not want to be in such close proximity," He stopped at this point as a ripple of laughter ran through the audience.

"When we have completed the leasing formalities, the house will be renamed, tentatively, 'The Manor'. And now," he concluded, "I propose that we adjourn to the annex for some much-needed refreshments."

As I followed Russell into the annex, a buzz of discussion filled the air. Here, rows of cups and saucers were set out on several white-clothed tables with cakes and biscuits on another larger one. Russell was constantly greeted by people he knew, and although I felt a bit awkward, a number of kindly souls went out of their way to introduce themselves and ask if I'd enjoyed the talk.

Then I heard Russell call my name. He was conversing with three others: a small girl who smiled at me in a friendly way; a tall, striking young man wearing black velvet trousers and a matching jerkin; and a slender young woman with huge grey-green eyes and masses of curling brown hair who stood next to the young man and was gazing tenderly up at him. It was obvious the two of them were considerably taken with each other.

The clothing of all three intrigued me. While not exactly fancy-dress, it was certainly unusual for Sydney. The brown-haired girl was wearing a long skirt reaching nearly to her ankles, topped by a deep red blouse and a brightly-coloured scarf. But strangest of all was the garb of the small girl standing quietly beside them – her faded cotton dress, though clean and pressed, had obviously seen better days and her leather sandals looked as though she'd made them herself (and later I discovered she had!)

"Ed," Russell said. "I've been talking to these three about our psych dissertation and how keen you are to study the workings of the TS."

"That's not quite how I'd put it," I demurred. They laughed and the small girl said,

"Don't worry, Ed, we know Russell very well. I'm sure we can all be of help to you. I'm Dora van Gelder, by the way, and these two are . . ."

"Antonia Vivian and Ambrose Mortimer," they said in unison.

Russell grinned. "What? Speaking as one?" he marvelled. "At this rate you'll soon be married!"

Everyone laughed and Antonia said, "We saw you writing in your notebook, Ed, and now we know why. We'll be very glad to help, won't we, Ambrose."

"Sure thing, only too happy to be of service," Ambrose replied with a smile, his voice a deep American drawl. He gave a slight bow, conveying irony or

American good manners or maybe both. Either way, I'd never yet met anyone as glamorous as Ambrose Mortimer or as beautiful as Antonia Vivian.

Admittedly, I did not operate in a wide range of social circles, being at this point limited to old schoolmates, university friends and members of the Stanmore tennis club younger set. And my sartorial sense was no less limited. The men I knew almost all wore three-piece suits on weekdays and at weekends changed into grey flannel trousers, neutral-coloured shirts and sports coats. The girls in my age-group tended to be more adventurous, with many adopting the New Look: short skirts, bright lipstick and hair worn in a boyish bob or shingle.

At first glance, Dora van Gelder seemed somewhat more conventional than her two companions. She stood quietly by them, looking on with a smile.

"Any relation to Mr van Gelder who gave the talk this evening?" I asked, aware that my question was banal, but needing to start somewhere.

"He's my father," Dora replied. "My family has only recently arrived in Sydney. I, on the other hand, came here a number of years ago." Since she looked only about fifteen, I wondered how this independent travel could have come about.

She laughed suddenly. "It's a long story," she replied, as though she'd guessed my thoughts, "which sometime I'll tell you. But first, why don't you read up a bit on Theosophy and note down a few questions. Then we could meet for afternoon tea and I'll enlighten you – hopefully," she said with another laugh. "Here, borrow one of these books and take a couple of our magazines – that'll get you started." Plucking a few items off the display-stand, she thrust them into my hands.

"What about coming here next Tuesday around four o'clock – that'll give us nearly two hours before the meeting." This was said more as a statement than a question, but it sounded good to me.

Across the room, Antonia Vivian and Ambrose Mortimer were saying goodbye to the throng of people around them. Nonetheless, they called across to me, "We'll help you too, don't forget!" and gave a friendly wave.

Russell was also ready to leave, so I stuffed the reading matter into my briefcase and went to join him, my head fairly spinning with all the new impressions, ideas and people I'd met in the past few hours.

On the train back to Stanmore, Russell was in high spirits.

"I always enjoy an evening with the TS crowd," he said. "Makes everything else look a bit plain, doesn't it?"

I nodded, intrigued yet also daunted by the task ahead.

CHAPTER 3

DORA'S STORY

A few days after the TS meeting, Dr Herbst handed back our psychology dissertation proposals with his comments attached. On mine, he'd written: 'Fascinating subject – my aunt was a TS member. Keep focus on topic, avoid digressions – lots to look into.'

My initial reaction was elation, followed by a sudden fear – maybe Dr Herbst knew a huge amount about Theosophy, as opposed to my almost total lack. And what did that '*was*' mean regarding his aunt? Did she die, or simply leave the TS? Was she a member back in Vienna or Berlin before the war, or was she right here in Sydney ready to pour scorn on my dissertation? Without wishing his aunt any harm, I did rather hope she was not around.

During the weekend, I examined the material Dora van Gelder had given me. And as I did so, I came to more fully understand Dr Herbst's words. There really was a lot to absorb and, perhaps due to my non-religious background, a fair amount of it seemed quite obscure, to put it mildly. By Tuesday I had a list of topics for Dora that barely scratched the surface – but at least it was somewhere to start.

At four o'clock I arrived at the TS building in Hunter St in a mood of keen anticipation. Quite apart from my Theosophical questions, I was intrigued by Dora van Gelder herself. As I climbed the stairs to the third floor, my surroundings didn't seem quite as strange now as they did the week before.

I tapped on the open door of the annex and was greeted by Dora, who was busily placing cups and saucers on one table while a middle-aged woman with a kindly, somewhat weather-beaten face was laying out cakes and biscuits on another.

"Hello, Ed. Lovely to see you," Dora said. "I'm sure you've got quite a few questions for me." Turning to the woman beside her, she went on, "Ed's doing a university dissertation on the TS and a few of us are helping him," and then to me: "Ed, I'd like you to meet Joyce Housman."

"How do you do, Mrs Housman," I said.

"Ed," she replied with a smile. "Please call me Joyce – we're nearly all on first name basis here at the TS."

"Thank you, Joyce, I will," was my response.

How different this was from my mother's social circle at Stanmore. These women, at their first few afternoon-tea parties, would address each other as 'Mrs so-and-so' until one would suddenly exclaim: 'Oh, *do* call me Barbara!' (or Hazel or Dorothy or Mavis). This was the cue for the others to proffer their first names, and they'd go back home happy in the knowledge they were now more than mere acquaintances. I'd never dream of calling any of these women by their first name, and in fact Joyce Housman was the first older person I'd ever addressed in this way.

Dora poured us both a cup of tea and we sat down at a small table near the door while Joyce bustled around in the background. I took out my list of topics:

Bishop Leadbeater
The coming World Teacher
Liberal Catholic Church
Dr Annie Besant
Reincarnation   The Masters

After reading through the list, she laughed.

"You have some big topics here, Ed, but some of them are part of larger ones – rather like those Russian dolls that all fit inside one another. And although you've come at a very busy time with the Communal Living project getting underway and the April Convention looming, I can assure you that Antonia, Ambrose and I will help you get a fair idea of what the TS here in Sydney's all about."

Overhearing this, Joyce added, "And count me in, too! Anything to do with the TS, I am delighted to help with."

"Thank you, Joyce, that is very kind of you," I replied gratefully.

"Oh, there's no need to thank me," Joyce responded, "I can talk about TS matters until the cows come home!"

Dora took a pencil from her apron pocket and drew a series of arrows on my list to link allied topics.

"I can tell you quite a lot about Bishop Leadbeater, who I've known since I was seven years old back in Java. After I came to Sydney I studied under him and later worked closely with him over several years helping with his correspondence. However," she went on, "the subject of Leadbeater can't be separated from some of your other topics like the Liberal Catholic Church, reincarnation, the coming World Teacher, and of course the Masters and the Esoteric Section. Joyce knows a lot about the Masters, so maybe she can help on that one." Here, she glanced across at Joyce who beamed and nodded.

"Then," Dora added, seeming to choose her words with care, "there are some topics I feel might be best tackled by Ambrose. And although education is not on your list, Antonia will be able to fill you in on the important educational aims of the TS and its role in changing the nation's psyche. She's training to be a teacher at our school, by the way."

Quite frankly, I hadn't given any thought at all to education. I soon learned, however, that Theosophists had a long-standing interest in new educational theories and putting them into practice in their schools like Morven Garden School located at Gore Hill, five miles north of the city. It was the first co-educational school in Australia and now had over a hundred pupils, including boarders.

The fact that Antonia was associated with the school sparked in me a sudden interest in education. She was, quite frankly, the most amazing person I'd ever met. But, enough of this – Antonia was clearly enamoured of Ambrose Mortimer, who exuded confidence and worldliness and obviously reciprocated her feelings. (I have mentioned this matter here simply because Dr Herbst had enjoined us never to ignore subjective, personal responses to external stimuli, as these intuitive reactions often contributed important information to the 'reading' of a situation.)

My short reverie was cut short by Dora asking, "What would you like to start on first, Ed?"

"Well, actually I'd really like to learn a bit more about *you*, if I may," I said, surprised to hear myself say this, as I was generally rather reserved in social situations.

Dora took my interest in her stride. "Certainly," she replied. "I enjoy telling people my life story because it really gives a picture of Theosophy – both in Java and here in Australia. You could say it's 'meat and drink' to me – well, not *meat,* of course – as a Theosophist, I'm vegetarian. Do you know, Ed, I've never eaten meat, fish or chicken in my life and I never will."

At that moment, I decided to simply note down every single thing that occurred and extract portions later for the dissertation. I was now plunging into the unknown, but at the same time I felt exhilarated. Who knew where all this would lead?

Briefly, here's what Dora told me. She was born in 1904 (which made her eighteen, not fifteen as she appeared) in Java, the largest island of the Dutch East Indies. Her family were Dutch colonial planters going back to the 1790s with interests in sugar, tea and coffee. Java was a racially inclusive society at its higher levels and Dora herself was partly Chinese. Her parents were very active in the TS and she often attended meetings at their home, so becoming accustomed from childhood to people of other cultures and faiths.

Over the years, her family had undergone a number of financial ups and downs, so she'd always been aware of change as an intrinsic part of life. This, as well as her daily meditation practice and her clairvoyant abilities, had helped her to adjust to being without her family when she'd come to Australia in 1916 at the age of thirteen. Useful to her also was the legacy of her father's preference for reasoned debate over emotion-based stances on topics under discussion.

I very much wanted to hear about her clairvoyant abilities, but she said,

"We'll come to that later – right now I want to get started on the topic of Bishop Charles Webster Leadbeate, known as CWL." She explained how she'd first met him in 1911 on his first tour of Java when she was a was seven years old and very shy. On his second visit in 1914, he became aware that she was clairvoyant.

I stopped writing and looked at her. "You mean you can see the future?"

Dora smiled, obviously accustomed to this question.

"Not exactly," she told me. "But I *am* able to see certain things going on around us that are not 'visibly obvious'. My mother and my grandmother are also clairvoyant, so for us it's quite natural."

I'd never met a clairvoyant person before and I wondered how far Dora's powers extended. She always seemed very composed, I'd noticed, maybe this was why. 'But can she read my thoughts,' I wondered, rather hoping she couldn't.

She laughed. "People always ask if I know what they're thinking," she said in what seemed uncannily like a response to my unvoiced question. "But to reassure you, Ed – it doesn't really work like that. At least, not with me."

She told me that education was one of CWL's enduring interests, and how he'd been the first principal of Ananda College, an English-Buddhist school for boys in Ceylon.[5] When he came to live in Sydney, he decided to gather around him a group of young people with special abilities. Aware of Dora's clairvoyance, he wrote to her parents in Java and asked if their daughter could join the small group of students who were to form the nucleus of the future TS school. Dora's parents left this decision entirely up to her and, after considerable meditation, she decided to take the plunge and go to live in Sydney. Arriving here at the age of thirteen with her Aunt Tet as guardian, she exchanged a comfortable life in Java with servants for a life in Sydney speaking little English and living with her aunt in a boarding house.

"Not many parents would have let their child choose something so momentous," I remarked.

"Very true. But they believed that if my 'inner-self' told me it was right to do it, then they would make it possible." She then described how she achieved this, saying, " 'I would . . . be quiet and meditate and then find out – in that quietness of mind – what my decision should be. If you feel that you have done that, even if you make a mistake, I think you get a sense of self-confidence. Because it isn't about what you do, but this inner sense of experiencing it – this inner certainty.' "[6]

---

[5] In 1972, Ceylon became Sri Lanka.
[6] Kirsten van Gelder and Frank Chesley. *A Most Unusual Life: Dora van Gelder Kunz: Clairvoyant, Theosophist, Healer.* (IL, Quest Books, 2015), 30-31.

Being the only girl among the seven boys taught by CWL and several tutors strengthened her sense of self-reliance, she told me, saying it was a matter of 'sink or swim' and that having chosen her life herself, she could never blame her parents for anything.

"But didn't you miss your parents and brothers?" I asked.

She told me she certainly did, but that her seven fellow-students became her family, spending much of each weekend together swimming, hiking and exploring Sydney.

Apparently, CWL was extremely secure in his own opinions and, because his own clairvoyant abilities were highly revered by the people around him, his word was rarely questioned. An example of this was his belief that shoes were not necessary in Sydney's climate and his insistence that Dora and the boys go barefoot, even in mid-winter.

At this, I looked up from the notes I was writing and, from my bemused expression, Dora realized further explanation was needed. CWL, she told me, believed that by wearing no shoes, the group of students would be in contact with the earth's current and, furthermore, become impervious to people's glances – in other words, develop the important attribute of complete unselfconsciousness.

I couldn't stop myself from glancing down at Dora's feet, and saw she was wearing a pair of ordinary sandals rather than the rather 'unusual' ones she'd been wearing the week before. Seeming again to divine my thoughts, she laughed and told me how her appearance evoked sympathy in some quarters as she was often mistaken for a refugee from the war in Europe while also occasionally attracting ridicule.

" 'Many people, particularly because I was a girl, came and offered to buy me a pair of shoes out of pity… I must admit we really were brought up in a very hardy way. Not only did we wear no shoes and stockings in the winter but we dressed in very few warm clothes. A sweater is all we ever wore.' " [7]

The more I heard of Bishop Leadbeater, the more intrigued I became.

"I'm really looking forward to meeting this man," I said, and repeated Russell Fletcher's words: 'Once seen, never forgotten.'

Dora laughed. "Certainly, Russell spoke the truth," she said. "You'll get to meet CWL pretty soon – right now, he's getting over a bout of bronchitis. He's nearly seventy now, you know."

"You mentioned earlier on that you'd worked for CWL for a time."

"Oh yes," Dora replied. "After the Great War ended, CWL used to receive many letters from people whose husbands, sons or brothers had been killed. Having heard that CWL was clairvoyant and believed in continuity of consciousness, they'd write to him asking if he could make contact with their loved ones and find out how they were doing 'on the other side', thereby hopefully gaining some solace in their loss. CWL would receive an enormous number of these letters and needed secretaries to take shorthand and type up his replies. He involved me in responding to this correspondence, and I drew on my clairvoyance to draft answers to the bereaved people. I did this for several years, but eventually told him I couldn't continue it – and he accepted this and never asked me to do it again. In the coming weeks, you'll be seeing and hearing a lot about CWL and his role in the Liberal Catholic Church."

Suddenly, a buzzer sounded and a man holding an electric megaphone walked past the annex, announcing: "We have just five minutes until the meeting will

---

[7] Ibid., 40.

commence, so if you can all please take your seats in the auditorium . . ."

I closed my notebook, thanking Dora for meeting with me and providing so much background.

"Now that we've talked about me," she said, "why don't we meet here same time next week and discuss some of the items on your list. In order to make any sense of what's currently going on in the TS, you'll need to understand the concepts on which Theosophy is based"

On the train back to Stanmore, I glanced through the notes I'd made. Although I felt a bit dazed from all the input, I also felt a sense of wonder at the thought that no-one else in the world could have experienced an upbringing quite like that of Dora van Gelder – and how different it was from my own.

CHAPTER 4

JOYCE'S STORY

The week flew by. Although I wanted to find out more about the Communal Living project and the approaching TS Convention, there was a lot I needed to know first. The next Tuesday afternoon, I tapped on the open door of the TS annex. There was no sign of Dora, but Joyce Housman was there, bustling around setting up the cups and saucers for after the talk. She was evidently expecting me, saying with a friendly smile,

"Dora will be along shortly. She's busy getting the Communal Living project underway at The Manor – that's the new name for the big house at Mosman. She suggested we might like to talk about the Masters until she arrives."

"Thank you, Joyce, that'd be very helpful," I replied. "I do need some enlightening there. I can't quite get the hang of the Masters, to tell the truth."

Joyce nodded understandingly, obviously no stranger to this type of ignorance.

"The Masters are an intrinsic part of Theosophy," she told me. "And they are very close to my heart, as a matter of fact. Now, open your notebook, Ed dear, and we'll get started. Tell me if anything's not clear."

Once started, Joyce was virtually unstoppable.

"In every culture, throughout history including today, some individuals seem to have moved beyond the general population in their understanding of the principles or laws that underpin existence," she explained. "These people, call them what you will – saints, great souls, mahatmas, shamen, wise ones – are found in all religious traditions and indigenous cultures. In the purity of their lives, they embody the wisdom of their clan, of their group, of the ages. In Theosophy, we call them 'Adepts', or 'Masters'.

"Theosophists believe not only in biological evolution but also in *moral* evolution. Madame Helena Blavatsky, who founded the TS in New York in 1875, was the first to introduce the Masters to the Western world. You see, Ed, the Masters *chose* Madame Blavatsky to be their 'vehicle' to bring their wisdom to the world of today."

I needed some clarification here.

"So, Joyce – were the Masters real people?"

"Of course," Joyce replied. "And not just *were*, but *are*. We have accounts by those fortunate enough to have actually seen the Masters and interacted directly with them, by letter or through actual visits." She paused, then went on in a rush, "But, Ed, in any important movement you'll always get a few dissidents – remember 'Doubting Thomas' in the Bible? But no-one can ever question *my* belief in the Masters, though I've not yet been fortunate enough to personally sight any of them."

My home background and university training had instilled in me the need to objectively examine any hypothesis put forward regarding unexplained phenomena. However, I knew that now was not the time to interrogate the veracity or otherwise of the topic presently under discussion.

"When Madame Blavatsky's groundbreaking work *Isis Unveiled* [8] was published," she went on, "it struck a chord with all the many people who were disenchanted with traditional Christianity and intrigued by psychic phenomena, Spiritualism and Eastern religions. Madame Blavatsky believed that the era of modern materialism was over, and for those who were seeking something

---

[8] See Glossary note under title.

beyond it, two sources of progress were available. These were, firstly, knowledge that had been lost to the world; and secondly, direct instruction by living Masters located in Tibet who could assume the human form in the interest of true religion.

"The TS does not *compel* members to accept the Masters," she continued. "Some people are deeply committed to the ideals expressed by them, others are less involved. Speaking personally, I can only say I have sometimes been inspired beyond my own knowing, and to me this understanding comes directly through the Masters."

I nodded, puzzled that belief in something described as 'intrinsic' to Theosophy should be a matter of personal choice; however, I reasoned that the same could probably be said regarding some of the views of Christians in relation to church dogma. And for all I knew, members of other religions might not believe holus-bolus in all the tenets of their faiths.

"The Masters – who are they, exactly?"

Joyce's face took on a serious expression. "There are a number of Masters, but only two – the Masters Kuthumi and Morya[9] – have extended their special protection to the Theosophical Society. They have retained the bodies of their last incarnations and they dwell in Tibet . . ." Here she paused, gazing into the distance with a misty look in her eyes.

"But it's not necessary to *physically go* to Tibet to access the Masters' wisdom," she went on. "They can be visited on the 'astral' plane. And, as I've said, they can manifest themselves to people who've reached a certain level of spiritual development. This is what I'm working towards now." She paused, and I could see she was steeling herself to say something more.

---

[9] Also known by slightly variant spellings.

"Edwin," she proceeded solemnly, "I should tell you this now – Madame Blavatsky in her own lifetime was a controversial figure, and she still is today. Some very hurtful things have been said about her . . ."

"Really?" I queried, "Why would that be?"

"I'd rather it came from me than you heard it from others," she replied. "Accusations of plagiarism regarding some parts of '*Isis Unveiled*' were levelled at her, and suggestions were made that certain of the Masters' letters were in fact written by Madame Blavatsky herself and others." Taking a deep breath, she plunged on, "But right down history, I think you'll find, any major advance has met with opposition. Just look at the struggles of the early Christian martyrs."

"These are very serious claims, Joyce," I murmured. "I appreciate your telling me of them."

Joyce, like many other Theosophists I'd observed, generally projected an air of well-being, but in the last few minutes I noticed she'd lost some of her customary good cheer. Feeling that a change of focus might be welcome, I thought I'd ask her if she'd be willing to talk to me about her life.

"Ed," she responded joyfully, "if you've got the time, I'd *love* to tell you!" She fetched us both a cup of tea and a piece of banana-cake and set them down on a coffee table alongside two capacious armchairs.

Settling herself comfortably, she announced, "What you see before you is a re-born woman. And I can thank Theosophy for this. If I hadn't become involved in this wonderful movement, I don't know where I'd be now.

"Up until the Great War, I was a happily married woman with four children, living at Kogarah. Then Eric, my husband, enlisted in the army – he was a real patriot, you see. Soon, he went off to fight in Europe and in 1916 I received the terrible news that he'd been killed in battle. My world simply fell apart, but of course I had to keep going for the children's sake. It was hard, Ed, I can tell you. But I was not alone in my anguish, of course, so many others had also lost people they'd loved.

"Then I heard from a friend how it was possible to receive messages from departed ones through séances and even real letters. I didn't feel up to attending a séance, to me that was very much dabbling in the unknown. But a letter, that was different . . . I asked my friend to find out who I should write to, and – I think you've guessed, Ed – it was none other than our beloved Bishop Leadbeater!

"Straight away, I wrote him a letter giving details of my husband and saying I just wanted to know if he was happy and not in pain, and to tell him how much our children and I loved and honoured his memory.

"I didn't know if I'd even receive a reply, but a few weeks later a letter arrived. I felt quite shaky as I opened it, but when I read what it said I felt an enormous sense of peace and joy that quite frankly, Ed, has never left me!" She gazed into the distance, and after a short interval I said, "If it's not too personal, Joyce, what did it say?"

"Oh, it was wonderful!" she replied, seeming to relive the moment. "It said my husband Eric was in a good place and no longer in pain. He would always love us and knew I would do the best for our children. It was signed 'Bishop C.W. Leadbeater'. I have the letter to this very day – it's one of my most treasured possessions.

"Later, I found out from young Dora van Gelder that at one time she used to help Bishop Leadbeater with these letters by contacting the departed souls using her clairvoyant skills. To me, this simply added to the magic of it all. After that, it was but a short step to attending one of Bishop Leadbeater's sermons at the Liberal Catholic Church in Redfern, then joining the Theosophical Society and meeting the most special group of people I could ever hope to know. My life has been transformed and I journey on through it in a state of peace, at one with creation."

When she had finished this story, we sat there in silence for a moment, and then I heard footsteps on the stairs and Dora appeared. She glanced from Joyce, whose flushed face reflected her intense involvement in her story, to me – who probably looked quite drained.

"Thank you so much, Joyce, for talking with Ed," Dora said. "I'm sure he's learnt a lot from you."

"I certainly have," I told her. "Joyce has explained about the Masters, and she's just told me how she became involved with Theosophy."

Dora gave Joyce an affectionate hug and, turning to me said,

"The cafe round the corner makes good coffee. Why don't we dash down there before the meeting."

"Great idea," I said and, thanking Joyce for all she'd told me, I gathered up my coat and bag and followed Dora out of the room.

As we entered the café, we were met by the delicious aroma of freshly-brewed coffee. It was fairly dark inside and decorated in 'European' style with rows of shelves holding enormous jars filled with different coffees and teas. High stools were arranged along both sides of narrow tables and towards the back of the room we found a couple of spare ones to perch on.

After we'd ordered our coffees, I found that Dora was keener to talk about her visit to The Manor than discuss Theosophical topics, and I was more than happy to do this.

"Will you be living there yourself?" I asked,

"Yes, of course," Dora replied. "This'll be the first time I'll be with my family since I came to Australia. There will be separate living areas for families, couples and individuals. In fact, we have a large group ready to move in right now. For my father, it's a dream come true.

"People will be amazed at the building," she continued. "It's on such a huge scale: three storeys high, a chapel in the basement, attics on the top floor and so many chimneys you wouldn't believe! In a few weeks' time, we'll hold an 'Open House' day, and you'll be able to see what we've achieved in such a short time."

"Thanks, Dora, I'd enjoy that," I replied pleasantly. While I was going through the medical course, I'd had to study pretty hard and hence my social life was fairly embryonic. In truth, I'd only ever been to a small number of parties, and these had been very staid events conducted under strict parental supervision.

"Would you'd like to bring your parents along?" she asked. "We really want to open our doors to the wider community – show that we're not some strange sect or cult, but simply people who are exploring the same aspects of life that concern everybody – except that we may take our investigations and commitment a little further."

"That's a very nice idea, Dora. I'll ask them about it," I said, though feeling that this very thoughtful extension of the invitation could be a trifle too much. Dad might fit in alright with the Theosophical crowd, as he always liked an intellectual discussion, but Mum might find it a bit too 'outre'. Mainly, however, I really wanted to enter this new social setting on my own without my parents in tow.

As we left the warm, coffee-laden atmosphere of the café, Dora exclaimed, "Ed - I nearly forgot! Ambrose has suggested you and he meet for breakfast at a café next Sunday morning. We – that is, Antonia and I – have asked him to fill you in on Bishop Leadbeater and the Liberal Catholic Church. And afterwards, you might like to come along to the Church and actually witness CWL giving a sermon."

I was delighted to hear of this offer from Ambrose.

"Yes – I'd love to," I replied. "When and where shall I meet him?"

"9 a.m. at Central Station under the clock on the main concourse," Dora informed me promptly. "And don't eat beforehand – you'll love the Greek food!"

At home during dinner on the Saturday evening, I told Mum&Dad I'd been invited to The Manor open day in a few weeks' time and I'd need bring some food. And while on the subject of food, I mentioned I wouldn't be needing any breakfast the next morning.

"That's not like you, Ed," Mum said, looking worried. "Don't you feel well?"

"I'm fine thanks, Mum," I replied. "But I'll have to leave here around 8.15 to meet a friend for breakfast in a Greek café near Central Station. And after that," I added piously, "we'll go to church."

Mum and Dad exchanged a glance, and Mum added in what she probably thought was a neutral tone, "What religion does your friend belong to?"

I explained that I was going to meet with Ambrose Mortimer and learn more about the workings of the TS, and later in the morning we'd wind up at St Alban's Liberal Catholic Church, Redfern and attend a mass there.

The words 'Catholic' and 'mass' seemed to cause my formerly Church-of-England mother some unease. She looked at Dad enquiringly and as usual he rose to the challenge. I actually think he enjoyed moments like this.

He leaned back from the table and began to speak.

"In 1916, Bishop James Wedgwood, of the Old Catholic Church, which was not connected to the Roman Catholic Church, by the way, visited Sydney from England. He already knew C.W Leadbeater and together they initiated a new church, the Liberal Catholic Church. Like the Old Catholic Church, the Liberal Catholic Church was able to ordain its own priests and bishops. Wedgwood ordained Leadbeater as a priest and consecrated him as Regionary Bishop for Australasia. These two are the driving force behind the Liberal Catholic Church, and with Annie Besant they devised a ritual modelled on the Roman Catholic mass but in English."

"How on earth do you know all this?" Mum asked admiringly. Dad laughed and explained that the Liberal Catholic Church building in Redfern was near his office and one day he'd picked up a pamphlet that was lying on the pavement outside and had read it on the train on his way home.

Mum was still not finished with the topic. "But what I don't understand," she said looking slightly perplexed, "is the connection between the Theosophical Society and this church."

Dad welcomed this query, as it enabled him to move smoothly into the second part of his speech.

"There's no formal link," he replied, "but the Liberal Catholic Church very much appeals to those Theosophists who miss the rituals of the faiths they used to belong to. Others, however, have totally rejected religious ceremonial and its trappings, and they are not at all enamoured of the Liberal Catholic Church, with its clerics in their priestly garb and the rituals they preside over. Bishops Wedgwood and Leadbeater enjoy a considerable following and have ordained a number of men as priests. Women, I might add, are not permitted to play an active role in the church."

By now, Mum's interest in the topic had been quenched.

"Thank you, Dad," she said briskly and stood up, looking a bit worried. I asked her if there was anything on her mind.

"I was just thinking you'd be better off having a nice plate of hot porridge before you go off to meet this Ambrose person tomorrow morning," she replied.

"Mum," Dad said heartily, "I doubt the boy will starve between Stanmore and Central Station. The Greek cafes round there do a very nice dish of eggs and bacon, you know."

Our house is small, and later that evening as I was undressing up in my room I couldn't help overhearing my parents talking in their bedroom next to mine.

"I do worry about him," my mother said. "He's an impressionable young lad and he hasn't seen much of the world."

"True," rejoined my father. "But that's because he's been studying fairly hard. I'd say now is just the time for him to spread his wings a little."

"But these The-os-o-phists . . ." Mum said doubtfully, articulating the word as if it were a strange lozenge she was tasting for the first time.

"Nonsense, Isobel," my father replied. "I'd much rather he was in with a group that was lively and actually thinking about the world than getting involved with a brainless sporting set."

Then my father started humming a little tune. I knew what it was, and so did Mum. It was the old Scottish folksong 'Raggle-Taggle Gypsies' which tells the story of a young girl who leaves her life of comfort to run away with a handsome gypsy boy.

After a moment, I heard my mother chuckle.

"No, Arthur," she said. "I *don't* think he's going to run off with the Theosophists!" and soon I heard their light click off.

CHAPTER 5

AMBROSE'S STORY, AND
SOME TS BACKGROUND

The next morning dawned clear with a touch of autumn in the air. I woke up early and heard Dad pottering around downstairs. As I came into the kitchen, he looked up from making a cup of tea and said, "Not wanting to cramp your style, Son, but I wonder what time you might get home later today?"

"Oh, round 3pm, maybe earlier," I replied. "Why?"

"I'd like your assistance with one of my projects."

"Which one?" I asked cautiously.

"The mice."

I groaned inwardly. I didn't mind helping out with the beans from time to time, but the mice were quite another thing. Apart from their rank smell, I'd recently been responsible for several mice escaping, thus compromising the validity of his study. Dad had taken the loss very well, but I knew he was disappointed. However, in true scientific spirit he built this setback into the experiment by adjusting its parameters to accommodate a certain level of mouse attrition.

"Certainly, Dad. You can always count on me," I said loyally, putting on my coat and picking up my bag.

On the train to the city, I glanced round at the other passengers. Some of the men were obviously on their way to a day of fishing, with rods and canvas bags for bait and the hope of a catch; while several families in their best attire looked to be heading for church. The closer we got to Central Station, the more I wondered how my discussion with Ambrose Mortimer would go. Having only exchanged a few words with him, I really didn't know what to expect. But at least he'd made time to meet with me.

Our train arrived at Central Station right on 9am. Entering the recently-completed station concourse, I enjoyed anew the feeling of airiness and light achieved by its mix of stone, steel and glass. 'I'm glad Ambrose never saw the old Central Railway Station,' I thought, recalling its dingy gloom.

Despite the travellers scurrying in all directions to reach their various platforms, I could easily spot Ambrose Mortimer standing directly under the large clock and scanning the crowd. He was a striking figure and I noticed more than one passer-by giving him a second glance. Today he was wearing a pair of checked plus-fours[10] with a rust-coloured shirt. A jumper was slung casually over his shoulders and the outfit was topped off by a wide-brimmed black felt hat.

Americans were a rare species in Sydney so I had no way of 'reading' his apparel in sociological terms. My own outfit of dark grey trousers, white shirt, and grey wool top-coat suddenly seemed woefully nondescript, if not dowdy, and for a fleeting moment I wondered if Ambrose would even notice me in the crowd.

I needn't have worried, for he waved and greeted me warmly, saying, "Hi there, Ed," and clapping me on the shoulder. "Great to see you! And dressed very appropriately for church, I see. I'm famished and I hope you are too. There's a good café, the Doric, nearby and their coffee's superb!"

We walked several blocks to the Doric café, and on reaching it Ambrose was greeted by the proprietor like a favourite son. High up on the wall at the back of the café,

---

[10] 'Plus-fours' are trousers that reach 10 cm (or 4 inches, hence the name) below the knees, popular for golfing and walking.

a neon sign announced in red, green and blue intermittently flashing letters, 'Fresh Fish, Fish & Chips, Ready to Serve'. The proprietor, whose name was Jim, called his wife over to meet us, then led the way to one of the booths with tables attached. Urging us to 'make yourselves at home', (though these booths, with their hard wooden seats and immovable tables were nothing like home), he handed us two slightly grease-splotched menus and hurried off to serve some other customers.

All the items on the menu seemed to be hearty lunch or dinner dishes, there was nothing remotely breakfast-like. I remarked on this to Ambrose, who laughed and said, "We're not having breakfast at home in Stanmore with Mum and Dad this morning, Ed, but I can promise you – whatever you choose, you'll enjoy it." We placed our orders and presently two huge platters arrived piled high with fried eggs, bacon, sausages, steak, onions and peas plus a large serving of potato chips. Ambrose was right – it certainly was delicious!

At the end of the meal, over a cup of thick Greek coffee, he produced from his shoulder-bag a silver cigarette case and from it took an elegant slim black cigarette with a gold tip. Never having seen anything remotely like this before, I must have stared, for he exclaimed, "Oh Ed, sorry! I didn't realise you smoke. Do have one," and he proffered the open case. I told him I actually didn't smoke, but was curious about the cigarette.

"It's a Sobranie," [11] he replied. "My father sent a few boxes over from the States, knowing I couldn't get them here." He lit the cigarette, inhaled deeply and settled himself a little more comfortably on the hard seat of the booth.

"So," he drawled. "What's on the agenda for discussion today, m'boy? The girls have asked me to fill you in on some sensitive aspects of the TS story, and of

---

[11] See Glossary: Sobranie cigarettes.

course I'm happy to do so. But first, why don't I put you in the picture on where I fit in to all this?"

As including biographical notes on my interviewees was now a definite part of my dissertation, this idea suited me down to the ground, and I was pleased that I didn't have to ask if I could do it. While Ambrose smoked his cigarette, I pondered how I'd describe him in psychological terms, arriving at: 'above-average intelligence; generally non-neurotic; some narcissistic characteristics; strong sense of self/entitlement; genial manner in social contexts'. Without having a general frame of reference regarding Americans, however, these observations could only be impressionistic.

"I'm here in Sydney as part of a two year-world trip, courtesy of my father in the States," he began. "His plan is for me to see the world, albeit through a Theosophical lens, then return to join the family firm, which I will describe as a hardware store . . ." He paused here, looking straight at me, and I had a strong sense that this eventuality was unlikely to come about – if Ambrose had any say in it.

"Fact is," he continued, "until I started on the trip I hadn't really focused on the TS, even though I was in it from birth. Obviously, this was a reaction-formation against my father's long-standing obsession with Theosophy and all that goes with it.

"I'm now on the last leg of the trip, having spent some months in India based at Adyar, the TS world headquarters, then on to the Dutch East Indies. After that I stayed a while in Perth, Western Australia, another stronghold of Theosophy. I lived with a group of Theosophists – and had a pretty good time, too, I might add," he said with a meaningful look.

I ignored this and simply asked how his father had first become involved in Theosophy.

"Easy question, easy answer!" he replied breezily. "In 1893, my father attended the first Parliament of the

World's Religions in Chicago, where he heard Mrs Annie Besant give a public address. He was mighty impressed by the 'New World View' advanced by this famous orator and activist, and from then on he radically changed our family's way of life. My mother, three older sisters and I became all-in Theosophists – vegetarians, advocates of cremation to anyone who wanted to hear about it, occult explorers . . . You name it, you can bet your bottom dollar we'd be on board."

It was hard to tell whether Ambrose had any personal commitment to the ideals of Theosophy, or if he was in it 'just for the ride', which he certainly seemed to be enjoying.

"Did your father continue with his business?" I asked. "Or was he completely taken up with Theosophy?"

He laughed. "Hell, no! Like so many enterprises run by Theosophists, the business flourished. This is no accident, by the way – Theosophists in general have inquiring minds and aren't averse to taking risks. This makes for large-scale success, or massive failure as the case may be."

"Do you know why Mrs Besant's speech made such a huge impression on your father?" was my next question. Ambrose started on another cigarette, called for more coffee and embarked on a short lecture – rather in the style of my father, I couldn't help thinking.

"During the 1890s throughout the English-speaking world and in Europe, people's earlier faith in progress, prosperity, capitalism and religion was giving way to disillusionment. A search for new values was on, and a range of movements such as Socialism, Spiritualism, Christian Science and Theosophy appeared. All had in common the search for a way of re-ordering an existence that was felt to be fragmented and spiritually unsatisfying.

"After the Great War of 1914-18, many more people joined the search for new ways of living, and this is why Theosophy is now really coming into its own, with Mrs

Annie Besant – sorry, *Doctor* Besant – as head of the world-wide movement."

I really admired Ambrose's eloquence and wondered if it was innate or acquired through the study of rhetoric while at school back in the States. Whatever the reason, the guy seemed never at a loss for words.

While Ambrose was taking a short break, I realised I needed to clarify his reference to Annie Besant as *Doctor* rather than *Mrs*. On his return to our booth, he explained that the Benares Hindu University in India had recently conferred an honorary doctorate on Mrs Besant for her work promoting educational opportunities for young people , and she now wished to be addressed as *Doctor* Besant.

"Have you ever heard Dr Besant giving a public address?" I asked.

"Sure have," Ambrose replied. "I've been to three of her lectures. She's a superb speaker – in fact she's been called 'the world's finest living orator'. She'll be coming to Sydney soon to deliver a number of public talks – definitely try and get along to hear her."

So, first Bishop Leadbeater – 'once seen, never forgotten,' – according to Russell Fletcher; and now here was Dr Besant – 'the world's finest living orator'. If these two Theosophical luminaries were even half as good as their devotees claimed, they'd be pretty impressive, to say the least.

Ambrose called for more coffee and glanced at his watch.

"Yes," he said. "There's just enough time left to put you in the picture on some of the current tensions in the Sydney TS. Then we can mosey along to the Liberal Catholic Church and you can attend the Mass."

"The Liberal Catholic Church and the TS . . . Where to start?" he said, as if to himself, then went on to explain, "Many Theosophists have a longing for ritual and, in response to this need, Mrs Besant worked with Bishop

Leadbeater to develop a program for the Liberal Catholic Church that incorporated religion, ritual and education. However, at the same time within the TS there exists a sizeable and very vocal group that regards organised religion as anathema. These members had rejected it years before and were deeply dismayed when they saw the growing involvement of the Liberal Catholic Church in the Theosophical movement.

"This group, known as 'the Dissidents', have recently formed the 'Theosophical Society Loyalty League' in order to re-assert TS traditional objectives and religious neutrality. They've also launched a magazine, *The Dawn*, in which they voice their dismay at the growing links between the Liberal Catholic Church and the TS – including, I might add, the use of TS lodge premises by the Church.

"Opposing the Dissidents is a strong cohort led by the Bishops Wedgwood and Leadbeater. Recently, a claim was made in *The Dawn* that it had evidence of 'moral corruption in high places'[12]. Since then, not surprisingly, antagonism between the two groups has heightened considerably.

"What sort of 'corruption in high places' are you referring to?" I cut in. "There are so many different types."

Ambrose laughed. "You never said a truer word, Ed. This particular corruption refers to a potentially extremely troubling situation that's been around for quite some time. What I'm referring to here is Bishop Leadbeater's interactions with boys he has tutored, and his advocacy of masturbation. This issue weighs heavily on a lot of people's minds, both here in Australia and elsewhere in the Theosophical world, particularly in the USA. I'll tell you more about it when next we meet. So now," he

---

[12] Roe, Beyond Belief, 264.

finished, "you can see why the girls nominated me for certain topics."

"Yes, quite," I replied. I was rather stunned by all this, not least by hearing the word 'masturbation' uttered. The topic and even the word itself were taboo in my social experience, although to be sure Dr Herbst seemed to have no such qualms about mentioning it in lectures, explaining that hearing the word spoken would assist us in overcoming a few of our many inhibitions.

"I can see now that beneath the surface camaraderie of the TS there's quite a lot going on," I remarked.

"You've sure hit the nail on the head, Buddy," Ambrose said with a wry grin. "And if we can just get through the Convention – only a week away now – without any major blow-ups, we'll all be mighty relieved."

Glancing at his watch, he observed: "Well, I guess it's about time we strolled on down to the church, where you'll get your first glimpse of Bishop Charles Webster Leadbeater in action. I'll give the service a miss, but if you're free afterwards, what about joining Dora and Antonia and me for a spot of lunch?"

"Sounds good to me," I replied.

We quickly gathered up our bags, paid for our food and set off along Regent St towards St Albans, the Liberal Catholic church. As we neared it, I could see a fair-sized crowd gathered outside. Catching sight of Antonia and Dora, Ambrose waved and said, "And there's the reason why I'm still in Sydney."

Then I said something so idiotic I could hardly believe my own ears: "You mean – Dora?" I asked.

Ambrose stared at me and laughed. "No, you idiot – Antonia! I'm besotted with the girl. I thought everyone knew that!"

"Oh yes," I said. "Antonia is marvellous . . . Dora's very nice too, of course."

"Of course," he agreed. After greeting the two girls, he bade us farewell and disappeared off around the corner.

Antonia and Dora asked me in a friendly way how my talk with Ambrose had gone.

"Very well indeed," I replied. "He was most informative, and our breakfast was marvellous!"

As we filed into the church, which was now filling up rapidly, I reflected on my stupid remark to Ambrose and recalled the words of Dr Herbst in one of his lectures: 'The subconscious mind has a mind of its own. Listen and learn from dreams and chance remarks – your own and other people's.'

CHAPTER 6

A LIBERAL CATHOLIC MASS, AND ANTONIA'S STORY

The sheer size and grandeur of the Liberal Catholic church surprised me, as well as how 'traditional' it appeared. With its pointed arches, steep-sloping roof and solid sandstone walls, it seemed like a smaller sister to Sydney's two great cathedrals – St Mary's and St Andrew's – that I often passed when walking through the city. [13]

This being my first-ever attendance at a church service, I decided to simply jot down everything that struck me. The church was cavernous, with stained glass windows casting shafts of coloured light through the dimly-lit interior. An enormous chandelier hung over the altar and the air was heavy with a rich and exotic aroma that I learned was incense. On both sides of a wide central aisle, the pews were packed with people of all ages and types. Among them I recognised a number of now-familiar TS faces, including Joyce Housman, who gave a friendly wave.

The service itself was lengthy, over two and a half hours, and involved much bobbing up and down, wafting of incense in little metal containers on chains, hymn singing, choral interludes and the tinkling of tiny bells at particular moments. In purely sociological terms, it was of considerable interest, but for me the most fascinating aspect was the sermon by the acting priest, the Right

---

[13] See glossary: St Albans Liberal Catholic church building, Sydney.

Reverend Bishop Charles Webster Leadbeater (CWL) himself.

As he strode down the aisle at the head of a procession of twelve red-smocked young boys, the Bishop was an impressive sight. A tall, strongly-built man with a long grey beard, he was attired in a full-length magenta robe. An enormous gold cross rested on his chest in company with several heavily-bejewelled gold chains and the highly-decorated mitre on his head seemed to yet increase the authority of his presence.

The theme of Bishop Leadbeater's sermon today was 'coping with the loss of loved ones'. He acknowledged the universal and personal pain of bereavement and offered to all who suffered, seeming as he did so to embody Holy Wisdom and Understanding in the mellifluous cadences that flowed from his mouth in a seemingly endless stream.[14] Now having seen CWL in action, I could readily understand how Joyce Housman had been moved by his eloquence during her dark days as a new war-widow.

When the service was over, we filed out from the gloom of the church into the bright sunlight of Redfern.

"Well, what did you make of that?" Dora and Antonia asked.

"Most impressive and interesting," I replied. This seemed to be sufficient, with Dora then announcing, "I don't know about you two, but I'm absolutely famished!" and, turning to me, "Ed – we're meeting Ambrose down at the café on the corner. You'll come with us, won't you?"

I glanced at my watch – it was now one-thirty.

"Just for a cup of tea," I replied. "Ambrose and I had a huge breakfast, and I've got to get back home to help my father with a couple of his projects."

---

[14] See glossary: Leadbeater, Charles Webaster (Bishop). voice recording, 1925.

The café was full – mostly families having large Sunday lunches of fish and chips, and country people enjoying their first square meal in Sydney after long train journeys. Ambrose was already there, in possession of a table for four, and he'd ordered a couple of plates of sandwiches. We sat down and when the food arrived, I arranged for two large pots of tea to be brought over to us.

"So, Ed, how did you find the service?" Ambrose drawled.

I replied in a similar vein to how I'd answered Dora and Antonia, then asked the two girls if they often attended services at the Liberal Catholic church.

"Oh, no, hardly ever," Dora answered. "Females aren't permitted to assist in rituals in the Liberal Catholic Church, and I'm not one to just sit by and watch other people doing things. We only came today because there was a rumour that Krishnamurti and his brother Nitya might be there, but apparently they've not yet reached Sydney."

During the past few weeks, I'd read and heard a lot about Jiddu Krishnamurti, the young boy 'recognised' by Bishop Leadbeater some years ago in India as the future World Teacher. Krishnamurti had been educated towards this role and now, at the age of twenty-seven, was emerging as a leading figure in the TS. I'd heard, too, how close he was to his younger brother, Nitya, who suffered from tuberculosis, or TB as it was commonly called.

"I'm sorry you have to dash off home, Ed," Antonia remarked as I finished my cup of tea. "What do you need to help your father with?"

I told them briefly about Dad's devotion to genetics and his experiments with beans and mice. They seemed to enjoy hearing about this, which surprised me somewhat as I viewed my home-life as very pleasant but quite ordinary.

Dora sensed my puzzlement and explained, "Ed, your life interests us because your background is not at all like ours. Although the three of us grew up with Theosophy in common, we were in very different situations – Ambrose in the States, Antonia here in Australia boarding at Morven Garden School and me on a tea plantation in Java."

As I got ready to leave the cafe, Antonia said, "Ed, I'd really love to meet your parents. What about bringing them to our Open House Day at The Manor next Sunday?"

Hearing Antonia's words, I experienced what in religious terms would be called 'an epiphany'. When Dora had suggested the idea earlier, I had no intention of inviting Mum&Dad to the Open House Day. Now I heard myself say warmly: "I think they'd *love* to come! I'll ask them when I get home."

I paid for the tea and was on my way out of the cafe when Antonia called after me: "Ed, wait! I haven't made a time to meet with you! What about one day next week?"

I stopped in my tracks and spun around, nearly bumping into a waitress carrying a tray full of plates.

"Oh, that would be excellent, Antonia. Thank you!" I replied. "When would suit you? And where?"

"How about Tuesday, in the TS building annex, around 4.30?" If Antonia had said "Midnight, on the moon," I'd have answered just as I did now: "Perfect. I'll be there!"

That evening at home over dinner, I gave Mum&Dad a run-down on my day's activities, editing some aspects of Ambrose's discourse that would definitely be too *outré* to mention to my parents. I told them that my new friends had invited us as a family to attend the Open House day at The Manor over at Clifton Gardens. They responded very favourably to the idea, and I remembered to tell them that everyone was asked to 'bring a plate'.

Mum immediately started thinking what she might cook.

"I know," she announced, "I'll make a batch of Scotch eggs and a dozen custard tarts. That should go down very well."

A doubt assailed me. "Mum," I said tentatively. "I have some reservations about the Scotch eggs . . ."

"What on earth for?" Mum demanded. "Everyone *loves* my Scotch eggs!"

Mum prided herself on her cooking, and for good reason. Her Scotch eggs, which were hard-boiled eggs covered with sausage-meat and then deep-fried, were delectable. I felt my way – we were in delicate territory.

"It's not the eggs themselves," I began, "It's the 'Scotch' part . . ."

Mum stared at me "Ed!" she said indignantly, "Are you telling me these people have some sort of prejudice towards the Scottish population?" (Some of Mum's ancestors came from Scotland.)

"No, Mum, settle down," I replied soothingly. "It's just that Theosophists are vegetarians. They couldn't eat the delicious sausage-meat surrounding the eggs, which I always feel is by far the best part."

This explanation mollified Mum and she said she'd work out something else to bring.

Dad, who'd been sitting there quietly, now spoke up. "Do you foresee any problems with the custard tarts, Son?" he asked.

I looked at him quickly and caught the glimmer of a grin.

"No, Dad," I replied evenly. "The custard tarts will be fine. Thank you for asking."

Two days later at the appointed time, I knocked on the half-open door of the TS annex and heard Antonia call, "Come in, Ed."

I entered the room to find her sitting on a small sofa with an easy chair drawn up beside it. The late afternoon sun shone through the window behind her, catching golden glints in her curling brown hair and making it glow like a halo round her head. For a second I stood transfixed by the sight of her, then quickly regained my self-possession and thanked her for making the time to see me.

"Oh, it's fine," she replied. "Dora and Ambrose have met with you and I certainly wasn't going to be the odd one out! I'm thinking," she continued, "it might be good to fill you in on the coming TS Convention and some of the identities who'll be there."

"Sounds excellent," I replied, sitting down in the chair beside the sofa and opening my notebook.

"As you know, our Convention will start next Friday and go though to Tuesday, with the Open House Day at The Manor coming in the middle on the Sunday," she said. "Luckily, it coincides with Easter, so that many interstate members can attend. As well, we'll have some overseas visitors, including Krishnamurti and his brother Nitya. The Open Day will be a great occasion to show off The Manor – everyone's heard so much about the house and the Communal Living project. You've invited your parents, I hope?"

I told her I had, and that they were looking forward to the day.

"Throughout the afternoon," she went on, "some visitors from the Convention will drop in. Bishop Leadbeater, who is living nearby while his rooms at The Manor are being made ready, has said he'll stop by, and we're very much hoping Krishnamurti and his brother Nitya will honour us with their presence."

"What about Dr Besant?"

"Unfortunately, she is still over in India, campaigning in a number of cities on Self-rule for the country," Antonia explained. "She'll arrive in Sydney on May 9 and of course we're all keenly awaiting the chance to hear her speak. The Town Hall has already been booked for her opening address and everyone who can get there will attend."

Now that I had a clearer picture of the approaching events, I felt able to move on to my next topic of interest – finding out more about Antonia herself. I outlined my plan to include in my dissertation several short biographies of young Theosophists.

"What a good idea!" she responded. "For some reason, people often think of Theosophists as really strange and also quite elderly. Any chance to show how wrong they are is most welcome."

After a short pause in which she seemed to be debating where to start, Antonia announced,

"Well, here goes: my life-story! It may take a little while, Ed, I hope that's alright . . ."

As she said this, she looked at me and I was quite lost for words. Luckily, she took my silence for assent as she then began her story without further ado. "My grandfather, Alexander Vivian, was a Scottish doctor who decided to come to Australia in 1865 after his wife, my grandmother, died in childbirth with her eighth child. In Scotland at that time, TB was prevalent, so he felt the warm climate would be good for his children and chose to settle in Brisbane. The new life turned out well for them – all the children succeeded at their studies, with several following their father into medicine; Paul Vivian, my father, was interested in science and became an analytical chemist. The family was very involved in the cultural life of Brisbane and, like many people at that time, took a keen interested in ethical and religious matters.

When the first Brisbane Theosophical study group was established in 1881, my father and several of his siblings joined it and this is where he met my mother, Clara. Her family belonged to another of the new religious groups,

Christian Science,[15] which was growing in popularity for many of the same reasons as Theosophy."

I nodded, recalling how Ambrose had mentioned Christian Science in his recent talk. Antonia could see from my face that all this was new to me but, being unaware of my non-religious upbringing, she couldn't know just *how* novel it was.

"My parents married young," she went on, "and within eight years they had a brood of five children, of whom I'm the eldest. During this time my father had become increasingly involved in Theosophy and decided the family must move to Sydney to be right at the hub of TS activity in Australia. He bought a large house in Mosman overlooking Mosman Bay, settled us all in it and was soon deeply engrossed in Sydney Theosophical life."

Antonia stopped at this point and I looked up from my notes. She appeared to be debating whether to add something. Then, taking a deep breath, continued:

"Ed, I am a believer in honesty in every part of life. So I will tell you the full story of what actually happened to us.

"In my mother's family, the women were extremely fertile and also liable to produce twins. For example, my grandmother gave birth to thirteen children including two sets of twins. It broke my mother's heart to see the huge toll all this childbearing took on her dear mother, and she dreaded the same thing happening to her. So – she decided to become celibate and told my father.

"His response was not at all favourable, and he soon made other arrangements in this respect. He joined forces with another Theosophist and within a matter of months they decamped to Western Australia, leaving my mother high and dry with the five of us children. To make matters even worse, father's focus on his religious and personal

---

[15] See glossary: Christian Science.

life meant he'd greatly neglected his business and by the time he left Sydney he was staring bankruptcy in the face.

"My poor mother – all alone, a long way from her family in Brisbane, with five young children, no money and nowhere to live as our house had been seized by the bailiffs. She had no idea what to do. Her education had been all literature, languages and music – not very useful at a time like this.

"Fortunately for us, the TS stepped in. My father's actions were viewed extremely dimly in TS circles, and members rallied round. They were just like a family and we will always be grateful to them. Morven Garden School, owned by the TS and located near St Leonards on the north side of the Harbour, took in all of five of us children as boarders and supported us entirely for the duration of our schooling.

"Our mother, Clara, rented a room nearby and went out to work. She contributed financially as much as she could, but without the assistance of the TS, my sisters and brother and I would have ended up in orphanages, very likely losing all contact with each other."

She stopped and, looking up from my notes, I could see how distressed she was at the memory of this time.

Soon, she continued her story. "These events have had a profound impact on how I view the world and human behaviour," she said. "At Morven Garden School I saw at first-hand how the two wonderful principals, Miss Lily Arnold and Miss Jessie MacDonald, put into practice the Theosophical approach to education. This was why I decided to become a teacher myself, and I now teach the younger children at Morven Garden School and live-in there as a boarding house mistress."

While I was noting all this down, I couldn't help admiring Antonia's honesty and directness – and thought how very different her life was from those of the girls I knew through university and my local tennis club.

She seemed to sense something of my thoughts, for she said in a comradely fashion, "You're probably coming across quite few new ideas these days, Ed, and anything that puzzles you, I'll be glad to help with."

"Thank you, Antonia," I replied. "I really appreciate that. You know, I'd very much like to visit Morven Garden School as part of my dissertation work, if that might be at all possible."

"Certainly," she replied, smiling. "Miss Arnold and Miss Macdonald always love showing visitors over the school."

At this moment, a buzzer sounded to announce the start of the TS meeting, so I thanked Antonia again for meeting with me and got up to leave.

"I'm so looking forward to meeting your parents at the Open House Day," Antonia said. "And by the way, my mother will be there also – I'll make sure you meet her."

CHAPTER 7

OPEN HOUSE DAY AT
THE MANOR

On the Sunday of The Manor Open House, Mum, Dad and I rose early in order to complete our various chores prior to embarking on our day out. Dad watered his beans, Mum tidied up the kitchen and I fed the mice. Mum had made a large fruitcake and two dozen custard tarts and was just packing them into a basket when there came a knock at the door.

It was The Aunts – bearing gifts.

"We thought we'd bring you a few more items for The Manor Open House," Aunt said, beaming.

"They're very light, just a batch of meringues and cream puffs," added Auntikin. "They won't weigh you down at all."

Aunt and Auntikin were small, birdlike women with rather severe haircuts, due to the fact that they cut each other's hair in order to save money towards their next overseas trip. Now, as they stood gazing at Mum, there was something almost childlike about their eagerness to please their elder sister.

Mum took the offerings and graciously thanked the Aunts for their contribution. Then, with many cheery exhortations to enjoy ourselves, they departed, leaving Mum&Dad to conduct their leaving-the-house ritual. They double-checked that the stove was turned off, all lights extinguished and every door and window safely locked. Finally, we were ready to go.

As we walked to the station, each holding a basket, Mum commented on how lucky we were to have such beautiful weather for, as she said, "Easter can be tricky, you know."

"You're right. I think a few other people down history may have felt that way," Dad said mildly, then quickly added, "We certainly *are* fortunate, it could have been April showers."

"That refers to England, actually, not Australia," Mum informed him.

On the train, Dad said reflectively, "You know, I think The Aunts might have liked to have come with us."

"Well, they weren't invited," Mum replied briskly. "We are going to The Manor by personal invitation from Ed's friends. It's not open to all and sundry, you know."

"Quite so," murmured Dad.

I enjoyed this type of exchange between my parents. Often, much more was going on than met the eye. In this instance, the unspoken topic was 'choices made in life' by Mum and her two sisters. Mum had married and produced a child, whereas The Aunts had remained single – 'spinsters' Mum called them, but certainly not to their face. They worked as secretaries in offices in the city and were currently saving towards their third trip to England. Mum&Dad, on the other hand, had never left Australia's shores, which Mum regarded as proof of their more sober, and hence superior, approach to life.

Now Mum had something more to say, "And besides, Ed is spreading his wings a bit – up till now he's led a very sheltered life and it's good that he's made these new friends who take an interest in the wider world, rather than mixing with a group of brainless sporting types."

"You're absolutely right," said Dad comfortably, settling down to read his weekend newspaper.

When our train arrived at Central Station, we made our way to the tram stop. Here, along with many others looking forward to a day out on Sydney Harbour, we caught a tram down Castlereagh St to Circular Quay, or as most people simply called it, 'the Quay'.

Ever since I was a child, I've loved the Quay. Residents of Stanmore who never ventured far afield could live out their whole lives unaware that Sydney is a maritime city. But once they'd journeyed ten miles north through the city and arrived at the Quay, they'd enter another world. A traveller from a landlocked European country arriving at Venice in the days of Christopher Columbus could not have felt their spirits lift more than mine whenever I arrive at the Quay and take my first deep breaths of the salt-laden air. To hear the chugs, clanks, whistles, shouts and bells of the cargo ships, passenger liners, ferry-boats and launches as they make their way across the Harbour gives me more pleasure than any symphony concert.

After leaving the tram, we made our way to wharf No.5 for 'Athol Wharf, Mosman'. When our ferry arrived, we watched admiringly as the deckhand flung a thick rope around a bollard and nonchalantly leapt across the wide, watery, heaving gap onto the wharf to put the gangplank in place. Conscious of his power, he then strolled over to unlock a padlock on the gate and release the waiting horde of passengers.

The crowd surged onto the ferry, albeit with some unmannerly pushing and shoving, and soon we were away. As the Quay receded behind us and we entered the main harbour, Mum&Dad talked about the bridge to be built one day that would link the southern part of Sydney to its northern shore.

"I believe things are finally underway to start the bridge," [16] Dad remarked.

"And not before time, either!" Mum replied. "It's going to make a huge difference to everyone living on the northside of the Harbour."

---

[16] See Glossary: Sydney Harbour Bridge.

Twenty minutes later, we disembarked at Athol Wharf and took a tram up the hill along Bradley's Head Rd. As instructed by Antonia, we alighted at Thompson St and from here walked down a very steep hill towards The Manor, each carrying some of the food: Dad with the fruitcake, which was square and fairly weighty; Mum with the custard tarts because she could be relied upon to get them there in one piece; and me with The Aunts' meringues and cream puffs – which in a way said a lot about us all.

Eventually, and not a moment too soon – Mum& Dad being somewhat tubby and not much given to exercise – we reached the crest of Morella Rd and there before us stood The Manor, in all its glory. We stopped and simply stared.

The house was absolutely enormous – a true mansion, three stories high with numerous chimneys, attic windows and wide verandahs. Surrounding it was a well-kept garden filled with flowering camellia, bougainvillea and plumbago bushes. Behind this imposing edifice, Sydney Harbour sparkled in the sun while a light breeze ruffled the eucalyptus trees nearby. Although I'd heard that The Manor was large, I'd no idea it would be quite so imposing. Suddenly, I felt a rush of admiration for the Theosophists, whose sense of daring and adventure had led to the Communal Living project.

We opened a creaking wrought-iron gate, made our way down a set of marble steps and crossed a wide, tiled verandah to reach the front door. This was a solid, 'baronial'-scale portal with stained glass inserts and a huge brass doorbell. I went to ring the bell, but before I could do so, Dora van Gelder appeared.

"Oh Ed," she said, smiling. "How lovely to see you. So you've brought your parents. Good for you! And loads of food, too, I see!" She opened the door fully and introduced herself to Mum&Dad, saying, "I'm Dora, a friend of Ed's. Welcome to our Open House Day!"

A moment later, Ambrose and Antonia appeared, greeting me with a clap on the back and a friendly hug respectively. After I'd introduced them to Mum&Dad, Antonia took the meringues and cream puffs from me with a smile.

"Good for you, Ed! Did you cook these yourself, I wonder?" she asked, We both laughed and a feeling of relief surged through me – the day would be alright.

Dora took charge of the rest of our food and led us into a large reception area that opened onto what seemed like some sort of refectory or dining room, with solid wooden tables on which a number of covered dishes had been placed. At one end of the room I spotted Joyce Housman among a group of women busy laying out plates and cutlery.

When Joyce saw me, she came straight over to us.

"And these are your parents!" she exclaimed. Turning to Mum&Dad, she said, "I'm Joyce Housman, a friend of Ed's. It's lovely to meet you both."

Joyce took Mum under her wing and soon they were chatting away like old friends, even addressing each other as 'Isobel' and 'Joyce'. Dad quickly found his feet and, holding a glass of non-alcoholic cider, gravitated towards a small group of men talking in an indoor conservatory filled with ferns and small palms. Beyond the greenery, a breathtaking view of Sydney Harbour could be glimpsed through the leadlighted windows.

A little while later the tinkling sound of a little bell called us to lunch. Around fifty people, including my good friend Russell Fletcher, converged on the reception area from various parts of the house and grounds. Russell bounded over to Mum&Dad and greeted them enthusiastically, then we all went into the refectory and filled our plates with a fine mix of exotic and beautifully-displayed food, most of which was totally new to me. Carrying our laden plates, we headed out onto the verandah where cane-lounges, easy chairs and large cushions were arranged. Many of the gathering were familiar faces from TS meetings. Others I'd never seen before, including some who obviously hailed from the Dutch East Indies or India.

As I was coming out of the refectory with my second helping of food, I heard my name called and turned to see a slim woman in her middle years smiling at me. She left the group she was sitting with and came towards me. Although I couldn't recall seeing her before, there was something about her that seemed faintly familiar.

"Ed," she said, "I've heard so much about you! This dissertation you're writing is going to be fascinating. I do hope I can read it when it's finished."

'Who on earth can she possibly be?' I wondered with a sense of near-panic. Obviously, she knew who *I* was. Then with smile she said, "I'm Clara Vivian, Antonia's mother."

Relief flooded through me. "Of course!" I exclaimed. "How nice to meet you, Mrs Vivian."

"Call me Clara, please, Ed," she replied. "Let's find a place and talk for a few moments. That is, if you're not already ensconced with others of your own age."

I assured her could easily be spared, and would love to talk with her. We found a place in one of the ground floor reception rooms and sat down on a large leather sofa. Now that I knew who she was, I could easily see the resemblance between Clara and Antonia. This augured well for Antonia, for Clara was a graceful, good-looking woman who bore little trace of the difficult years she'd gone through in the past.

For something to say, I remarked on Antonia's somewhat unusual name.

"She's called after my mother, a wonderful woman." Clara explained.

Now it all came back to me: "You mean, the one who had thirteen children including two sets of twins?"

"Yes," she said with a smile. "You must be a good listener, Ed, if you remembered Antonia telling you that."

Naturally, I gave no indication that every single word Antonia had ever said to me was etched into my heart, and proceeded with a pleasant conversation in which I asked about the names of her other children.

"After Antonia comes Helena, and you can guess where that comes from . . ."

"Madame Helena Blavatsky?"

"Spot on," she said with a laugh. Then comes Pauline, named after her father. And next there's David, a fine lad and nearly grown up now. He was named by his father after a close friend." I noticed Clara didn't refer to her former spouse by name or use the term 'husband'.

"And finally comes Christina. This was my choice entirely – I just loved the name."

After we'd talked for a short while Clara said, "Well, Ed, I'd better let you get back to your friends, and I must rejoin my group of Co-Masons – we're having a great debate on the pros and cons of educating boys and girls together."

"What's your view on co-education, Clara?" I asked.

"Oh," she replied. "I'm very much in favour of it. My children have all attended Morven Garden School so I've been lucky enough to see close-up how it works."

"If Antonia is any example of co-educational schooling, then I'm all for it too," I said smoothly.

"Oh Ed!" she exclaimed. "What a nice young man you are. I'm so happy to have met you and I hope we'll meet again before too long."

"I feel exactly the same way," I replied.

Just as we were finishing lunch, there came a flurry of excitement – Bishop Leadbeater had left the TS Convention to drop by and see how things were going here at the Open House. Wearing full clerical rig-out and surrounded by a gaggle of young people, the Bishop exuded geniality and goodwill to all as he made his grand entrance. Although he was warmly received by many of those present, I observed that others kept their distance – simply greeting him with a polite nod and continuing their conversations.

'Are these the Dissidents who Ambrose told me about?' I wondered. As for the Bishop, although I knew he was in his mid-seventies and not in the best of health, he seemed to absolutely radiate energy and love of life. I saw with interest the delight he took in the company of the youths around him, throwing his head back to laugh appreciatively at their jokes and greatly enjoying the general stir his visit had created.

About an hour after Bishop Leadbeater and his retinue had departed, Krishnamurti with his brother Nitya and their entourage arrived. For all of us at the Open House day, this was undoubtedly the highlight. Not being a TS member, I remained in the background, but it was enough to observe them even from afar.

Krishnamurti was slender and extremely good-looking with huge brown eyes and shining jet-black hair falling nearly to his shoulders from a centre parting. He was beautifully dressed and comported himself with a dignity that made his every gesture memorable. I have no idea what was going through his head, but he gazed upon us all with what appeared to be reserved yet benign tolerance.

His brother Nitya was smaller than Krishnamurti, and stayed fairly close to him throughout their visit. He, too, was impeccably well-presented right down to his black leather shoes, which positively gleamed. Although I knew Nitya's health was not strong, he looked as though he was enjoying this afternoon gathering of like-minded people.

Fairly soon after Krishnamurti and Nitya had departed, Dad appeared and suggested it might be time to take our leave. Ambrose, who was with me, sprang up saying, "May I give you and Mrs Best a lift down to the ferry wharf? And I have a suggestion – how about Ed here stays on for a while and I drive him back home to Stanmore? My friend Antonia and I are visiting friends nearby at Lewisham this evening and we could easily drop him off home."

Dad was pleased to take up Ambrose's offer to drive them to the ferry. The walk up the steep hill to the tram-stop was not an appealing prospect, especially after lunch on a warmish day. He looked over at Mum, who was sitting in the middle of a group of women engaged in an animated discussion on nutrition. Healthy eating was one of Mum's great interests and clearly it was close to the hearts of the others, too.

"I think we're about to go vegetarian at our house, Arthur!" Mum called to Dad gaily. He told her Ambrose would take them both to the ferry wharf now and drop me back home before dinner. So, after thanking everyone for a wonderful day, Mum&Dad went out front of The Manor to wait for Ambrose, with me bringing up the rear holding the now-empty baskets.

CHAPTER 8

BEFORE THE TS CONVENTION SESSION

Presently, Ambrose drew up at the wheel of his car. He cut a dashing figure, sporting a peaked cap, leather driving gloves and goggles pushed high on his forehead. I recognized the vehicle as an 'Australian Six', a very handsome convertible with a spare tyre on each side of the chassis and wheels with steel disc hubcaps, a definite style improvement over the wooden spokes of most cars on the road.

'Lucky devil,' I thought. 'Looks like the hardware store back in the States must be doing quite well.' I helped Mum&Dad into the car, then waved them off and went back inside.

As the afternoon wore on, I met so many interesting people that by five o'clock I was quite pleased when Ambrose said it was time we made a move. He located Antonia and, after thanking everyone for a wonderful day, we went out to the car. Ambrose suggested I sit beside him, saying Antonia preferred to sit in the back.

As we got going, I remarked on the fact he had an Australian car. He glanced across at me and grinned. "So … what'd you think I'd have?"

"Oh, probably something American like . . . um . . . a Lincoln, maybe?"

He laughed. "I'll have you know, Ed, back in the States I have a Duesenberg Model A Phaeton just waiting for me to come back and take her for a spin! This car's my father's idea. His motto is 'When in Rome, do as the

Romans', so he told me to get myself an Australian car – hence this Aussie Six."

Then he and Antonia chanted the Aussie Six slogan: "Made in Australia, by Australians, for Australia."

"What does the 'six' in Australian Six stand for?" Antonia asked. I was wondering the same thing.

"Six cylinders," Ambrose replied knowledgeably.

He was a confident driver and knew his way around Sydney. We drove to Gladesville and crossed to the southern side of the Harbour by way of the punt at Bedlam Point, then took Parramatta Rd towards the city. As we motored through the older part of town towards Stanmore, Ambrose said, "Ed, I'm wondering if you'd like to attend one of the TS Convention sessions with me tomorrow. You'll not be bored, I can promise you."

I was surprised and pleased to receive this invitation and accepted it readily. Besides being an interesting experience in itself, it could well yield valuable material for my dissertation.

"Maybe we could meet before the session so I can brief you on some of the issues that will likely be raised," he suggested, adding soberly, "more's the pity."

I'd never heard Ambrose speak in this serious way before, and it occurred to me that maybe this was why he'd been so helpful in taking Mum&Dad to the ferry. Whether or not this was the case, the fellow was brimming with social finesse and it always seemed to serve him well.

From the back seat of the car, Antonia said in a cautioning way, "Ambrose, these are simply *rumours* about Bishop Leadbeater. We must always be careful not to spread stories about people that we cannot verify."

Ambrose turned and glanced at her quickly. "Dear Antonia," he replied, "I admire your high-mindedness, but . . ." and then to me: "Ed I think you may find that after tomorrow's Convention session there'll be quite a few 'changes in the group dynamics' of the Sydney TS.

Also, you're the only person I know here who's quite outside of this complicated web of events, and I find that quite refreshing, I can tell you."

By now we were approaching Stanmore, so I gave him directions to Ethel St and as we drew up outside my house we agreed to meet the next day at a café near the TS building an hour before the session. Then I walked up our front path and entered a very different world – my home life with Mum&Dad.

The two of them greeted me cheerfully, with Mum saying: "Oh Ed, you've just arrived in time for dinner – I've cooked a very nice roast chicken with baked vegetables and beans from the garden."

"Sounds delicious, as always," I replied, realizing with surprise I was actually quite hungry. Despite the thoughts that were spinning around in my head, I was also thinking that Mum really needn't have mentioned the beans, as we had them for dinner every single night of the year, courtesy of Dad's genetic experiments. Sometimes the thought even crossed my mind that our own genes might be affected by the amount of beans we consumed.

Mum&Dad were delighted with their visit to The Manor, both of them commenting on the stimulating and unusual people they'd met. Mum said how much she'd enjoyed talking with a group of women who actually took nutrition seriously, unlike her bridge group whose main culinary interest was the latest cake recipes. Dad related the chief points of a discussion he'd had with several tea-planter Theosophists from Java on the current state of world tea and coffee markets.

They were also pleased that Dora, Antonia and Ambrose had introduced themselves. Dad had talked genetics with Ambrose, who'd impressed him with his knowledge 'for a layman', as Dad put it. Antonia, according to Mum, was 'a delightful young woman and a very good match with Ambrose'. As for Dora, she got top marks from both of them for her independent approach to life and the straightforward, no-nonsense way she faced the world. 'A girl after my own heart,' was Mum's verdict.

I mentioned that I'd had a nice chat with Antonia's mother, Clara Vivian, and Mum asked if I'd met Antonia's father.

"No," I said. "He, ah . . . evaporated . . . a number of years ago, I believe . . ."

Dad laughed. "Very Theosophical. I suppose he just de-materialised, turned into ectoplasm or something."

"Yes, something like that, I imagine," I said with a vague grin, and the moment passed without further enquiry from Mum.

All in all, the day had been a great success, though as I went up to my room after dinner I couldn't dispel a sense of unease. Unless some peace could be brokered between the Dissidents and the Loyalists, the Sydney Theosophical Society seemed headed for a rough ride in the very near future.

The next afternoon, which was Easter Monday and a Public Holiday, I met with Ambrose at a café near the TS building. He ordered coffee for both of us and lit up one of his Sobranie cigarettes.

After taking a long drag on it, he said reflectively, "Ed, this trouble in the TS that's now reaching crisis point has been brewing for a considerable time. As I've mentioned, there are concerns on two fronts, namely: the increasing role of the Liberal Catholic Church in the TS, and the allegations of immoral conduct within the church. And perhaps we can say here that both of these concerns coalesce in – the Right Reverend Bishop Charles Webster Leadbeater.

"This isn't simply just a Sydney matter," he continued, "Certain TS members in America and elsewhere are closely watching developments and actively involving themselves, too, by communicating with law enforcement agencies over here. However, leaving aside the personalities concerned, the issues strike at the core values of Theosophy and what it stands for: the search for truth in all matters; the nourishing of the higher levels of the human psyche; and the 'neutrality' of the TS in regard to conventional religion."

. "Tell me about this 'overseas involvement' you referred to. What's it based on? Checkable facts or simply hearsay?"

With a dramatic flourish, Ambrose pointed to his shoulder-bag, which he'd slung over the back of his chair. "Right here," he said, "I have a number of documents, including one I've compiled myself, which I am pretty sure will answer your question. Soon enough, if I'm not mistaken, there'll be a flurry of activity in the press – news stories and letters to editors from all the major participants in this fracas. After all, as we say in the States, 'the juiciest scandals involve sex or religion', and this one's got both. The pity of it is that no-one's been able to find a way through this tangled web of problems, and this is what has led to some of the people involved feeling that their only course of action is to go public."

He paused for a moment then said, brightening, "But hey, here's a bit of good news for you. Because all this stuff seems destined to appear in the daily newspapers, you'll have no problems regarding confidentiality in your dissertation. You'll have so much great material to quote! And speaking of which – your dissertation, I mean – I hope I'll be the first to read it, given the huge amount of assistance I'm providing."

I laughed, assuring him he'd have the first crack at it if he wanted to, then asked, "What are the precise allegations regarding Leadbeater?"

After stubbing out his cigarette in the ashtray on the table, he replied, "Questions had been raised about Leadbeater's moral conduct in regard to young boys going way back to his early days," he said. "But in 1910 while he was living at Adyar in India and involved in the education of the young Krishnamurti, he was accused by Krishnamurti's father of involving his son in 'immoral practices'. These accusations were dismissed by many as simply being part of a desperate ploy by the father and his advisers to prevent Krishnamurti and his brother Nitya being taken to England by Annie Besant to be educated."

"For Krishnamurti's future role as the coming World Teacher," I cut in.

"Exactly. And although all this happened – or did not happen – a long time ago and in another land, there have been subsequent rumours down the years involving Liberal Catholic clerics and certain practices. I've made a summary of these allegations, which you can add as an appendix to your dissertation if you so wish."

One thing was puzzling me. "But how could what you've just told me ever come to be printed in the Sydney newspapers?" I asked. "Maybe this type of thing can be published in America, but here in Australia we're rather strait-laced. I don't know whether you've noticed this at all."

Ambrose grinned. "I certainly have! It's way different from the States. When I was over in Perth last year I took a girl out once and practically had to marry her!" He gave a mock shudder and continued. "It's an awkward topic to talk about, especially in mixed company, but you might find a few euphemisms useful, such as: 'unnatural vices' and 'immoral tendencies'. As time goes on, you'll build up a quite a repertoire – my favourite right now is 'pernicious practices'."

We laughed, then he said, "And because you're certainly going to be asked whether Theosophy condones or even promotes these practices, I'll be kind enough to tell you what I say." In a sanctimonious voice, he then intoned: "There is nothing in the teaching of Theosophy that advocates this type of behaviour, and anyone promoting it has no place in the TS."

"Very effective!" I exclaimed. "I'll need to have some ready answers for people who know about my dissertation topic. I don't think my mother would feel able to allude to the subject even obliquely – if she even knew of it – but I expect my fellow psychology students won't hold back with their ribald remarks."

"Quite so," agreed Ambrose. "The pity of it all is that it makes for an enormous distraction from what the Sydney TS hopes to achieve through the Convention and the coming visit of Dr Besant.

"Fair enough. And how is Bishop Leadbeater handling all this?" I asked, hastily adding, "No pun intended, of course!" We both laughed uproariously and I recalled how Freud (or Jung) had written on the role of laughter as an indicator of tension as well as a diffuser of it. Here, it seemed to be doing both.

"Oh," replied Ambrose. "Leadbeater freely admits he's advocated masturbation to boys as a way of relieving tension, and also as a deterrent to forming undesirable liaisons with women. He does, however, deny that he's had boys in his bed."

"What do you think will transpire this afternoon?" I wondered.

After pausing for a moment, Ambrose replied, "You may recall my speaking of Mr T.H. Martyn, former General Secretary of the TS out here and now head of the Dissidents group – "

"Who are very much against Bishop Leadbeater and the Liberal Catholic Church," I cut in.

"Exactly," Ambrose replied, ignoring my interruption. "So – just to refresh your memory, Ed, on what I've told you before: the Dissidents have a number of areas of concern. Firstly, they oppose what they see as 'the cult of personalities' that's blossomed under the two Liberal Catholic bishops, Wedgwood and Leadbeater. Secondly, they feel that occult advancements in the Esoteric Section of the TS are being awarded too freely, and to people who have not earned them through assiduous and dedicated work on their moral advancement. And, last but not least, they are also very concerned at how intertwined the Liberal Catholic Church is becoming with the TS – it's even getting known as 'the TS church', apparently, which really raises the hackles of those TS members who value the neutrality of the TS towards all traditional religions, Christian and non-Christian."

"What about the coming World Teacher?" I asked, reasoning the Dissidents would probably have a position on this matter, too. And having actually been in the presence of the coming World Teacher – namely, Jiddu Krishnamurti – only the day before at The Manor Open House, he was in the forefront of my mind.

"Well, that's another contentious topic within the TS, which we might leave for another time," Ambrose continued, sounding somewhat weary. "It's all very worrying, like a volcano about to erupt. The pity of it is, that everything that's been worked for so hard, trying to establish the TS as a serious and legitimate organization with strong ethics and a vital message for the world, may be entirely undone by a sordid scandal that now seems impossible to avert."

He glanced at his watch and sighed. "Oh well, time now to go in there and see what will unfold."

On this note, we picked up our bags, paid for our food and made our way to the TS headquarters at 69 Hunter St.

CHAPTER 9

THE TS CONVENTION SESSION, AND AFTER

When we arrived at the TS building, it took us a while to get into the auditorium due to the number of people waiting outside for the session to commence, word having spread that it was likely to be fiery. Nearly all the leading figures of the Sydney TS were present including Mr Martyn, as well as a number of interstate delegates and of course Krishnamurti and his brother Nitya.

The session commenced in an orderly fashion with several routine items discussed and voted upon, and it was only after these had been dealt with that the atmosphere became heated. A prominent delegate rose to his feet and put it to the meeting that a vote of confidence in Dr Besant and Bishop Leadbeater should be passed.

From this point onwards, the meeting entered a prolonged state of eruption. Fierce debate ensued, with some participants proclaiming that while they could endorse Dr Besant, they emphatically could not support Bishop Leadbeater. Various delegates made impassioned speeches for and against the motion, including Mr Martyn, leader of the Dissidents, who explained very cogently the reasons why he could not vouch for the integrity of Bishop Leadbeater (who was present throughout the session and appeared unperturbed by the fracas surrounding him). Staunch defenders of CWL had their say, including Krishnamurti, Nitya and Fritz

Kunz[17], an American Theosophist who'd known CWL for many years. Krishnamurti was particularly vehement, saying that he and his brother Nitya knew CWL better than nearly anyone else in the room, so he could speak with some authority. He attested to CWL's greatness of spirit and roundly condemned those who spoke ill of him, observing that 'his clairvoyance may be doubted but not his purity'.[18]

The discussion raged for over two hours, with delegates passionately speaking their minds on the topic. Old skeletons in cupboards were exhumed, including the court case in Madras in which allegations of improper conduct by Leadbeater were made by Krishnamurti's father. Eventually, the resolution was carried: 86 votes in favour, 15 against.

When Ambrose and I emerged from the building at the end of the session, it was already early evening. We made our way towards Wynyard Station in silence, each wondering what the scene we'd just witnessed might portend for the future of the Sydney TS. Ambrose was first to speak, saying, "Have you got time for a bite to eat, Ed? Or do you have to go home and help your father with the beans or the mice?"

"Thank you for your concern, Ambrose," I replied ironically. "Fortunately, my time's my own for the next few hours, and I'd be delighted hear your thoughts on the session."

We ducked into a nearby café, ordered something to eat and got straight into discussion.

"86 votes in favour of Besant and Leadbeater, versus 15 opposing," I mused. "The Dissidents were really trounced, weren't they!"

---

[17] Fritz Kunz and Dora van Gelder later married.
[18] Mary Lutyens, *Krishnamurti: the Years of Awakening* (London: Order, 1984) 143 (quoting Krishnamurti in letter to Lady Emily Lutyens, April 22, 1922)

"Well, it would appear so," Ambrose replied. "Though as a social scientist, Ed, you'd know of course to carefully scrutinise statistics and look beyond the obvious. Of the approximately 400 people present at that particular session, only about 120 were delegates and therefore eligible to vote. The 15 who voted against the resolution were 14 members of the Sydney Lodge (amounting to 50% of Sydney Lodge delegates) plus one delegate from Tasmania who represented the unanimous view of his lodge."

"Hmm," I commented. "An impressive analysis. Thank you, Ambrose. So, what you're suggesting is that members from far-flung lodges and those from overseas might not be quite as aware of the situation as local members?"

"Precisely. And they also might consider it bad form to add fuel to someone else's fire," he replied. We talked about the meeting for another half hour, really as a way to digest the dramatic events we'd witnessed.

"And now for the last bit of business for today – the documents," Ambrose announced. He reached for his bag and from it produced a sheaf of papers. Handing them to me with a flourish, he said, "Take your time going through these. They'll provide you with a lot of background on why the TS in the USA has a certain interest in what's happening over here. I'd say it'll be a couple of weeks before things really fire up. Dr Besant's arrival in Sydney will trigger the next burst of activity, if I'm not mistaken. I've said it before and I'll say it again – this furore's not going away any time soon."

As we left the café, I thanked Ambrose for all his help, adding, "You've been tops!"

He laughed. "I love the way you Aussies talk, you sound so *British!*"

On the train back to Stanmore, I glanced through Ambrose's papers and realized how helpful they'd be. The most illuminating document was a timeline detailing allegations of sexual misconduct involving Bishop Leadbeater, with the first entry going back to 1906. The dossier contained so much meticulously-supported information that for the first time in our acquaintance, the thought crossed my mind that Ambrose's involvement with Theosophy might be deeper than I'd realised, and that his sojourn here in Sydney might not be quite so artless as it appeared.

The next morning at university, I walked towards the Psychology lecture hall in deep thought regarding my dissertation. Try as I might, I simply could not arrive at a way of organizing my complex and often contradictory notes into a cohesive whole. As I crossed the main quadrangle, I heard my name called and looked up to see Dr Herbst coming my way.

"How's the dissertation going?" he asked without any preamble. "I hear there's quite a ruckus going on in the TS at the moment. Talk about 'a change in the group dynamics'!"

"I attended yesterday afternoon's Convention session, and the discussion was pretty impassioned" I told him. "But I'm rather flummoxed about how to deal with it, what approach to take . . ."

Dr Herbst nodded. "Good to see you're getting stuck into the fieldwork, but keep in mind you are a psychology student, not an historian. Your job is to simply describe what you observe, note how participants articulate their viewpoints and what degree of influence this may have on the working of the group, and vice versa.

"You'll need to examine the language choices made, the strategies adopted in the pursuit of various aims, the techniques employed to gain advantage over adversaries – that sort of thing. Remember: you are a social observer, you are *not* there to make a judgment on any positions taken by individuals within the group." I nodded – this advice made a lot of sense.

"If you view your material through this prism," he finished, "I think you'll find your way through the maze of contradictions, rumours, downright lies and good intentions that you'll encounter."

One thing bothered me. "But – wouldn't that put the dissertation more in the realm of linguistics rather than psychology?"

Dr Herbst looked pleased. I felt I'd asked exactly the question he wanted, for off he went again: "If you take psychoanalysis, what does that consist of? Mainly hundreds of hours of talk which yields insights on motives, underlying influences, secret ambitions, fears, transference and so on.

"As Sigmund Freud once said: 'Words have a magical power. They can bring either the greatest happiness or deepest despair; they can transfer knowledge from teacher to student; words enable the orator to sway his audience and dictate its decisions. Words are capable of arousing the strongest emotions and prompting all men's actions.' "

"Profound," I commented.

"And here's another quote you might find helpful as you put your dissertation together: 'The art of being wise is knowing what to overlook.' "

"Profound again," I observed. "Said by whom?"

"William James," Dr Herbst replied, and with that he moved on to speak with some other students.

I was intrigued at how much Dr Herbst knew about the goings-on at the TS, but even more, I was astonished at his clear understanding of the nature of my dissertation dilemma. The pearls of wisdom from Freud and William James had cut to the heart of my quandary, and I felt very special to be the recipient of them, courtesy of Dr Herbst.

This feeling evaporated, however, when I entered the lecture hall and saw the very same quotes written up on the blackboard and referred to by Dr Herbst as he gave everyone else in the class the same advice he'd given me.

At home that evening, I copied out the quotes and taped them to the wall above my desk. Next, I drew up a number of headings to categorize and then cross-reference the communications of the main participants in the current 'TS troubles', as they were now termed.

With Dr Besant due to arrive in Sydney on May 9, I had several weeks in which to familiarize myself with her extensive history of political and theological activism. I also needed to gain an understanding of how she rated Theosophy in relation to Self-rule for India, her current chief cause. Her lecture schedule in Sydney showed this topic occupying a goodly number of her thirty-four scheduled talks and lectures.

Theosophy, I found, was still extremely close to her heart – she'd been associated with the TS since the days of Madame Blavatsky and still had vital business to achieve in connection with the coming of the 'New World Teacher'. The more I read about Dr Besant, the more impressed I became with her political acumen and courage in speaking out on the injustices she perceived around her.

Having made official visits to Australia in 1894, 1908 and 1913, Dr Besant was no stranger to our shores. During these sojourns she had keenly observed Australia's unique culture and, although very positive regarding the psychic potential of this antipodean continent, she had observed some important negative aspects which she felt compelled to raise.

In 1914, when asked if she had a message for Australia, she replied that she did have, and it had three parts. Firstly, Australia must nurture its professional, artistic and middle classes, not simply be a nation of manual labourers. Secondly, safe leadership was required when imposing democracy in order to engender in the population a reverence for great ideals, a love of country and a spirit of self-sacrifice – that is, self-control was needed. Lastly, racial prejudice must be overcome.

This third point was obviously a reference to the 'White Australia Policy', which came into force following Federation in 1901 and was designed to keep Australia white and British. While many in the (white) population were presumably content with this state of affairs, it was viewed by others as deeply insulting and unfair to minority groups such as Chinese, Indians and South Sea Islanders who over several generations had worked, paid taxes and gone to war for Australia. As for the Aboriginal people of this country, their status and rights were even lower than that of any other group. With the first of the three objects of the TS being: 'To form the nucleus of a Universal Brotherhood of Humanity, without distinction of race, creed, sex, caste or colour', Dr Besant made it a point to speak out against racial prejudice whenever she could.

My next focus regarding Dr Besant was to gauge her position on the current 'unrest' within the Sydney TS. To this end, I examined a number of her recent communications to her followers through the prism suggested by Dr Herbst, that of language choices made. Dr Besant's prose style and content, I found, displayed a penchant for a quasi-Biblical turn of phrase, redolent with ancient echoes that imbued her words with a time-hallowed gravitas. The histrionic quality of her discourse was underpinned by a number of rhetorical techniques such as repetition, contrast and emotive adjectives.

In alluding to her long association with Theosophy and her closeness to the now almost mythical figure of Madame Blavatsky, Dr Besant had a trump card and she played it hard. That she'd actually known and worked with Madame Blavatsky and Colonel Olcott made her presumably more closely in touch with the fundamental principles of the TS movement than almost anyone else alive today, apart from her long-term friend and ally C.W. Leadbeater.

Dr Besant was fortunate in having ready access to a vehicle for her thoughts and ideas, through the monthly TS journal, *'The Theosophist'*. She used it to address her followers directly, in a way that was personal and involving, as can be seen in the concluding passage of her article entitled *'Whom will Ye Serve'*:

' . . . This last word I say to you, brothers of the T.S. You are free men and women. Use your freedom as you will. Rely on your own judgement. Choose your own path. But I pray you, in the name of Love and Honour, do not countenance the filthy slanders printed in America, for these are born of hatred and of falsehood, and are against all decency. Even ordinary newspapers do not use language so coarse and defiling, which can give pleasure only to uncleanly minds, and are of a piece by those used by the persecutors of Occultists in the past, and in our days used of H.P.B. (Madame Blavatsky), and of those whom she regarded as her successors in teaching. The disregard of all the canons of gentlemen in the use made of private letters, is a mark of the same origin. Trust and confidence are shattered where such betrayals are made.

'Choose ye whom you will serve. The cause of Brotherhood, of Love, of Truth, or that of disintegration, venomous hatred and falsehood: in a very real sense, will you choose Christ or Barabbas? I stand as the chosen Head of the Theosophical Society, chosen not only by the Society, but also by its true founders and by their Agents. To those who know anything of Occultism I say, that I

stand as the servant of the hierarchy, obeying
Their Will and doing Their work, as H.P.B.
bade me declare. Either I am Their agent, or I
am a liar and a blasphemer. Take me as you
will.'

Annie Besant,
The Theosophist, March, 1922

During this rather strange 'waiting for the storm to
break' interlude, I met up with Ambrose, Antonia and
Dora on several occasions at a coffee-shop close, but not
too close, to the TS building in Hunter St. Our
conversations always had the same refrain: how
unfortunate it was that this 'trouble' should erupt right
now and distract from the serious and timely issues the
TS was working on – like the economic challenges facing
individuals in this new, post-war era of the 1920s, and the
need to focus on 'ways of being' that nourished the higher
aspects of the human psyche. Our discussions always
ended on the same hopeful note: when Dr Besant would
arrive in Sydney, she'd sort things out.

CHAPTER 10

CHANGES IN THE GROUP DYNAMICS

On the morning of May 9th, I mentioned to Mum&Dad at breakfast that I'd be joining my Theosophical friends to welcome Dr Besant as her train arrived at Central Station. Dr Besant's original plan had been to attend the Sydney TS Convention, however her departure from India had been delayed by urgent business relating to Self-rule.

When she arrived in Australia there was TS business to attend to in Perth and other Australian cities, and this was how it came about that she'd travelled right across our continent by train. The journey was long and arduous, involving four train-changes due to the lack of a uniform rail gauge across the country. It was a gruelling trip for any traveller, let alone a woman now aged seventy-five.

"What time will Dr Besant arrive at Central?" Dad asked. When told she was due at 9.30 am, he said he'd try to catch a glimpse of her as he walked through the station *en route* to his office. "It's not often we have such a noteworthy visitor to Sydney," he remarked.

When the Melbourne-to-Sydney Express pulled in at Central Station, it was a surprisingly vigorous woman who emerged from her carriage to greet the waiting crowd. The official welcoming party comprised Bishop Leadbeater in full regalia surrounded by a group of boys and several girls, as well as many TS identities including Krishnamurti and Nitya. The two brothers had spent the past ten days in the Blue Mountains west of Sydney, where it was hoped the fresh air might improve Nitya's health, his TB having recurred

Dr Besant was an interesting figure: short, rotund and swathed in white garments from head to toe. With gracious equanimity, she accepted the adulation of the crowd, the huge bouquets of flowers and the popping of the press photographers' flashbulbs, then departed in a black limousine for her hotel.

"Whatever will happen now is in the lap of the gods," said Antonia, who was standing next to me. This seemed to sum up the general mood.

The next time we all met up was a week later at a crowded TS assembly at the Kings Hall. This meeting had been called in order to support Bishop Leadbeater within the TS and the Liberal Catholic Church. The auditorium was packed, word having got around that a 'bloodletting' was imminent.

Throughout the meeting, a strong atmosphere of dissent was evident, with many of those present feeling they were not given the chance to air their views. Mr Martyn was eventually granted leave to speak and, standing on a chair in order to be seen as well as heard, was applauded vigorously by his supporters.

He described how, while in England the year before, he'd met with Dr Besant with the express purpose of discussing the topic of clerical immorality within the Liberal Catholic Church, of which he had in his possession an item of written evidence. To his surprise and disappointment, Dr Besant refused to engage with him at all on this subject. Her stance, and its contrast with her public championing of the fearless pursuit of truth, had caused him to seriously question her integrity.

Another of Mr Martyn's concerns was the matter of the Liberal Catholic Church and its increasing association with the TS. He told his listeners that, in his view, the Liberal Catholic Church 'struck at the very root' of TS neutrality towards organized religions. He concluded his address by expressing the hope that when Dr Besant came to know the whole story, she would forgive herself for having made certain statements in the recent past.

A motion condemning disloyalty was then rushed through, reported the next day (May 18th) in the newspaper *Truth* as: '. . . A vote was taken for and against, and although the scribe of *Truth* used all his astral and physical sight, it was difficult to say which side had won . . .' [19]

Immediately following the meeting, Mr Martyn put into action his intention of contacting the newspapers with his concerns regarding clerical immorality and minors.

Dr Besant responded to this public airing of the TS's personal business swiftly and decisively. First, she said that anyone with concerns about moral probity matters should contact the police, then she expelled the Loyalty League members from the Esoteric Section and split the Sydney Lodge into two separate entities. A new home, Blavatsky Lodge, was created for the Loyalists, with Sydney Lodge to now be the domain of the Dissidents.

Naturally, the press had a field day at the expense of the Sydney TS. The story attracted extensive coverage over the next few weeks, and considerable space was provided in their Letters section for the airing of various views.

Some newspapers took a general slant on the topic, with headlines such as 'Theosophical Split, Stormy Meeting Last Night' (*Daily Telegraph*), 'A Night Out, Theosophists' Wild Meeting' (*The Sun*) and 'Theosophical Storm, Bishop Leadbeater Upheld' (*Daily Mail*). Others took an unpleasantly coarse approach, with headlines such as 'Where Leadbeater Bishes' and

---

[19] John Cooper, Theosophical Crisis in Australia: the story of the breakup of the Theosophical Society in Sydney from 1913 until 1923. (Sydney: University of Sydney, 1986), 248.

'Leadbeater a Swish Bish with Boys'[20]. Krishnamurti and Nitya came in for their fair share of attention, too, with 'Dandy Coloured Coons' being one particularly offensive reference. [21]

The *Daily Telegraph* dispatched a journalist to attend a service St Albans, the Liberal Catholic church. His report included the following:

'. . . Bishop Leadbeater, clad in a stiff gold robe, wearing a high scarlet and gold mitre, and carrying a gold crozier, passed among his flock waving a white-gloved hand, upon which is his bishop's ring, in Apostolic blessing.

'One was remarkably struck by the great lack of simplicity, which completely faded from one's mind before the Oriental splendour and the words of high thought and mystic suggestion which fell from the lips of the priests . . .'[22]

After three turbulent weeks in Sydney, Dr Besant returned to India, describing her trip to Sydney as merely an interlude in her work, 'and not a very pleasant one.'[23]

Within the TS, the predominant mood was one of shock and sadness. Deep rifts appeared among members and these cut across a number of cherished beliefs and long friendships. Ambrose, Antonia and Dora were greatly affected by the events but could get no respite from them, with Ambrose and Dora residing at The Manor where debate often raged far into the night, and Antonia living-in at Morven Garden School where the latest events were constantly dissected by parents and staff.

---

[20] Ibid., 243.
[21] Lutyens, Krishnamurti,145, quoting from a Krishnamurti's letter to Lady Emily Lutyens 2.6.22.
[22] Cooper, Theosophical Crisis in Sydney, 1968, 253.
[23] Ibid., 280

Although I had a lot of university work to do over the next week, I was of course wondering how my TS friends were getting on. I didn't need to speculate for long, however, as one late afternoon when I emerged from a psychology tutorial I found the three of them waiting for me.

"We thought we'd give you a surprise!" Ambrose said, with Dora adding, "And we wanted a break from 'things Theosophical', too."

"Let's go get us all a drink," Ambrose suggested. "Where do you-all hang out here on campus, Ed?" I explained that the answer was 'nowhere', for in fact there was no place within the university grounds where male and female students could congregate in this way.

Ambrose stared at me. "You've gotta be kidding . . . you're not telling me it's . . . *segregated*, are you?"

I had to tell him that this was indeed the case. He shook his head in disbelief and murmured, "Quaint custom," as though filing it away for regaling to his friends when he returned to the States. I explained that mixed groups of students usually gathered off-campus at one of the nearby public houses, or 'pubs', as they were called, in Glebe Point Road, and so we set off for one of them.

The pub we entered was, at this hour, rapidly filling with university students, office workers and a sprinkling of locals. We managed to find a spare table and, after getting our drinks and eats, we settled in to discuss the current state of play in the TS. Most members were still trying to absorb the events in this unpredictable drama which was still unfolding via articles and letters to the newspapers penned by the leading lights on both sides.

One fresh development was the voluntary visit to the Police Department by a group of Leadbeater's 'boys', both past and present, including Krishnamurti and Nitya. They were interviewed by several detectives with 'reporters' (possibly official note-takers) present. Each one of them emphatically denied ever witnessing or participating in any activities of an immoral nature involving Bishop Leadbeater.

"The saddest thing about this whole wretched business," Antonia remarked, "is how everyone involved is acting out of genuine concern for what they feel is best for the Society. And the result? A deep rift that may never be healed." This was so obviously true there was no point in saying anything further and we all stared gloomily into our drinks.

Then a voice said, "Mind if I join you?" and we looked up to see Dr Herbst advancing upon us, a brimming schooner of beer in his hand.

To my surprise, Ambrose answered: "Of course, Max." Quickly getting to his feet, he fetched another chair and placed it between Dora and me.

As I had no idea that the three of them even knew Dr Herbst, let alone were on first name terms with him, I sat there in shock.

"You know Ed, of course," said Ambrose.

"One of my star students," Dr Herbst replied in his typical sardonic way. "At least I can vouch that he's doing his dissertation fieldwork," and they all laughed.

I must admit I felt quite disconcerted at finding myself in such an informal context and close proximity with Dr Herbst. Fortunately, he stayed only a few minutes, mainly talking with Dora about how her father, Karl van Gelder, was coping at The Manor with so many differing viewpoints under the one roof. I was totally silent while Dr Herbst was with us, but no-one seemed to notice.

After he'd gone, I said, "I can't believe you called him 'Max'!" and they all laughed.

"What'd you think we'd call him – Maximilian?" Antonia asked.

"His full name is Herr Doktor Maximilian von Herbenstein," Dora enunciated. "He shortened it when he came to Australia after the War. We've known him for a while now, he seems to quite like mixing with Theosophists and he's a good friend of my father's. Both being Europeans, they enjoy comparing notes on some of the strange customs in this barbaric paradise they've landed in."

"Like segregated cafes for male and female university students," drawled Ambrose.

As we were getting up to leave, Antonia suddenly said, "Oh, Ed! We haven't told you our news! You'll never guess, so I'll tell you," she continued, her eyes shining, "Ambrose and I are going on a long sea voyage to India and then across the Pacific Ocean to America!"

I gazed at them both with a courteous, expression. "What, together?" I asked.

Antonia laughed. "No, certainly not! My mother would never allow that. We will be travelling in a group of twelve married Theosophists with their children, strictly chaperoned, I can assure you. And because I'm a primary-school teacher, I'll be employed during the voyage to supervise the children's lessons. Then when we reach India I'll be teaching them at Adyar, where we'll stay before going on to The States!"

"How wonderful! What a great experience!" I exclaimed, sounding suitably enthusiastic. "And when will all this come about?"

"Very soon. In fact, we'll sail in two weeks' time," replied Antonia. "It's all a bit of a whirlwind, but it'll be wonderful to get away from Sydney with all this trouble swirling around.

"We'll be having a farewell party," she continued, "to which of course you're invited. You'll receive an invitation pretty soon."

As I set off for Redfern Station to catch the train back home to Stanmore, I felt strangely melancholy. Although I'd known the three Theosophists for just a few months, things would not be the same with two of them gone. A few days later, the invitation arrived, requesting the pleasure of my company at a 'Going-Away Party' to be held a large Kings Cross hotel on the next Thursday evening from 5 to 7pm.

CHAPTER 11

AN ENDING, AND
A BEGINNING

The next day at university, Russell Fletcher told me he'd been invited to the farewell party too, and we agreed to go there together. So, on the appointed evening, Russell and I took a tram from the university into the city, then walked the five blocks up William St to Kings Cross, or as most people called it, 'The Cross'. I told Russell I wasn't going to stay for long, citing pressure of assignments, and he said he'd leave when I left, being under various kinds of pressures of his own.

We located the hotel easily enough and were ushered into a large, brightly-lit reception room. Here, a pianist was playing loud music on a honky-tonk piano while several couples gyrated madly on a small circular dance floor. I was surprised to see so many guests, but apparently the Theosophical group bound for India had combined forces to host the party.

Antonia and Ambrose were completely surrounded by well-wishers so I just waved to them across the room and chatted with a number of people, including Antonia's siblings and her mother, Clara. I was not enjoying the party, however, and after a decent interval, judged I could take my leave. Elbowing my way through the crowd to Antonia and Ambrose, I wished them 'Bon Voyage' and was just turning to go when Antonia caught hold of my hand.

"Don't forget us, Ed," she said. "We won't forget *you* – you're a very special friend, did you know that?"

"I'll miss you both," I replied. "Send me the odd postcard, won't you."

"We surely will!" Antonia told me. And then she kissed me – on the cheek.

Ambrose hugged me, saying, "Ed, you know what? I call you my 'Aussie brother' – and we'll be friends for life! Get through your studies and come see us in the States!"

"I certainly will," I replied warmly, my heart sinking. Obviously, they weren't planning to return to Sydney any time soon.

As Russell and I left the hotel, I noted that the music emanating from the pianola had changed and now the saccharine strains of 'In an English Country Garden'[24] wafted through the air. I'd never liked this song and it struck me as particularly ironic that my exit from Antonia's life should be accompanied by its syrupy cadences.

The next afternoon the ship, with its cargo of Theosophical passengers, steamed out of Sydney Harbour – whereupon I plunged into an extremely peculiar and unwelcome mental state. To myself, I frankly admitted I was 'lovelorn', and thanked my lucky stars I was sane enough to recognize the absurdity of my state and able to observe my symptoms with at least a modicum of clinical detachment.

Several weeks passed. Apart from the world seeming strangely lack-lustre, which was something I'd never experienced before, I had completely lost interest in food. It didn't take Mum long to notice this, and one evening at dinner she announced: "Ed, I'm worried about you. You're not eating much these days and you're looking a bit peaky."

---

[24] Composer: Australian-born Percy Grainger.

Luckily Dad came to my rescue, saying stoutly: "Nonsense, Mum, he's the picture of health. Probably working a bit too hard, but it was his own choice to keep on with the study this year."

I made a mental note to eat more during family meals. It was imperative that no-one should divine my inner state. Antonia had never given the slightest indication she regarded me as anything more than a friend and, moreover, it was clear she had eyes only for Ambrose Mortimer, and he for her.

I applied some of the TS maxims to myself, including 'Find happiness through service to others', so I went out of my way to be more helpful to the people around me. It worked to a certain extent and at least it kept me occupied.

One day Dad and I were in the garden pruning the bean-stalks when he said out of the blue, "Of course, nature abhors a vacuum."

I turned and stared at him.

"Meaning?"

"Oh, nothing really," he replied mildly. "You'll miss your friends for a while but others will come to take their place."

"Of course," I replied. "In the summer break I'll go out a fair bit, I imagine."

To the outside world, I carried on as if nothing untoward had happened. But inside, I felt quite bereft. I tried to 'look on the bright side' but I was unconvinced. Now that I'd completed my dissertation fieldwork, there was no pressing need to attend the Tuesday night TS meetings. However, I did go from time to time and enjoyed catching up with Dora and Joyce Housman and a few others I'd got to know. I also attended some of the Monday evening psychology talks, and occasionally saw Dr Herbst there. One evening as we were both leaving, he told me he enjoyed the TS psychology discussions because he found them generally 'more invigorating and open-minded' than those he had with university colleagues.

I tried to make the best of my miserable situation by acknowledging I'd now gained a keener awareness of certain aberrant mental states and read the poignant case-histories of patients chronicled by Freud, Jung and William James with much more more empathy. Their testimonies of personal anguish certainly put my own small difficulty into stark relief. As well, the routine of life at home with Mum&Dad had a useful stabilizing effect.

Several months passed. In November, with my dissertation now submitted and out of the way, I embarked on a determined campaign to gain greater social experience – namely to get to know a few girls. I re-appeared at my local tennis club, attended a number of Christmas parties and did in fact achieve some of my aims – in short, I was no longer quite the callow youth I'd been at the start of the year. Gradually, I regained my mental equilibrium, but catching sight of a young woman on the train who slightly resembled Antonia, or even walking past one of the cafes we'd frequented as a group could trigger a nostalgic daydream.

In late December, a letter bearing American stamps landed in our letterbox. It was addressed to 'The Best Family' and, in her neat handwriting, Antonia had written:

> Dear Mr and Mrs Best and Ed,
>
> How are you all? Sydney seems so far away and we do miss all our friends. The sea voyage to Colombo was magical with various stops along the way – so exotic!
>
> From Colombo we travelled up the east coast of India by train and after five days arrived at

Adyar, near Madras.[25] What a beautiful place – I'd heard about it ever since I was a child, of course, but never dreamed I'd ever be there!

The highlight of our stay at Adyar was – our wedding!! Ambrose suddenly got the idea that we should be married and so it was all arranged, in a matter of days. I wore a beautiful sari lent to me by one of the residents, and Ambrose was resplendent in a rather odd mixture of Indian clothes – anything that would fit him, really. There were about 50 guests and during the balmy evening we feasted and danced under a full moon. Our only regret is that my family and our Sydney friends were not here to share the happy occasion with us.

From India we travelled by boat to San Francisco, a beautiful city that's a bit like Sydney. I enjoyed the trip, apart from getting seasick – I'm obviously not a great sailor! We have decided to stay for a while at the Theosophical 'commune' in the Ojai (they pronounce it 'O-high') Valley here in California. And you won't believe who's also here – Krishnamurti and Nitya and their inner circle!! They're some distance from us and rather keep to themselves, but it is wonderful to know they're our neighbours!

Yours,
Antonia and Ambrose Mortimer

P.S: Ed – I am hoping Sydney friends will write to me when they are not too busy. I'd love

---

[25] In 1969, Madras became Chennai.

to hear how you're going and the latest TS news.
Our address is: and then came their address.

"Well I never!" exclaimed Mum when I told her about the wedding. "That was quick work, wasn't it! They only left Sydney a few months ago. Did you have any inkling this was in the air, Ed?"

"No, none at all," I replied.

I glanced at Dad, who was looking thoughtful. "What's going through your head, Dad?" I enquired.

"Oh, nothing really," he answered. "I was just wondering if a wedding ceremony conducted in that fashion in India would be considered legal in the state of New South Wales, Australia, that's all."

"Well," said Mum. "So long as they're happy, that's really all that matters. Do write to the girl, Ed, she's a long way from home and I'm sure she'd love to hear from you."

Mum displayed Antonia's letter on the mantelpiece over our fireplace and showed it to The Aunts the next time they visited. After a few weeks I took it up to my room and, carefully noting down the address, stored it away with my dissertation notes. The letter was like a postscript to a now-finished chapter in my life . . .

PART 2
1923 to 1925

CONTENTS

CHAPTER 12

JANUARY – JUNE 1923

I was longing to write to Antonia, but curbed the impulse until after the New Year. On January 3, 1923 I posted my letter to the address in the Ojai Valley, California, USA where Antonia now resided with her husband, Ambrose Mortimer. The letter contained news of recent events in Sydney, particularly those pertaining to the TS. I also mentioned that Dr Herbst had responded favourably to my psychology dissertation, awarding two other students and me the top marks for the year. I told her that 1923 would see me let loose on the general public to work as a novice doctor in a family-care practice and ended by saying if she wished to hear more about Theosophical topics, I'd be happy to research them. This wouldn't be at all onerous, as I intended to keep up my links with the TS by attending some of their Monday evening psychology lectures.

Although internally I felt somewhat flat, my conscious decision to turn my mind off Antonia and get to know other girls was paying dividends. Interestingly, a certain amount of Ambrose's confidence and general savoir-faire seemed to have rubbed off on me, judging by the number of invitations to parties and dances I received. Starting work as a new doctor in a busy general practice was also good for me. Seeing people with serious physical and/or mental problems coping heroically with their lot in life put my own self-inflicted state into perspective.

In due course, a letter arrived postmarked California and addressed to me. Antonia wrote that despite missing her family and friends in Sydney, she was enjoying her new life with Ambrose in a Theosophical community in the Ojai Valley. She'd mentioned in her previous letter that Krishnamurti, his brother Nitya and entourage were also living in the valley. Now, she wrote that Krishnamurti was undergoing some sort of strange 'Process' that involved considerable physical pain and mental anguish and left him completely drained after each episode.

Then came what was for me far the most interesting part of her letter:

On the boat across the Pacific Ocean from India to San Francisco I suffered from severe seasickness. It improved somewhat when we finally landed and for a few weeks in the Ojai Valley I felt fine except for bouts of nausea. Ambrose was very kind, but I couldn't help feeling bad that I wasn't the same healthy, energetic girl I was in Sydney.

I decided to go see a doctor and told him of my vague symptoms, finishing with the words: "I don't know, maybe I haven't really adjusted to married life . . ." He examined me, then said, "Well, Mrs Mortimer, I think you've adjusted very well to married life – you're approximately five months pregnant."

When I heard this, I almost fainted! Truly, you could have knocked me down with a feather! The doctor wrote something on my patient card and announced: "Baby is due in four months' time."

I managed to gasp out, "But I can't be five months pregnant – I've only been married three months," whereupon he said nothing but gave a little smirk which I found extremely offensive.

I staggered back home and told Ambrose the news. He was just as shocked as I was and he also knew the due date the doctor had told me couldn't possibly be correct. After a few days, we telephoned his parents over in Connecticut with our news. They were ecstatic, saying they'd always longed to be grandparents and had given up on Ambrose's three older sisters ever settling down and producing the next generation.

We ourselves don't feel quite so enthusiastic, as the thought of 'starting a family' was not remotely in our minds. Still, we are adjusting to our new status.

Everyone around us is jubilant and this helps a lot. As they say over here, 'Life sure does pack a few unexpected punches'.

Please say hello to your parents and tell them our news. Keep well, and do write when you have a spare moment.

Yours
Antonia

PS: Ambrose says "Howdy and come visit with us over here soon." (I'm starting to sound quite American myself, would you believe!)

I re-read the letter several times, ending up with a helpless sense that, as the months passed by and life took its course, Antonia was receding further and further away. I told Mum&Dad about the baby news and they were pleased, Mum more than Dad because she loved the thought of a new baby. Dad simply remarked, "Quick work, but good luck to them." I realised that my best and, in truth, my *only* course of action regarding Antonia was to write friendly letters keeping her informed on the events unfolding in the TS.

During the next few months I attended a few meetings of the Dissidents at the Sydney Lodge and also of the Loyalists at Blavatsky Lodge. Both Lodges were confident in their views, but I grew weary of trying to sift fact from rumour, which was well-nigh impossible as each camp was equally outraged by the actions of the other.

Theosophists in general are thoughtful and articulate, which can lead to prolific and impassioned communications, both spoken and written. Wishing to gather some different perspectives on the furore, one evening after finishing work I visited the Public Library of NSW and spent an interesting few hours reading through the press coverage on the TS 'troubles' of 1922.

Although I found the cynical and sneering tone of much of the reporting in the *Daily Telegraph* and *Truth* quite tiresome, it did provide another window on the events of the previous year. At least with newspapers, I could simply stop reading them and take a short walk outside the library when needed, which was preferable to being cornered by a steamed-up Theosophist wanting to air a passionately-held view on the current state of play.

Apart from the central issue of Bishop Leadbeater and the Liberal Catholic Church, there were other matters of concern for many TS members. It seemed that every topic I researched contained a mass of contradictions, one example of this being the way in which Dr Besant was perceived.

I still saw Dora van Gelder quite often, although she was very busy with her meditation and health groups. Dora had been greatly impressed by Dr Besant when she'd attended some of Dr Besant's public lectures in Sydney. According to Dora, Dr Besant '. . . had such a tremendous presence when she spoke . . . The power of her expression made you feel that here you were in the presence of a great person but also much bigger than she actually was . . . When there was a tremendous uproar she was a very, very quiet person. A person can be a great orator and yet convey the presence of quietness. . . she projected quiet, peace and strength – and no excitement whatsoever. She never responded in a violent way; with all the waves of opposition, none of that ever appeared. Whatever she said was firm and at no time was ever antagonistic. She just stated the facts and I was enormously impressed by her quiet strength.'[26]

A very different view of Dr Besant, however, was expressed by an ex-TS identity – Mrs Alice Leighton Cleather. Mrs Cleather's association with Theosophy went back to 1887, when, as a young married Englishwoman with two sons, she'd met Madame Blavatsky and become her loyal disciple. Although by 1899 Mrs Cleather had rejected organized Theosophy, her devotion to Madame Blavatsky and all she stood for never wavered. Having closely studied Blavatsky's writings, she could speak with authority on this subject and had made her own contributions to the field of 'Theosophia'.

Mrs Cleather maintained that Annie Besant had tampered with Madame Blavatsky's writings for her own ends and, being the sole possessor of some original Blavatsky material, she was in a strong position make this claim. On the question of who might succeed Madame Blavatsky as head of the TS, Mrs Cleather's answer, reputedly, was: 'No-one.' She viewed all possible contenders for the role including the front-runner, Mrs Besant, as quite unworthy of the honour. Naturally, this did not endear Mrs Cleather to Annie Besant.

By coincidence, soon after I'd read about Mrs Cleather in a *Truth* article, I bumped into Dr Herbst, (or 'Max' as I now called him, being no longer his student) at a TS lecture and asked if he knew of her.

"Mrs Alice Cleather? What a character!" he responded delightedly. "Do you know, I met her just a few months ago. She was here in Sydney with her companion, Mr Basil Woodward Crump. He's an ex-barrister twenty-one years her junior who's published on the subject of

---

[26] Van Gelder and Chesley, A Most Unusual Life, 53-54.

Wagnerian opera as seen through Theosophical eyes. The two of them travel the world giving slide lectures with a musical accompaniment."

"How enterprising," I remarked, having really no idea about it.

Max, however, had more to impart. "Mrs Cleather's had an amazing life. She told me how in 1918 when she and Basil Crump and her son were travelling to India, their ship was sunk by German torpedoes. The three of them managed to scramble into a lifeboat and were rescued, then simply continued on with their adventures in India. Not bad for a woman of seventy-two, eh?"

Mrs Cleather and Mr Crump arrived in Sydney in February 1923, ostensibly for their health but, in some people's view, more to meddle in TS matters. Soon after their arrival, they were invited to speak at Sydney Lodge and, in line with Mrs Cleather's general distain for everyone in the TS, she had some caustic words to share on the subject of Dr Besant and Bishop Leadbeater, both of whom she'd known since the 1880s:

'So long as Madame Blavatsky was alive, Mrs Besant was all right because Madame Blavatsky was the master mind (sic). However, when Madame Blavatsky died, Mrs Besant's ambitious spirit got the upper hand. It was always her ambition to be a world teacher.'

As for CWL, her verdict was: 'Leadbeater is a menace to the growing generation'. [27]

Blavatsky Lodge reacted swiftly to Mrs Cleather's 'slanderous words' by voting for the expulsion of Sydney Lodge from the section, and its leaders from the Society. In June, Sydney Lodge's charter was formally withdrawn and the Esoteric Section diplomas of twelve prominent members cancelled. This action was indeed drastic, and indicated how bitter the rift in the TS had become.

---

[27] Reported in *Truth* newspaper 18.2.1923, cited in Cooper, Theosophical Crisis in Sydney, 1968, 321.

By now, I'd learned a bit more about the Esoteric Section, or the ES as it was often called. Established in 1888 by Madame Blavatsky, the ES was an intrinsic part of the TS, an inner section devoted to the Society's third Object, namely: 'To investigate unexplained laws of Nature and the powers latent in the human being'. TS members could apply to join the ES and, upon being accepted, embarked on a course of training to facilitate their progress along the Spiritual Path, with diplomas issued at various stages. Members of the ES were bound by an oath of secrecy and loyalty to the head of the Society.

One evening over a cup of coffee after a TS psychology lecture, I asked Max what he knew about the ES. As a non-member, he naturally did not know its innermost intricacies, however he did offer this:

"Say what you will about Madame Blavatsky, she was a very astute old lady. She knew that since freedom of thought and belief was a central tenet of the TS, there was a tendency for people to drift away from the Society once the initial excitement wore off. In other words, it was all a bit vague. The concept of the ES was the work of genius, with its clearly marked stages along the Spiritual Path.

"When the ES became part of Blavatsky Lodge," he went on, "the Sydney Lodge lost quite a chunk of its 'pulling power.' As I often say in lectures, never underestimate human beings' need for structure and a sense of belonging. These are strong uniting instincts, yet ones that, paradoxically, can tear groups apart."

His observation brought to mind a newspaper clipping from the *Brisbane Telegraph* I'd come across at the Public Library recently. I opened my notebook and read out what the Brisbane Lodge Secretary, Mr G.W. Morris, had to say about the 'Sydney troubles' of 1922:

"... The basis of the trouble in Sydney is to my mind this: we have in our Society what is called the Catholic type, and also the Puritan type – the very antithesis of each other. The Catholics wanted a church, with the old ritual included, and it was given them, based on the Theosophical spirit which permits freedom of thought to every individual. It was to avoid any clash with the Puritans that the church was made a thing separate from the Society itself. And yet, you cannot separate the church from the society in spirit, because every member of it is a Theosophist."

"Couldn't have put it better myself," Max responded, and on this note we finished our session for the evening.

As I walked through the now-quiet streets towards Wynyard Station, my thoughts turned to Max. Any conversation with him was bound to be interesting, yet almost everything I knew about him came from others. Although he must be in his fifties, he never 'pulled rank' on life experience or superior academic standing. Definitely, he was 'a cat that walked by himself,' who seldom mentioned anything of his personal history or current life. However, for a clear-sighted appraisal on any topic you might name, you could always count on Max Herbst.

By the time I'd taken the train to Stanmore and made my way home to Ethel St, it was after ten pm and Mum&Dad had retired for the night. Mum, however, had left a postcard addressed to me on the kitchen table where I'd be sure to see it when I came in.

CHAPTER 13

LETTERS ACROSS THE OCEAN

Antonia's postcard contained the news that she and Ambrose would be moving from California to live with his parents on the east coast of USA in Greenwich, Connecticut before the birth of the baby. A letter would follow, but she did want friends in Australia to know that she'd soon have a new address, and she'd love to find a few letters awaiting her when they reached their new home.

I was delighted to hear from Antonia, and wondered how she felt about moving again so soon after arriving in California, and what it'd be like living with Ambrose's parents. The only way to find out was to write another letter, something I'd been planning to do anyway. Accordingly, even though it was now quite late in the evening, I wrote Antonia a fairly lengthy account of some recent TS developments.

Although she might already know from others much of what I wrote about, I was keen to maintain the thread of our common topic. I related how Bishop Leadbeater's name had been removed from the foundation stone of the King's Hall building, now home to the Sydney Lodge, and how Dr Besant had described this deed as 'a very petty and childish action, but one showing a strange depth of hatred.'[28]

As well, I told her about Mrs Alice Cleather and Mr Basil Crump and their visit to Sydney, and how outraged

---

[28] Cooper, Theosophical Crisis in Australia, 1986, 214.

Theosophists had described her as 'the vitriolic ex-Theosophist' and her published views as 'scandalous attacks'. [29]

Soon after posting my letter, I attended an occasion I thought Antonia might like to hear about, so dashed off a note while it was fresh in my mind:

Dear Antonia

This is just to fill you in about a recent event.

At 3.30 pm on Thursday June 28 about 100 people assembled on a steep and rocky site at Balmoral Beach to witness the 'turning of the first sod of earth' ceremony by Bishop Leadbeater to mark the start of building work on the Star Amphitheatre. The day, although fairly chilly, was sunny with a brisk breeze coming in straight off the Pacific Ocean through the Sydney Harbour Heads (in other words, we froze!).

The crowd included a number of TS identities, many of whom were 'Founders' – i.e people who've already fully paid for their seats in the auditorium. I didn't see a lot of familiar faces, probably as it was

[29] Ibid., 332.

my account will be the first to reach you.
a weekday, but this may also mean that

With the wind whipping at his purple cassock, Bishop L wielded a hefty shovel to do the honours regarding the sod. After this, the Founders formed into a large circle inside which Bishop L faced the four points of the compass giving Readings at each one and then did the same from the centre of the circle for the zenith and nadir. Before each Reading, the gathering chorused, "May the Angels of the (North, South and so on) bestow their blessings". And in the middle of the ceremony an inquisitive wallaby bounded through the clearing. Everyone was thrilled and of course viewed it as an omen for success.

Bishop L recited (in Pali) the Buddhist 'Three-fold Refuge' and the 'Five Precepts', then the ceremony closed with a chorus of "Thanks be to GOD". The gathering then dispersed rapidly, eager to get out of the now icy wind. It was an occasion marked by great collective goodwill towards a very courageous venture.   Yours, Ed.

From time to time, I enjoyed attending a TS psychology lecture on a Monday evening and then adjourning to a nearby café. Naturally, we'd have preferred to hold our discussions at a pub over a glass of beer, but this was out of the question. By law, hotels closed their doors at 6 pm, a fact often cited by 'foreigners' as evidence of Australia as a country of philistines.

One evening Max, who'd also been at the lecture, said he'd like to consult me 'as a medical man' about a certain individual. I told him I was not competent to diagnose illnesses sight unseen, and probably never would be, but Max waved aside my protestations saying, "Your psychology degree equips you with a much greater understanding of human nature than a person with only a medical degree, you know that."

I conceded he was correct on this point and, after ordering some coffee, we made our way to a quiet table. Here, Max explained that he'd been asked to give his opinion on some mysterious symptoms exhibited by a young man in another country.

"Quite a tall order, I'd imagine," I remarked. "Have you ever met this person?"

"Several times down the years," Max replied. "I am able to provide a case history of sorts which may assist you in diagnosing what's up with him."

"How have you acquired your information?" was my next question.

"Let's just say I've been contacted by a 'concerned friend', and leave it at that, shall we?" he replied. "I will simply refer to the young man as 'X'."

"Very well. Please proceed," I told him.

"X is now aged in his late 20s. He was born in another country, spoke a different language and had a different religion. His mother died when he was about eleven and he was then brought up by his father and older siblings. Money was always fairly tight. He is very close to his younger brother, whose health is currently poor. X himself had a few illnesses as a child, including malaria. At the age of thirteen, he was taken up by a group of foreigners who inducted him into their belief-system and subsequently took him and his brother away from their father to be educated overseas. X was well looked after by his guardians, who ensured that the two boys received a sound education, X being trained to take up a high-ranking role within the guardians' organization, and his brother studying law. All was proceeding as planned until X suddenly began to experience a mysterious condition whereby he now suffers recurring bouts of intense pain and mental torment, for which there appears no physical cause or remedy. Now – Ed, what would you say? What do you think is the matter with this young man?"

"I wonder if I'm the right person to consult, Max," I demurred. "Wouldn't this be more in the line of territory for some of your more esoteric friends – you know, maybe do a séance, or a spot of astral travel? What kind of a doctor would I be to diagnose someone sight unseen, in another country and without the benefit of any medical or psychological test results?"

"Settle down, Ed," Max replied robustly. "Just look around you and you'll see we're in a café, not a clinic or consulting room. Simply tell me what you think, off the top of your head. That's all I ask of you."

"Right-oh then, I will," I replied, and after a minute said cautiously:

"Several aspects stand out here, the main one being that this young man has experienced a number of dislocations and losses in his early life – death of mother, change of language and religion, loss of father and replacement by people of a very different culture and even appearance, though you've not been specific on this. Throw into this brew some serious medical episodes and you have quite enough valid reasons for this young man to feel somewhat discombobulated."

" 'Discombobulated'? Meaning – what?" Max asked. "I thought I knew most of the English words, but that one's new to me."

"It's a fancy way of saying 'confused'," I told him.

He laughed. "Is that so? Well, I certainly agree – he has every reason to feel confused. So now – do you think this strange malady is physical in origin, or psychological, or a bit of both?"

"There are enough factors present for some kind of psychological trauma that has now come to the surface and is being expressed physically," I replied.

"Because he feels unable to deal with something in his life in any other way?" Max queried.

I nodded. "Quite possibly, but at the same time there could be any number of physical reasons for this . . . ah . . . 'process'."

When I uttered the word 'process', it struck a chord in my memory.

"Wait a minute, Max!" I exclaimed, "You're not talking about . . . Krishnamurti, by any chance, are you?"

Max looked at me in surprise. "I certainly am. But how did you guess?"

"Because someone else used the word 'process' recently to describe a similar set of symptoms experienced by Krishnamurti and, pairing that with the case history of 'X', it suddenly all clicked."

Max laughed. "Miraculous. I'll buy you another coffee on that one, Ed."

While he was organizing for the coffees to be brought to our table, I looked at the clock. Although it was getting quite late, I thought if we stayed talking for another half hour I'd learn a lot. When Krishnamurti had come to Sydney the previous year, I'd observed his courteous and somewhat detached demeanor at a number of Theosophical gatherings. Then later I'd seen the vehemence of his defence of Bishop Leadbeater when questions were raised concerning CWL's moral conduct. I remembered being surprised at the contrast in his bearing.

Max returned carrying a plate of potato chips and told me the coffee would be along soon. As I helped myself to a handful of chips, I asked him to expand on his brief account of Krishnamurti's life.

"I will," he said, "but it's going to take longer than you might think, and look – they're getting ready to close up shop."

It was true – the café staff were busily stacking chairs and moving tables ready to mop down the tiled floor. We gulped down our coffees and agreed to meet for lunch at the Sydney University Union during the next week.

When I arrived back home, a letter from Antonia lay on the kitchen table. Eagerly, I tore open the envelope and read what she had to say:

Dear Ed,

Thank you for your letter – it is wonderful to know the latest news from Sydney. Apologies for the delay in writing, but a lot's been happening.

To continue from where I left off – as you know, I was not impressed by the doctor I saw back in California and neither were Ambrose and his parents – his father apparently has no faith in anyone on the West Coast of America – "A bunch of cowboys," according to him.

We came East because Ambrose's mother and father (who insist I call them Narne (pronounced NARN) and Pappi in readiness for their new roles) felt strongly that we should stay with them until the birth. Narne said she knew of a marvellous 'baby doctor' and

I was thankful to go along with her suggestion. We travelled in a very luxurious train for several days right across America to Grand Central Station, New York City where a chauffeured car was waiting to take us to Greenwich, Connecticut, about an hour and a half's drive north. I can tell you, Ed, it was sheer bliss to have everything taken care of like this. When we arrived at Narne and Pappi's house (which was extremely large), they were waiting out front for us, beaming with welcome.

Narne's 'baby-doctor' turned out to be a gem – kindly, knowledgeable and polite. When I waddled into his consulting room he probably thought I was going to give birth on the spot, but he masked any surprise admirably and simply asked questions about my general health and when I thought the baby might be due. To my embarrassment, I burst into tears and sobbingly told him that the baby could only be due nine months after our wedding day. He listened to this in a courteous way (unlike that quack back in California!), then examined me and asked one question, "Is there a history of twins in your family, Mrs Mortimer?" To which I answered, "Yes, my grandmother gave birth to two sets of twins."

"Well," he replied. "I have a strong hunch that you are following in your grandmother's footsteps. If I'm not mistaken, you are expecting twins."

Well, Ed, for the second time since arriving in America you could have knocked me down with a feather!!! The doctor calculated the due date, warning that twins often arrive early, and said to come back in a week's time.

I tottered out to the waiting room and told Ambrose, who went white with shock but quickly recovered. When we arrived back home and shared our news with Narne and Pappi, they were absolutely thrilled – again far more than Ambrose and me, but their joy was lovely to behold.

So – to cut a long story short we, Antonia and Ambrose Mortimer, are now the parents of twins – Ambrose (named after Pappi, and also of course after my Ambrose) and Ingrid (which is Narne's real name) – who are now 3 weeks old. (Born exactly 9 months after our wedding day, I might add!) Ambrose is still in shock at his swift transition from carefree Sydney bachelor to 'married man, father of twins'. Sometimes he looks at me with a bemused expression, but I just laugh and say 'It's all beyond my control!'

We plan to visit Sydney to show off our two little bundles of joy as soon as they're old enough to travel. Narne and Pappi are the envy of their friends and make me feel like the cleverest girl in the world. Still, even though all is good here, I'd really rather be back in dear old Sydney!

Do write soon, Ed.

Yours,

Antonia

PS: Be sure to tell your parents our news!

I must admit to a feeling of shock when I read the letter, followed by a sense of how ridiculous this was. I already knew that Antonia Vivian, now Mrs Ambrose Mortimer II, was expecting a baby, so what earthly difference did it make that she'd now produced two? I acknowledged that the twins compounded a situation that I wished in my heart to deny, and the sooner I accepted that Antonia was now even further away than she'd ever been, the better it would be for my general sense of well-being.

In short, I needed to do what Mum advised anyone who showed self-indulgent weakness: 'Just buck up and snap out of it!'

CHAPTER 14

OLD HISTORY, AND NEW EVENTS

The next Wednesday I went to the University Union building to meet Max Herbst for lunch. I was really looking forward to this, as our conversation the week before had increased my interest in the somewhat enigmatic Krishnamurti. After we'd placed our food order, I asked Max if he'd heard about Ambrose and Antonia becoming parents of twins over in the USA.

His response was interesting: "That'll cramp Ambrose's style a bit, I'd imagine."

"How do you mean?" I asked neutrally.

"Oh, just that before he met Antonia he was quite the young man about town, and you don't need to be a psychologist to wonder if a few tensions might emerge following his rapid transformation into 'family man, father of two'," he replied sardonically, or possibly not. I didn't prolong the subject and we settled down to discuss the matter in hand, namely the early life of Jiddu Krishnamurti.

Max had obviously given the topic a bit of thought, for he said, "You did a good job with your psychology dissertation, Ed, but on some aspects of Theosophy your understanding was sketchy, to say the least."

I knew only too well what he was talking about – those parts in my dissertation where, like many a student, I'd carefully crafted passages that I fervently hoped would mask gaping holes in knowledge.

"Overall, however," he went on, "your work was of a high standard, and the aim of the dissertation was not to explore the belief system of the group studied, but rather to report on its internal dynamics. You happened to study the Sydney section of the TS at probably its most turbulent time so far, and you conveyed its zeitgeist very effectively."

"Thank you, Max, but – what is 'zeitgeist'?"

Max laughed. "Feeling a bit discombobulated, are you?"

"Just a little. It sounds like a German word . . ."

"Of course," he replied, a tad superciliously. "German contains the most extensive social science vocabulary of all the European languages – though naturally I cannot comment on Eastern and African languages."

"Well, naturally not," I murmured. Max could be a bit pompous at times, but overall he was extremely good value, which more than cancelled out any pedantic longeurs that featured in his discourse.

"'*Zeit*' means 'time' and '*geist*' means 'spirit'. The dictionary definition is: 'the spirit of a specific time. But," he continued, "if you want to really understand Krishnamurti, you'll need to gain a deeper understanding of Theosophy. However, you may feel you've learnt more than enough to last you several lifetimes, or maybe I should say 'incarnations'." Here I gave an obliging smile.

"It's up to you, of course, but I personally find it an interesting subject, which is one reason I keep in touch with the TS folk, 'unusual' though some may be. Quite apart from Krishnamurti's inborn 'essence' that permeates his every thought and action, as it does with us all, he is the product of a unique set of circumstances. Who knows how his story will unfold, but it's bound to be intriguing. In fact, I'd go so far as to say that the future of the TS rests very largely on the way Krishnamurti handles the role that fate – via the triumvirate of Blavatsky, Besant and Leadbeater – has dealt him."

I was curious to know how Max's familiarity with the TS had come about, and he was quite happy to tell me:

"I have an old and dear woman friend who discovered Theosophy a number of years ago in England and became a great devotee of Madame Blavatsky. My friend's husband grew very concerned about his wife's 'fixation with all things Theosophical,' as he put it, and sought my assistance as a psychologist to find out what was going on. I attended a number of TS meetings in London and later in the States and became interested in Theosophy as a phenomenon, rather in the same way that William James was fascinated by religion."

"And what became of your friend?" I asked. "Did she remain in the TS? What did you say to her husband?"

Max laughed. "Oh," he said, "she's still deeply involved with Theosophy and has transferred her former fixation on Madame Blavatsky onto Krishnamurti. I told her husband that, on the whole, Theosophy was a benign interest for his wife to have and one that had the potential to enrich his own life, too. This settled him down and the two of them have gone on to experience some of the positive aspects that a Theosophical attitude to the world can impart."

After a moment's pause, he continued,

"I've been thinking that, given the amount of TS history we need to get through, it might be better to spread it over several lunches, say two or three weeks apart, rather than hitting you with too much all at once."

This suited me down to the ground. Although I greatly enjoyed meeting with Max and talking with him on the 'psychological plane', I also had a few other things on my plate at that time. Getting time off in the middle of the day was no problem, as my roster at the General Practice involved seeing patients in the morning and running an early-evening clinic, which meant I was free in the middle of the day.

I told Max this sounded like a sensible plan, to which he replied, "Well, today I propose to touch on two topics, the TS's Esoteric Section, and The Masters – both of which could benefit from further elucidation, yes?"

I nodded, reasoning it would be best to let Max run on these topics, even though I'd probably heard some of it before.

The 'tutorial' commenced with some observations on Madame Blavatsky.

"Blavatsky has always been a controversial figure," he stated. "Since her death in1891, she has gained an almost mythical standing within the TS. This is due to the magnetism of her personality, her message to the world and her copious writings – including her best-selling book *Isis Unveiled*. To her followers, she's a woman of utmost integrity and the possessor of occult powers derived from the highest spiritual sources. To her detractors, she's an unscrupulous and dangerous fraudster and plagiarist.

"In 1888, Blavatsky established the Esoteric Section as 'a society within the TS'. When members had been in the TS for two years, and if they were 'of good repute' and had done some work for the Society, they could apply to join the Esoteric Section. If accepted, they had to swear an oath of secrecy regarding their membership and undertake to lead a balanced life centred on 'harmlessness, good will and altruism'. Meditation, self-purification, study and service were their aids to progression along the Spiritual Path.

"A central concept in Theosophy is the belief in evolution through a number of lives until perfection is reached and the soul is freed from *karma*.[30] The soul is then ready to embark on the Path of Discipleship, then on

---

[30] Karma: the inexorable law of consequence of good and bad actions over different lifetimes.

---

to Adepthood and finally to membership of a group of select beings who direct the world.

"According to Theosophical lore, some Adepts, or 'Masters' as they're often called, choose to maintain human forms. Two of these, the Master Moriya and the Master Kuthumi, are closely involved with the TS and reside in Tibet. Actual physical visits to Tibet are not necessary, however, due to astral travel, and some Masters are also able to materialize at various earthly locations."

"Very convenient," I commented. "To me, all this sounds quite hierarchical, almost bureaucratic. Of course, my non-religious background may hamper me here."

Max laughed, "Well, I'm not a Theosophist myself, I'm just describing the belief system of a particular social group," he said easily. "In most religions you get hierarchies – look at Christianity: angels, archangels, ghosts, earthly manifestations of deceased people, the Holy Spirit . . . And what about the 'pagan' faiths with their multitude of gods, demi-gods, 'kitchen gods', 'garden gods' and so on? The world's awash with them!"

His observations reminded me of how Dora van Gelder had spoken of the spirits that lived in her garden in Java and the many local deities that would need to be placated or thanked at various times. To Dora, these beings were simply an intrinsic part of the environment around her.

I then asked Max how astral travel actually 'operated'.

"If we knew how it works, why the whole world would take it up and we'd all be in disarray – everyone would get into it – no more need for aeroplanes, letters or telephones," he replied, "let alone passports and visas! We'd all be dropping-in on each other for intercontinental discussions, though there'd have to be some way of closing the door on unwanted astral visitors.

"Now, to be serious," he went on, "The term 'astral travel' is used to describe how the soul, or 'astral body', can detach itself from a person's physical body and then travel throughout the world and even the universe."

"As a psychologist, Max, what's your view on it?" I asked. After a moment Max replied, "Some individuals have reported experiencing astral travel when under the influence of hallucinogenic drugs or while in an hypnotic state. I personally have never travelled astrally and there is no scientific evidence for astral travel – as yet, that is."

At this point, a waiter approached and asked if we wanted another cup of coffee. After it arrived and Max had drained his cup, he resumed the 'tutorial'.

"Following that little digression on astral travel," he said, "let's get back onto the Masters. Above the Masters are some even higher beings, who can take on a human body to guide the world though extremely difficult times. According to Madame Blavatsky, one of these beings, the Lord Maitreya, came to the world as Jesus Christ and she believed the time was approaching when another great teacher would come to show the world the Way. Dr Besant and Bishop Leadbeater are convinced that the time is now ripe for this momentous event to occur, and this is the driving force behind much of what they currently say and do."

Max could tell from my glazed expression that I'd now had quite enough for one session, so he concluded it by saying, "Next time we meet, in two weeks from today, the focus will be on Bishop Charles Webster Leadbeater. And I can promise you, we will not be discussing such lofty topics as the Masters and astral travel."

After leaving Max, I set off across the campus towards Redfern train station to get the train back home to Stanmore. After several minutes, I heard my name called and turned to see Russell Fletcher coming up behind me. I was always pleased to see Russell and once we'd got on the train we spent the next fifteen minutes bringing each other up to date on recent events in our lives.

I told Russell how I'd attended some of the TS psychology lectures recently, had got to know Max Herbst a bit more and in fact had just been lunching with him. I ended by asking Russell what he knew about Max.

"Scarcely more than when we finished studying psych with him," he replied. "And by now you probably know him better than I do. Apparently he came to Australia after the War, following a pretty bad time and I don't think he has any family here. Seems a bit of a loner, though on good terms with everyone – and fiendishly intelligent, of course."

After a bit more chit-chat, I mentioned Ambrose and Antonia and the birth of the twins.

Russell laughed. "All I can say is, I hope Ambrose remembers the heady days when he first arrived in Sydney and we had many a night out on the town . . . Of course that was before Cupid shot an arrow into his heart and he fell for the lovely Antonia Vivian."

I gave a worldly chuckle in response to this news, and our talk then turned to other topics. On an impulse, I invited Russell to come home for dinner, and he took up the offer readily.

When we arrived at my place, Mum opened the door and was delighted to see Russell.

"Oh, Boys," she said. "You've just arrived in time for dinner!"

"What's on the menu tonight, Mrs B?" Russell enquired.

"Meat-loaf, roasted vegetables and green beans from the garden, followed by an apple crumble with baked custard," Mum answered promptly.

"Sounds absolutely delicious," Russell said. "You're a lucky devil, Ed, to have a mother who's such a great cook!"

"Flattery will get you everywhere, young Russell," Mum beamed, then to me, "Oh, by the way, Ed, there's a letter from Antonia for you. I put it on the mantelpiece in the sitting-room."

Russell glanced at me with a slightly raised eyebrow, which I studiously ignored. The meal, albeit extremely tasty, seemed interminable. Mum, Dad and Russell had a lot to say to each other and I joined in, mentally counting the minutes until Russell would go. I helped Dad with the washing-up and finally the time arrived when I could snatch the letter from its place on the mantelpiece and hurry upstairs to read it in my room.

CHAPTER 15

ANTONIA'S LETTER, AND SOME TS HISTORY

Once up in my room, I tore open the envelope.
Antonia had written:

10th December, 1924

Dear Ed,

This is going to be quite a long letter, celebrating the fact that I have now got through the first few months with the twins – who by the way are totally delightful and doing well.

We are now settling into our new life here on the East Coast living with Narne and Pappi.

Greenwich, Conn. must be one of the nicest places on earth to live. By car, it's about an hour and a half north of Manhattan and looks out over Long Island Sound. Many of the houses have lawns going down to the water, some with their own dock (a 'jetty' to us Aussies) for their yachts. Narne and Pappi's house is huge, rather like an English country house, I imagine, with beautifully-kept gardens, fountains and so on.

Pappi and Narne both have cars (or 'automobiles') – Pappi has a very imposing black Studebaker Lite 6, while Narne's is a more sporty Wills Sainte Claire roadster – lemon yellow with black trim! I am telling you this, Ed, because everyone here is absolutely mad about cars – and no wonder, with USA the hub of the world's automobile industry.

Do you remember Ambrose's 'Aussie Six' car? Well over here it wouldn't even rate a second glance. And would you believe – Henry Ford, founder of the Ford Motor Company, is a Theosophist!

You'll probably recall how Ambrose used to say his father owned a hardware store. Well – turns out 'Mortimer's Hardware' is the largest hardware chain on the East Coast of the U.S. of A. Pappi is a serious Theosophist (Narne also, but she's more interested in meditation and yoga) and he often says what a proud day it'll be when he can change the name of Mortimer's Hardware to 'Mortimer and <u>Son's</u> Hardware.' All Ambrose says to this is, "Well, Pop, I got a deal of living to do before that day dawns . . ."

We have a constant stream of visitors (Greenwich folk who Narne and Pappi have known for years and Theosophists from NY City) who come to 'pay their respects to the twins' and meet the brand-new Australian daughter-in-law.

Three generations under the same roof does have its moments, I can tell you, but overall I couldn't wish for a better American family. Having three people in the house all named Ambrose has caused some confusion, however, with Narne saying something like, "I think Ambrose might need his diaper changed," and my Ambrose replying in a squeaky baby-voice, "No, my diaper's fine, thank you Narne." So – to avoid this type of mix-up, we now address the Mortimer dynasty like this: Pappi is 'Ambrose I', my Ambrose is called by his name, so no change there. Then, we started calling Baby Ambrose (ie Ambrose III) 'Three' and the nickname has stuck. We just call him 'Three'.

You won't believe it but – Ambrose and I have to get married – again! Pappi's attorney (lawyer) believes our Adyar wedding may not be legal over here, so we're going to 'tie the knot' once more, as passports need to be arranged for the twins and me.

We joke about it – Ambrose calling me 'an unmarried mother of twins' and I say he'll soon be 'a twice-married father of two'!

We're planning to visit Sydney in a few months' time when the babies are a bit bigger. We're looking forward to it immensely, Ambrose in some ways even more than me, if that's possible. He finds life here somewhat restrictive, with Pappi always seeking to involve him in the business and me occupied with the babies so much of the time. He even hints that maybe we'll stay in Australia, which is something I can only dream of. I do enjoy it over here but, as the saying goes, 'East, West, home is best.'

Do write again soon, Ed – one of the most lovely things when we first arrived here was the sight of your letter sitting there on the table in Narne and Pappi's reception room.

Please say a big 'Hello' to your parents.
Antonia

Antonia sounded like she was getting along pretty well over there in the States. Of course, living in the lap of luxury with congenial in-laws would obviously be a huge help. But having heard Max and Russell's remarks about Ambrose prior to Antonia, and learning that the 'hardware shop' was in fact an empire with Ambrose as the unwilling heir-apparent made me wonder what his current frame of mind might be. Whatever was happening to them, it was far away and in another land and I had my life to lead here in Sydney. I was enjoying my work as a doctor and, all things considered, my life was satisfactory – in most respects . . .

Max Herbst had said that C.W. Leadbeater would be the topic for discussion at our next lunch so, as the agreed-on day approached, I was curious to hear what he'd have to say. When I arrived at the University Union cafe, he was already there and got down to business straight away.

"There's a lot to tell, and it goes back many years, involves a number of countries and quite a few people – living and dead. What you saw when Krishnamurti rose to his feet at the TS Convention session last year in strong support of CWL was, in a way, a culmination of many past events."

"I'm all ears," I replied. "Pray get started on it, Max."

And so for the next couple of hours, Max waxed eloquent on the history and activities of Charles Webster Leadbeater, whose early life and times I've summarized here:

> CWL was born in England in 1847 and as a child spent some time in Brazil with his family, in which time his father died and his brother was murdered by bandits. He studied at Oxford University, but left prior to graduation due to family financial pressures. In 1878 he became a Church of England curate. Keenly interested in occultism, in 1883 he joined the TS and a year later met Madame Blavatsky. He was accepted as her pupil, left the Church of England, adopted vegetarianism and followed her to India. Here, he developed his psychic powers and became a Buddhist, then went to Ceylon and taught at a TS-supported school for Buddhist boys, ending up as principal of Ananda College.
>
> After five years in the East, he returned to England to tutor two boys with family connections to the TS: George Arundale, who is now a powerful figure in the TS hierarchy, and one of his

Singhalese pupils, C. Jinarajadasa, who CWL believed was a reincarnation of his murdered brother. Jinarajadasa has remained close to CWL and at various times down the years has played a prominent role in the TS.

In 1884 Mrs Annie Besant, then a 30-year-old separated clergyman's wife and mother of two, joined the TS. In 1890, she and CWL met at a London TS meeting and a lifelong friendship followed. The two enjoyed an interest in occult investigations and astral travel, even on occasion (astrally) visiting The Masters in Tibet together. However, down the years, their relationship has been severely tested on several occasions.

At this point in Max's mini-lecture I remarked, "I wonder what that might have been about," to which Max replied:

"No prizes for guessing," and pressed on with the story, a bit like the Ancient Mariner in the famous poem. But like the wedding-guest, I had no way of stopping him, nor any wish to do so.

"Although CWL was riding high in the TS as a speaker, writer, clairvoyant and teacher – particularly to groups of young boys – there was talk linking him with immoral practices. Rumours of this type had been around ever since his curate days, but they came to a head in the USA during 1906 when two separate complaints were made by parents of boys he'd taught. It was alleged CWL had encouraged the boys in the practice of masturbation. Further, a coded sexual message had come to light, though this was later claimed to be a forgery.

"How did CWL react to these stories?" I asked.

"He has never denied advocating masturbation as a preventative, pre-emptive measure, viewing it as a lesser evil than, for example, young men visiting prostitutes and contracting venereal disease, developing a guilty involvement with erotic thoughts or getting involved with women at too young an age.

"Mrs Besant was shocked by what she heard, and CWL promised that within TS circles he'd desist from advocating the practice. The American Section of the TS sent a Commission to London on the matter and the President, Colonel Olcott, was obliged to request CWL to appear before the Council of the British Section to answer the charges. However, just before the meeting, CWL resigned from the TS,[31] saying he wanted to spare the Society the negative publicity that would most certainly ensue.

"When Mrs Besant heard that CWL had admitted to not only advocating masturbation but also that he may have demonstrated 'indicative action', she was aghast. She immediately distanced herself from him, even questioning their mutual occult experiences. As members of the Esoteric Section, both she and CWL had by this stage advanced a considerable way along the Path of Discipleship and were now high Initiates who had taken each step together in the presence of the Masters.

"And therein lay the crux of Mrs Besant's moral quandary. Because 'absolute sexual purity' was one of the first requirements for Initiation, CWL could not therefore be an Initiate. And if that were the case, her visions of standing before the Masters with him could only have been delusions."

"Hmm," I said. "Quite a dilemma. I can see her reasoning . . ."

"Yes," replied Max. "Hard to fault her logic. But after a period of estrangement," he went on, "the two resumed their friendship – to the relief of both, no doubt."

"It must've caused a huge upset within the TS," I commented. "In those days, the topic was almost beyond

---

[31] May 16, 1906

speech. Even now it's seldom broached – except by you, Max, in your psychology lectures . . ." I added with a grin.

Max laughed. "To you, being so enveloped in the Australian 'culture', it must be hard to imagine that these 'taboo' topics are quite freely mentioned in some circles elsewhere in the world – namely London, New York, Berlin . . ."

"Thank you for that insight, Max," I replied in the direct way two people who know each other well can converse. "You've often expressed the opinion that Australia is a backward country populated by philistines. And yet – you remain here. Why is that, I wonder?"

Max gave a slightly rueful smile. "I ask myself that question quite often," he replied. "But even though Australia comes with colossal bigotry, prejudice and so on, there's something very beguiling and energetic about this country and the people here. This is why, overall, Australia's a far better place to be than many others."

"Well," I replied graciously, "your presence here is our good fortune." Max bowed his head ironically and we continued our discourse.

"After resigning from the TS, CWL lived quietly in England. Although the loss of his livelihood and reputation after twenty-two years' involvement with the Society must have come as a shock, he seemed completely unperturbed and totally unrepentant. He never resiled from his position regarding masturbation and, assisted by his numerous supporters, he continued teaching privately and writing – totally unruffled by the scandal he'd generated.[32]

"At the start of 1907 Colonel Olcott, still President of the TS, became ill. Annie Besant was generally viewed

---

[32] For a compilation of correspondence during this period, see Pedro Oliveira. CWL Speaks: C.W. Leadbeater's correspondence concerning the 1906 crisis in the Theosophical Society, 2018.

as his obvious successor. However, it was recognized that if Mrs Besant became President, CWL would re-enter the fold. This prospect generated strong opposition, particularly in the American Section. Nonetheless, important forces were in support of Mrs Besant –it was Colonel Olcott's wish and also that of the Masters that she'd succeed him.

"At the behest of the Masters, the dying Colonel wrote to CWL apologising for his previous harshness. According to Mrs Besant and Mrs Marie Russak, a wealthy American Theosophist who cared for Colonel Olcott during his last days, the Masters were present at his deathbed and the two women saw them.

"In June 1907, Mrs Besant was elected to the Presidency with a large majority, and eighteen months later CWL was readmitted to the Society, though he never again held a formal position within it. He requested permission to go to India and reside at the Society's headquarters at Adyar and this wish was granted."

At this point Max stopped, saying, "I feel the need for another cup of coffee and I'll get you one, too, if you like." I indicated this would be welcome, then before he went to get the coffees he said, "Oh, and by the way, I've heard your friends will be back here in Sydney before too long."

"Oh, yes?" I said nonchalantly. "Which friends do you mean?"

"Ambrose and Antonia," he replied. "Last night I had dinner with Antonia's mother, Clara Vivian, amongst others." He strolled off to get his coffee, leaving me in a state of burning curiosity.

When he returned, holding two cups of steaming coffee, he said,

"I've been thinking – there's a lot more to tell about Krishnamurti and CWL, and it has a strong bearing on what's happening now and, more importantly, what will happen in the near future. I think we should call it a day now and push on with the story next week.

"Our topic will be: how it came about that Krishnamurti met CWL and Mrs Besant, and how this meeting changed Krishnamurti's life for evermore."

Although I'd have liked to continue our discussion, I did understand Max's reasoning, so I just said: "Certainly, Max. Wild horses couldn't stop me from hearing the next instalment of this saga."

CHAPTER 16

KRISHNAMURTI'S EARLY LIFE, AND NEWS FROM USA

The next week at the appointed time, I arrived at the Sydney University Union café to find Max already there. I got us some coffee and cakes and after exchanging a few pleasantries we got started on the topic in hand, namely the early life of Jiddu Krishnamurti.

"Adyar in 1909 was an interesting place to be," Max began. "At the start of the year, Krishnamurti's widowed father, Narianiah, brought his family to live there and took up duties as a clerk in the TS office. Three weeks later, CWL arrived from England and set up house in a comfortable bungalow in the compound. With him were several male assistants whose main job was dealing with the mountain of correspondence generated by CWL.

"One evening, CWL took a stroll by the shores of the Adyar River and watched a group of Indian boys bathing. On returning to his bungalow, he announced that 'one of the boys had the most beautiful aura he had ever seen, without a particle of selfishness in it'.[33] When the lad was identified as Jiddu Krishnamurti, there was surprise among those who knew him, for he was not considered very smart at all and was physically rather scrawny. Interestingly, this was not the first time that Krishnamurti had been seen as special: before his birth, his mother had a premonition that her son would be noteworthy in some way; and the astrologer who cast his

---

[33] Lutyens, Krishnamurti,, 21.

horoscope the day after he was born confirmed that he'd become a very great man.

"Having now identified Krishnamurti as the likely vehicle for the new Lord Maitreya, CWL made himself responsible for the training that would be needed to prepare the boy for this vital calling."

"Pretty impressive," I murmured.

"Yes," agreed Max. "But here I'd be remiss if I didn't mention that Krishnamurti was not the first boy CWL had identified for the role of the new World Teacher. A few years before in the USA, he'd singled out another lad, one Hubert van Hook, for the role. Hubert's parents were Theosophists, his father being General Secretary of the TS in America from 1907 to 1911. When CWL named Krishnamurti as the vehicle for the new World Teacher, this naturally caused some confusion, for Hubert and his mother were already on their way from the States to Adyar to commence his training. Somehow, things were smoothed out. Hubert's mother liked Krishnamurti and his brother Nitya and the three boys spent a lot of time together."

"Two candidates for Lord Maitreya? Isn't that a bit rum?" I mused.

"Ed," Max said patiently, "perhaps I should explain something here. I'm aiming to tell you about events in the TS that have a bearing on what happens later. These occurrences may not always be straightforward, unequivocal or subject to the laws of logic and rational discourse. In hearing about them you may encounter ambiguity, contradiction and phantasmagoria, so I suggest you take it all in your stride."

"Point taken," I replied. "But ... *phantasmagoria*? What a marvelous word!"

"Yes, I thought you'd like it," Max replied. "Comes from the French *phantasmagorie* and means 'a sequence of real or imaginary images like that seen in a dream.' It's a term used in psychotherapy to describe what a patient actually comes out with, pertaining to the patient's subjective perception or recollection of an event rather than anyone else's view on it."

"Then what happened?" I asked.

"CWL began to clairvoyantly investigate and write up Krishnamurti's past lives, which eventually numbered over thirty. These incarnations were referred to by the generic name of 'Alcyone'. CWL's collected notes appeared as '*Lives of Alcyone*' in the *Theosophist* starting from April 1910 and were widely read by Theosophists and non-Theosophists alike.

"As directed by the Masters, CWL saw to it that Krishnamurti and Nitya were taken out of their father's care and educated in Western ways. This involved teaching them privately at Adyar, cutting their long hair, de-lousing them, attending to their teeth and of course intensively tutoring them in English. From numerous accounts, Krishnamurti did not seem to be a natural scholar, whereas Nitya, three years younger, was much quicker on the uptake and more alert than the rather dreamy Krishnamurti.

"Matters of personal hygiene became the province of CWL, who introduced the boys to Western-style bathing involving nakedness and washing between the legs. This approach was very different from the Hindu practice where the loincloth remained on while water was poured over the head. And it was not too long before this new style of bathing became the source of much trouble.

"In carrying out his instructions from the Masters, CWL was well aware of the need for prudent behavior concerning young boys, given the events of previous years. His main focus, of course, was Krishnamurti's spiritual development, and he reported to Mrs (as she then was) Besant that he'd taken Krishnamurti and Nitya on an astral expedition to meet with Master Kuthumi, who had put them both on Probation."

"Refresh my memory here, please, Max," I cut in. "Tell me again about Probation."

Max sighed, and I wondered if he was starting to feel I was as slow on the uptake as Krishnamurti was said to be.

"Probation is the first step towards Discipleship in the TS and involves the successful facing of difficulties of various types which test an individual's moral strength," Max explained patiently. "Usually, this phase lasts around seven years. The next step is Acceptance, when the pupil becomes united with a Master and thus is part of the Master's own consciousness.

"These two first steps, Probation and Acceptance, pave the way for the First Initiation. At this point, the pupil gains membership of the Great White Brotherhood, although four more Initiations must take place before becoming an Adept." [34]

"Thank you," I said. "Pray continue. I am well aware that my ignorance is a real test of your own moral strength, and I apologize unreservedly for it."

Max smiled benignly, perhaps demonstrating his own mastery over the irritants of the transitory world, and went on, "Every night of Krishnamurti's Probation, CWL would take him on an astral visit to the Master in Tibet for a short session of instruction which the Master would then summarise into a few sentences. The next morning, Krishnamurti would have to write down the Master's words, which he found extremely difficult to do. CWL tidied up his notes a little, claiming his involvement only extended to correcting spelling and punctuation.

"In November 1909, Krishnamurti met Mrs Besant for the first time when she visited Adyar. He and Nitya waited in the garden while she and CWL talked together

---

[34] See Glossary: Esoteric Section of the Theosophical Society.

privately, then were summoned by CWL with a loud call of 'Coo-ee!'." [35]

On hearing this, I glanced sharply at Max to see if he wasn't pulling my leg. It seemed distinctly odd that 'Coo-ee' would be used in faraway India by an Englishman sending for two Indian boys. My bemusement was not lost on Max.

"Yes, Ed. Thought I'd drop that one in – CWL had picked up the word during his 1905 visit to Australia and Krishnamurti recounts hearing the call in a letter he wrote to his dear friend Lady Emily Lutyens."

I had a question here: "How did you get access to this information, Max? Are these letters published?"

"Not yet," Max replied smoothly, "but one day they will be. Krishnamurti and Lady Emily are very close – she's like a mother to him. [36]

"Now, back to the story. During Mrs Besant's three-week stay at Adyar, she saw Krishnamurti and Nitya every day, admitted them into the Esoteric Section and arranged for them to sleep in her room after she'd departed for her next public lectures elsewhere in India.

"A short time later, CWL 'brought through' instructions from the Master to the effect that the boys' father, Narianiah, must accept that his sons no longer belonged to him, but rather to the world, and that henceforth he must not interfere in any aspect of their lives. The two brothers were to be kept completely separate from all other boys except Hubert van Hook and only ever mix with Theosophists. Furthermore, their room must be kept free of contamination by any female, apart from the woman who cleaned it."

"Hmm – pretty strict," I commented.

"Well, that's the way it was," Max replied. "However, Krishnamurti and Nitya were given bicycles

---

[35] See Glossary: 'Coo-ee'
[36] Lutyens, Krishnamurti, 29.

and enjoyed cycling, always chaperoned of course, and they swam and played tennis with Hubert van Hook. By all accounts, Hubert had quite a lot to put up with. CWL believed that negative forces could emanate from inanimate objects and for this reason he would not allow Hubert to touch any of Krishnamurti's possessions such as his tennis racquet or bicycle."

"Interesting concept," I commented. "And did this belief of CWL's pervade any other aspects of life at Adyar?"

"I'd say it did," replied Max. "I've heard that he ordered the room next to Mrs Besant's be cleaned and whitewashed in preparation for the boys to occupy it. In a letter to Mrs Besant he said, and I quote: 'It absolutely will not do to have such a depleting figure as Mrs Lubke (the occupant of the room) permeating the atmosphere where they sleep'.[37]

"In less than one year after their mother's death, these boys' lives had undergone enormous and irrevocable changes. Obviously, they missed their mother greatly and, in a letter to Mrs Besant, Krishnamurti asked if he could call her 'Mother', telling her that now he had 'no other mother to love'.[38]

"On the last day of 1909, CWL telegraphed Mrs Besant with important news: Master Kuthumi had informed him that Krishnamurti had passed through his Probation and was now ready to become an Initiate. Furthermore, the Master was going to accept Krishnamurti as his own pupil.

"As Probation usually lasted seven years and it was only five months since Krishnamurti had commenced it, this was indeed amazing. CWL was very keen for Mrs

---

[37] Ibid., 43, fn 2, letter from C.W. Leadbeater to A.Besant, 8.1.1910.
[38] Ibid., 31, letter from Krishnamurti to Lady Emily Lutyens,
    24.12.1909

Besant to attend the ceremony (astrally) at Master Kuthumi's residence in Tibet and she expressed her joy at the news.

"And so," Max continued, "for around thirty-six hours, Krishnamurti and CWL remained secluded in Mrs Besant's bedroom at Adyar. Krishnamurti lay on Mrs Besant's bed with CWL beside him on the floor. Outside the door, Nitya and one of CWL's assistants maintained a vigil to ensure no-one disturbed them. Nourishment, mostly in the form of warm milk, was provided at intervals. According to all accounts, Krishnamurti left his body and participated in a wonderful ceremony, emerging from it feeling extremely well and profoundly happy. CWL asked him to write down what he remembered of the experience, but Krishnamurti was very tired so CWL wrote it from notes he'd made and had it typed up. These notes formed the basis of '*At the Feet of the Master*' and were later published, gaining a huge readership worldwide and translated into more than twenty languages. Everyone involved in the event including Narianiah, the boys' father, expressed delight at what had transpired.

"However, friction was emerging between CWL and Narianiah, who wanted more contact with his sons. And as time went on, this discord escalated. Narianiah was aware of past rumours about CWL and young boys, and he was deeply disturbed by gossip he'd heard regarding unseemly incidents involving CWL and his charges.[39] Mrs Besant, too, was deeply worried by these reports, and felt that the best course was to persuade Narianiah to transfer the boys' legal guardianship to her, which he did.

"But Narianiah was still not at all happy about events and, wishing to remove all influence of CWL from the boys' lives, took High Court action in Madras. In this matter, Narianiah did not act alone, having financial and

---

[39] Ibid., 40.

moral supporters including Theosophists in America who had strong reservations concerning CWL's moral probity.

"Legally speaking, it was not necessary for Narianiah to prove CWL's immorality in the court, a well-grounded fear was sufficient. Although he had agreed to Mrs Besant's guardianship of the boys, he emphatically did not want it transferred to a person about whom he had serious doubts. Furthermore, he objected to the deification of Krishnamurti as the next 'Lord Christ', as publicly announced by Mrs Besant. And last but not least, he did not believe Krishnamurti was the author of '*At the Feet of the Master*'.

"By 1913 the two boys were in England with Mrs Besant, and Krishnamurti was aged seventeen. After a complicated and prolonged legal battle, custody of the boys was ordered by the court to revert to their father. Mrs Besant then appealed the outcome and won."

Max stopped here, saying, "A lot's been written about this history, and it remains a controversial topic. What I've told you is a compressed version, but it's enough to give you the gist of the matter, and it's quite enough for today. "

"Phew, heady stuff." I remarked.

Max nodded. "But we must remain social scientists to the core and simply observe these phenomena in a detached way, as William James *et al* would have us do."

"Oh, absolutely," I agreed. And so the session concluded, on a note of scientific objectivity that was typical of Max.

I set off for home in a thoughtful mood. My reading of William James's *The Varieties of Religious Experience* had familiarized me with a number of case-histories relating how sundry individuals had 'found God'. But the story of Krishnamurti, involving as it did 'being discovered' by CWL, was very different from the heartfelt testimonies of those who were in torment and actively searching for 'Him' on their own account.

I tried to imagine how it must have been for the young Krishnamurti, closeted for all those hours in Mrs Besant's bedroom with CWL instructing him in the lore of the Masters, those godly beings. Although they'd have had the benefits of ceiling fans at Adyar, the atmosphere in the room must have become decidedly hot and humid as the hours unfolded, and CWL was an exceedingly forceful personality with strongly developed occult powers . . .

Secondly, I did rather wonder at my own 'lack of religious temperament'. Without being melodramatic, I saw myself like a colour-blind man with a love of colour, fascinated by what he could only read and hear about. In his book, William James devoted a whole chapter to a type of person he described as 'healthy-minded', characterized by a matter-of-fact, no-nonsense, even dismissive attitude towards religion. To tell the truth, I could more readily identity with this personality-type than many others described by James.

In fact, perhaps I was a little like William James himself for, as he explained in his introduction to *The Varieties of Religious Experience:*

'My personal position is simple. I have no living sense of commerce with a God. I envy those who have, for I know that the addition of such a sense would help me greatly. The Divine, for my active life, is limited to impersonal and abstract concepts which, as ideals, interest and determine me, but do so but faintly in comparison with what a feeling of God might effect if I had one . . .' [40]

I reflected on my current interests. I was intrigued by the story of Krishnamurti's life and fascinated by the

---

[40] William James, *The Varieties of Religious Experience.* (London, Longman, 1902), Introduction xxiv.

Theosophical Society in Sydney and I saw no reason to desist from this. As for Antonia – I certainly did 'hold a torch for her' and probably would for the rest of my life. However, I had no intention of becoming a celibate, a hermit, a mystic or any other variety of human being. Rather, I imagined I'd always count Antonia and Ambrose among my friends and in due course I'd meet someone nice and marry her. And life, as they say, would go on.

By the time my train drew in to Stanmore station I'd had my fill of introspection. This was a healthy-minded reaction, typical of the admittedly limited group I belonged to – courtesy of genetics, upbringing and, some would say, karma . . .

CHAPTER 17

THE BABY-VIEWING LUNCH

By the start of 1924 Russel Fletcher and I had now completed a year working as doctors, both also armed with a degree in psychology. I enjoyed working in a General Medical Centre several suburbs from Stanmore and getting to know my regular patients, whereas Russell preferred the constant drama of the emergency department in a large city hospital. He worked a rotating shift that left him free to develop some of his business ideas, which he said were coming along nicely.

On the home-front, our main news was – we had acquired a telephone. This modernism had long been resisted by Dad on the grounds he already had a telephone in his office and didn't want our quiet home-life disturbed by the constant jangling of a phone. Mum had tried a number of strategies to get him to change his mind, including the suggestion that she and I make several visits to his office each week and do our calls from there. This was patently ridiculous, but it showed how keen she was to become a phone-owner with a number she could give out to her friends. In the end, it was Mum's argument that as doctor I must be always available to patients *in extremis* that swayed Dad; and once we'd got the phone, none of us knew how we'd managed before!

Ambrose and Antonia plus twins would arrive in Sydney sometime soon, so I decided to write a letter to Antonia in Greenwich Conn. and include my telephone number, hoping she'd receive it before she left for Australia.

My letter mainly updated her on the activities of the two Sydney Theosophical groups, Blavatsky Lodge and the newly-formed Independent Theosophical Society (ITS), formerly the Sydney Lodge. Both were energetically pushing ahead with programs to appeal to a wide range of interests and age-groups: psychology lectures, public-speaking classes, a sewing guild for young children and Lotus Circle and Round Table (somewhat akin to Christian Sunday School). I mentioned that TS members were steadily drifting from the ITS to Blavatsky Lodge where, if accepted, they might join the Esoteric Section and embark on their spiritual journey.[41] Finally, I told her how the TS had now started broadcasting music and Theosophical talks from a transmitter located in an outbuilding in the grounds of The Manor, a project spearheaded by Mr Karel van Gelder, Dora's father.[42]

A few weeks later, a postcard landed in our letterbox addressed to 'The Best Family', saying:

Dear Mr and Mrs Best and Ed

We are now in Sydney and settling in at The Manor for the coming few weeks. On Sunday 6th April we're holding a 'baby-viewing' lunch 1pm onwards to show our friends our two little darlings. Do hope the three of you can come. Ambrose can pick you up from the ferry wharf. Please phone The Manor to r.s.v.p. and let us know which ferry you'll be on. Looking forward to seeing you!

Antonia and Ambrose (The Manor's phone number is .....)

---

[41] By edict of Dr Besant, the ITS was now precluded from involvement in the Esoteric Section.

[42] This was the inception of radio station 2GB, owned and managed by the TS.

Mum&Dad were very pleased to receive this invitation, and Mum threw herself into the preparations – replying to the invitation, finding out when the best ferry would leave Circular Quay for Athol wharf, deciding what food we'd bring and buying a couple of little gifts for the twins. I gave her the telephone number of The Manor and left her to it, not wanting to appear over-interested. Also, I wanted my first contact with Antonia to be face-to-face rather than as two disembodied voices on a phone.

Mum decided to bake a nice batch of pumpkin scones, which on the Sunday morning she carefully packed in a hamper together with the presents for the twins. At 11am we set off for The Manor with ample time to walk to Stanmore Station, take the train to Central and a tram down Castlereagh St to Circular Quay. A ferry leaving at 12.30 would get us to Athol Wharf by 12.45 and she'd left a message to this effect at The Manor so Ambrose could meet us.

Our travel arrangements worked smoothly and when we arrived at Athol Wharf, Ambrose was there waiting for us, standing beside a car that struck me as being very similar to his old 'Aussie Six' (and in fact *was* his former car, it having been put in storage ready for his return). True to form, his attire – green shirt, red kerchief knotted round his neck, and a black velvet waistcoat – was strikingly different from the sober clothing of everyone else in sight.

He greeted us warmly just like the Ambrose of old, but now, after eighteen months, I felt there was something a little different about him. 'He's probably thinking the same about me,' I reflected, recalling the naïve young student I was when first we'd met two years earlier.

Turning to Mum&Dad, he said, "Do you know, Mr and Mrs Best, I call your son 'my *best* Aussie buddy' – get it? And puns aside, he really is! Ed, you're looking marvellous – must be your mother's cooking . . . I'll have to come and get some medical advice from you on how to stop smoking – Antonia's very strict about no smoking near the babies."

"And rightly so," declared Mum from the back seat. I refrained from telling Ambrose that my father still had to go to the furthest corner of our backyard to enjoy his evening smoke.

A few minutes later we arrived at The Manor. Although by now I'd been there several times, its enormous size and magnificent position overlooking Sydney Harbour never ceased to amaze me. We climbed out of the car, opened the creaking wrought-iron gate, made our way down the marble steps and crossed the tiled verandah, Dad holding the hamper in one hand while gallantly proffering the other to Mum.

The massive front door was open, and through the fly-screen door I could make out a throng of people in animated conversation. A figure detached itself from the group and came towards us.

"Ed!" Antonia cried, giving me a hug. "I can't believe it! Lovely to see you! And Mr and Mrs Best – I'm *so* glad you could come. I know you've already met a number of our friends, and today I hope you'll get to know yet more."

Joyce Housman and Antonia's mother, Clara Vivian, appeared. They took control of the hamper from Dad and exclaimed with delight at the scones.

Mum took out the presents for the twins saying, "Lead me to these beautiful babies. I can't wait to see them!" and this was the last we saw of her for quite some time.

One of the men Dad had met nearly two years before at the Manor Open House day brought him a drink and they seemed to more-or-less continue their discussion from where they'd left off.

So that left me – gazing at Antonia, who was gazing back at me. Maybe it was only for a split second, but it had to stop.

"How was your trip back to Sydney?" I asked in a pleasantly normal sort of way, and Antonia replied in like fashion. Having now broken the ice, as it were, we entered into a well-mannered conversation with Antonia thanking me again for my letters and saying how delightful it was to receive news from home when one was overseas.

"And now, come see the babies," she announced, leading the way to a room nearby in which stood two cots side by side. Bending dotingly over one twin she said, "This is Ingrid, named after Ambrose's mother." Then, lifting the mosquito net from the other cot, "and here is Ambrose, or 'Three' as we call him."

I knew all this about the names already from one of her letters, but I certainly wasn't about to butt in and tell her so. While Antonia talked and I duly admired the twins, two robust and soundly sleeping infants, I was able to observe that she, like Ambrose, seemed a little different. 'As would be expected,' I thought, 'They've undergone many new experiences in a short space of time and also become parents – it'd be very odd if they remained exactly the same.'

Then Antonia announced, "Ed, You must come and meet Narne and Pappi Mortimer!"

"Oh?" I said in surprise. "Are they here, too?"

Antonia laughed, "Yes – they decided to come with us – they'd heard so much about Sydney and what a wonderful time we had here. And they love it. To tell the truth, I really think they couldn't bear to be parted from their only grandchildren."

She led me out to meet Narne and Pappi who were relaxing outside on deckchairs, gazing out at the Harbour. They leapt to their feet when we appeared, and on hearing my name, Narne exclaimed in a broad American twang,

"So you're Ed Best! Do you know, Ed, we used to put your letters on the hall table in our foyer back in Greenwich Connecticut and you'll never believe how Antonia's eyes would light up when she came in and saw one!"

Antonia smiled in her beautiful way. "Yes, Ed," she said softly, "it was *so* good of you to write. Especially as you're now a busy doctor."

"How do you do, Mr and Mrs Mortimer," I said, but my words were brushed aside by Narne.

"Ed, please!" she cried. "Call us 'Narne and Pappi'. We're the proudest grandparents in the whole world!"

There was no way I could not comply with this, and soon I'd almost forgotten they'd ever had any other names. Hitherto, I'd scarcely given Ambrose's parents much thought, quite frankly. To me, they were just shadowy figures far away in the USA. But now, here they were, living and breathing, standing right in front of me and impossible to ignore, even if I'd wanted to. They must have been about sixty, but looked more like mid-forties, simply radiating health, vitality and enjoyment of life. I knew they'd been vegetarians from way back – maybe that's what did it.

Narne was tall, suntanned and lithe, her hair in a thick tawny plait going halfway down her back. She was dressed in garments that looked to be of Indian origin, and I recalled Antonia saying in one of her letters that her mother-in-law did a lot of yoga and meditation. Pappi was short and stocky with a direct, matter-of-fact manner – clearly no fool and, from what I'd heard, a very astute businessman. Ambrose definitely took after Narne, and in fact I could see nothing at all of Pappi in him. Furthermore, I couldn't quite see Ambrose running the hardware empire Pappi had so lovingly built up.

A few minutes later we were called to lunch, which was laid out on platters in the refectory room on the large wooden tables that I remembered from the Open House day lunch at the Manor to celebrate the start of the Communal Living project. I helped myself to a large plateful of vegetable curry and rice, then checked on Mum&Dad to see if they were having a good time. They were: Dad talking with Mr van Gelder about the power of broadcasting to reach mass-markets and Mum chatting in a group that included Joyce Housman and Clara Vivian.

Towards the end of the lunch, Max Herbst appeared. After eating and having a glass of (non-alcoholic) cider, he was led off by Antonia to view the babies. A short time later, he emerged from the 'nursery' saying: "Ed – let's get out for a bit. I need a smoke." The Manor, as well as being vegetarian and alcohol-free, was also a no-smoking zone.

We walked along the street for a short way and presently arrived at a small park where we sat down on a bench under a large jacaranda tree. Soon, Ambrose appeared. "I thought I might find you two here," he said, grinning. "The Manorites call this park 'Smokers' Corner'."

He quickly lit a cigarette and, after exhaling a long plume of smoke, said reflectively, "You've got no idea how great it is being back in Sydney. There's something about this place that makes me – I mean *us* – want to stay here forever."

"Despite our strange, barbaric customs?" I asked.

Ambrose laughed, "I'll have you know, Ed, the U.S of A has certain barbarisms too, and some of them are less benign than yours, I can tell you."

"I agree," echoed Max, "and that goes for Europe, too." Then he added, "As for you, Ed, the sooner you go abroad the better. When's it going to be, I wonder?"

"In a couple of years," I replied. "First, I've got to get myself established as a doctor."

Max groaned *"Get established!* If that's your attitude, you'll *never* go."

"No," I said decisively. "You're wrong there, Max. In two years' time I'll be off and away."

"I very much hope so," he murmured, cleaning out his pipe with a handy twig.

When Ambrose had finished his cigarette, he left us to go back to The Manor and greet some newly-arrived guests. Max's eyes followed his retreating back and between puffs at his pipe, said thoughtfully, "I think the boy feels trapped."

"Could be," I replied, then changed the subject by asking when we might meet for our next Krishnamurti tutorial.

"Why not right now?" Max suggested. "It's pleasant out here in the park, and food and drink's laid on close by. We've both got to be here for a while longer, so we might as well make the most of it." Being used to Max dropping in and out of groups at a whim, I was a bit puzzled as to why he thought he needed to stay on. But no matter, having now made contact with Antonia and knowing Mum&Dad were enjoying themselves, I was very happy to sit out here with Max and talk of Krishnamurti.

"Remember how we discussed Krishnamurti's strange and debilitating 'Process'?" he began. "It's very stressful for him and also for those around him, so I hear, and in fact CWL is so worried he's sent Dr Mary Rocke[43] over to California to check on his physical state, see that his body's not getting overstrained. CWL, like everyone including Krishnamurti himself, is quite mystified by this Process."

"Hard to know exactly what it's all about," I mused. "It could be psychosomatic, physical, related to some childhood illness, or a bit of everything. I'd love to examine him and run a few tests and so on, see if anything showed up."

---

[43] See Glossary: Dr Mary Rocke.

"Well, Dr Ed," replied Max. "I doubt you'll ever be in a position to do that. Between these episodes, Krishnamurti seems to be able to carry on with his Theosophical work and is now taking more and more of a leading role in events. As well he should – after all, he *is* the vehicle for the new World Teacher."

I could never tell what, if anything, Max believed in – his public persona being so enigmatic, worldly-wise and world-weary. There was definitely a 'keep out' sign regarding personal topics, but I was a believer in taking people as they come, unless they indicate they want to 'get something off their chest' as Mum would say. I enjoyed my meetings with Max and was starting to see him as a friend.

We'd only been talking for a short time when Dad appeared, having been directed to the park by Ambrose. I introduced him to Max, who he'd not met before, and after a bit of small-talk Dad suggested it was 'time to make tracks', that is, to leave. We walked back to The Manor and I said goodbye to Antonia, Narne, Pappi and various others.

Ambrose was to take us to the ferry wharf, but there was no sign of him. I scouted around and, surprisingly, found him out in the garden sitting in a deckchair reading a book. On seeing me, he jumped to his feet, saying, "Just having a breather from the crowd, you know how it is? So – you're off now, are you, Ed, buddy? Go get your parents and I'll meet you out front with the car."

A few minutes later he appeared at the wheel of the Aussie Six and we all got in, Mum &Dad expressing their thanks for sparing them the walk up the hill and the ensuing tram ride to the wharf. On the way, he said, "Ed, I really want to meet up with you for a meal and enjoy one of our long talks. This coming week's going to be a bit hectic – I'm actually looking round for a house to rent, give us a bit more space to ourselves. Next weekend's no good either, I'm off camping in the Blue Mountains with a couple of friends. Should be a good break, an 'Aussie wilderness experience' with a bit of canoeing thrown in, if the streams are flowing. But after that, my time's all yours."

"Any evening you're free, just phone and we can meet for dinner," I replied. "And by the way, I really enjoyed meeting your parents – they're amazing!"

Ambrose glanced across at me briefly. "Yes," he replied. "They *are* amazing . . . and that's part of the problem."

Presently we arrived at the wharf, only to see the back view of the ferry as it steamed off towards the city. Ambrose did not seem at all unperturbed. "There'll be another along in forty-five minutes," he said easily. "Let's just sit here in the car, admiring the view and talking about – whatever . . ."

"That sounds an excellent idea." Mum said. "Actually, Ambrose, there *is* something I've been wondering about. At lunch today there was a lot of talk about something called 'The Amphitheatre' and do you know, I didn't have the faintest idea what it was."

"Mrs B," Ambrose said, smiling. "That's because you haven't been mixing enough in Theosophical circles. The Star Amphitheatre at Balmoral Beach is one of the Sydney Theosophical Society's greatest concepts, a truly breathtaking vision." Glancing at his watch, he continued, "I know – let's drive over to Balmoral now to see the site and I'll tell you all about it on the way. We'll be back here well in time for the next ferry."

I had in fact told Mum&Dad how I'd attended the 'Turning of the First Sod' ceremony at the Amphitheatre building site in June the year before, but apparently Mum had forgotten all about it.

Ambrose confidently guided the Aussie Six up the hill from the ferry wharf, along the spine of Mosman village and down a steep, winding road towards Balmoral Beach. On the way, he gave us a bit of background on the

Star Amphitheatre, usually simply called 'The Amphitheatre'.

"It's an enormous structure, built in the Grecian Doric style. When it's completed in a few months from now, it'll seat two and a half thousand people with room for another thousand standing," he told us. "It's the brainchild of members of the Order of the Star[44] which was established by Annie Besant in 1911 in order to prepare the way for the new World Teacher."

"So – this Order of the Star . . . is it part of the Theosophical Society?" asked Mum.

"There's never been an official connection between the two organisations," Ambrose explained. "However, there is a considerable overlap in membership. To put it another way – a number of Theosophists are *not* members of the Order of the Star. Some don't agree with its promotion of the coming World Teacher and won't have a bar of it. However, there's an equally strong ground-swell of support for the idea of the Amphitheatre, where the new World Teacher will address the multitudes who come to hear him speak. It'll also be a great location for other cultural events like operas, lectures, plays and concerts to be enjoyed by anyone who cares to come along."

"And who *is* this 'new World Teacher' exactly, Ambrose?" Mum wondered.

"His name is Jiddu Krishnamurti, often referred to as 'Krishna'," Ambrose replied.

He stopped the car in front of an enormous, unfinished building that looked straight out through the Sydney Harbour heads to the Pacific Ocean beyond. The view was absolutely breathtaking and Mum&Dad were silent for a moment. Then Dad said, "Cripes – very impressive indeed!"

---

[44] Formerly known as the Order of the Star in the East.

Mum seemed simply at a loss for words. I felt a surge of admiration for the sheer courage, tenacity and audacity that had led to this enormous physical statement of belief. Say what you will – this crowd did nothing by halves!

Then the accountant in Dad spoke up: "Who's financing it, by the way?"

Ambrose laughed. "I thought you might ask that, Mr B, so here's how it came about. First of all, Dr Mary Rocke, an English medical doctor who's been a lifelong Theosophical supporter, purchased three adjacent blocks of land here. Then the Order of the Star took out a loan of 4,000 pounds and sold subscriptions to seats. By this means, they raised the money to engage an architectural firm to design a three-storey building containing a stage, a chapel, a tea-room, a meeting hall and a library.[45] It's been described by members of the Order of the Star as 'a symbol in stone of that which our daily lives should be: simple, pure, clean, dignified'[46].

"Beautiful," murmured Mum. "And when will it be completed do you know, Ambrose?"

"Fairly soon, I imagine," Ambrose replied. "The builders had to excavate deep into the sandstone rock for the foundations and that took quite a time, but now they're making rapid progress. Hopefully, it'll be in use by next year's TS Convention in April."

"Most impressive," said Dad again, and he spoke for all of us.

"Well, we'll have to make sure you attend the grand opening," Ambrose said, turning the car around ready for our return trip to the ferry wharf.

---

[45] See Glossary: Star Amphitheatre, Balmoral, Sydney.

[46] Jill Roe (ed.), *Twentieth Century Sydney: Studies in urban and social history.* (Sydney: Hale & Iremonger in assoc. with Sydney History Group, 1980), 102.

"Thank you so much, Ambrose," said Mum. "Seeing the Amphitheatre has been a real treat – the icing on the cake of a lovely day."

"Well, Mrs B," Ambrose replied. "It's all due to you, for asking about the Amphitheatre."

As we drove down the hill, we could see the ferry steaming towards the wharf.

"Well done!" said Dad. "And thank you from all of us."

"Not at all," replied Ambrose. "It was my great pleasure to be with you. And Ed, let's meet up for dinner week after next – I'll phone when I get back from the Blue Mountains."

He took off the red kerchief that was knotted round his neck and, as the ferry chugged its way towards the city, we watched him wave it until he was just a speck in the distance..

Mum&Dad said they'd enjoyed every single part of the day.

"And your friend Ambrose," Mum said. "What a nice young man! Do you know, I think marriage and fatherhood have really brought out the best in him, don't you think so, Dad?"

"Oh, absolutely," Dad replied.

I didn't dare look at Dad. We both knew the sight of Ambrose and Antonia's twins would have set Mum wondering when babies might come into her own life, something that could only occur via – me.

CHAPTER 18

AMBROSE

The next week passed quickly at the General Practice. I heard nothing from Antonia and Ambrose, nor did I expect to. They had a lot on their plate, what with finding a place to live, showing Narne and Pappi the sights of Sydney, and caring for the twins. I, too, was quite busy, having met up with friends after work several nights in a row.

On the morning of Sunday 13th of April I woke up late, around nine, as I'd been out the night before. Mum&Dad, both early risers, had already been up for a while. I could hear the sound of Dad out in the garden snipping away at some shrubs he was pruning, and I knew Mum was in the laundry doing the washing.

The phone rang and, being the only one inside the house, I went into the hall to answer it. A voice I couldn't quite place said,

"Is that you, Ed?" to which I answered,

"Yes, speaking."

"It's Clara Vivian, Ed," said the voice. "Antonia asked me to contact a few friends . . ."

"Is everything alright?" I asked, and then blurted out, "Is it Antonia?"

"No, Ed," Clara replied quietly. "It's Ambrose. I have some terrible news, and it's very hard to tell you . . ."

I knew her words were said in order to prepare me for something pretty awful. "Tell me – what is it?" I said.

After a pause, in which I could hear her take a deep breath, Clara said, "Ambrose has been killed . . . in a canoeing accident in the Blue Mountains."

At these words, wave after wave of shock passed through me and for a few seconds I felt I was going to pass out.

"Ed?" Clara said. "Are you still there? . . . Are you alright?"

I found my voice. "Yes," I replied. "It's just . . . the most horrible, horrible thing . . . I can't believe it . . . How did it happen, do you know? It must be terrible for you to have to tell this news . . ."

"Everyone's devastated. I'm at The Manor now and we're all wandering around as though we're in a dream, or rather, a nightmare . . .

"Ambrose and two friends went to the Blue Mountains yesterday on a camping and canoeing trip. They arrived around midday, had lunch by a river and took turns taking the canoe out on the water. It was a lovely sunny day but, unknown to them, higher up in the mountain a sudden storm had sent a torrent of water cascading downstream in a huge surge. Ambrose was in the canoe when the wave hit, and he was swept downstream and over some rapids. The canoe overturned and Ambrose hit his head hard on the rocks. His two friends dragged him from the water, but it was too late. He was killed almost instantly."

I listened in silence, then found my voice. "I can't believe it," I said. "Of all the people I know – Ambrose, the one most full of life . . ." I could not continue, my words were completely inadequate.

With an enormous effort I stopped thinking about myself and asked: "Is there anything I can do? Would you like me to pass on the news to other friends?"

"Oh, Ed," Clara said quietly. "That would be *very* good of you. Making these calls is tearing me apart," She gave me half a dozen names and phone numbers which I noted down numbly.

"And Antonia? What state is she in?" I asked.

"She's in shock, of course, and I'm very worried about her," Clara told me. "I feel she hasn't really taken it all in. She's just quietly going about looking after the babies as if nothing has happened. It's as though she's in a trance. She's feeding them herself, you know, but I'm worried the shock will dry up her milk supply . . ."

"Would you like me to come over to the Manor and see how she is?" I asked. "After all, I am a doctor now."

"Oh, Ed," Clara replied. "If you could do that I would be *so* grateful."

"I'll just make the calls and leave straight away. I'll be there in about two hours."

When I got off the phone I sat down at the kitchen table with my head in my hands, and this is how Mum&Dad found me when they came into the house. They immediately knew something terrible had happened. I told them the news, and they stood there, too stunned to speak.

Dad was the first to recover. I told him of the phone-calls Clara Vivian had asked me to make, that she was worried about Antonia and how I was going over to The Manor to see if I could be of any help.

"Alright, Son," he said quietly. "Give me the list of names and I'll make the telephone calls. But first, why not phone Russell Fletcher? He's got a car now, I remember you telling me. Maybe you can ask him to drive you over to Mosman. It'll save time and it'd be better if you're with a friend and not alone at a time like this. If you like, I'll phone Russell now while you get yourself ready to go."

Mum, with tears streaming down her face, said, "Ed – I'm going to give you some food to take with you. Nobody at The Manor will be in any fit state to think about cooking."

"Thanks, Mum," I replied and hugged her with tears in my eyes. I found I could only take in the news in little bursts, then I would focus on some mundane, trivial thought, and then flip back to the dreadful reality.

Dad rang Russell, told him quietly what had happened and asked him if he could drive me over to The Manor. Russell was as shocked as we were, naturally, but immediately offered his assistance, saying, "Tell Ed I'll be over in fifteen minutes."

I hastily got ready and, still in a complete daze, made my way out to Russell's car clutching three baskets of food from Mum. On the way over to Mosman, we didn't talk much – it was all beyond words.

When we reached The Manor, there were quite a lot of people there, milling around in the house like zombies. Clara greeted me and said that Antonia was asleep at the moment, which she felt was a good thing. The twins were being cared for by several of the women residents, and Narne and Pappi were up in their room, completely given over to grief.

Russell and I went out into the garden. "I don't know about you, Ed, but I could do with a smoke right now," he remarked. "Do you want to take a walk along the street and we can have one?" The idea was certainly tempting, but I didn't take him up on it. Soon, I'd be talking with Antonia and I didn't want to do so reeking of tobacco at a time like this.

Presently, Clara came and told me that Antonia was now awake and would like to see me. She mentioned again her concerns about Antonia's milk supply. I had only a fairly general understanding of lactation matters, but reasoned that sounding calm and confident was the way to go. Time would tell whether or not Antonia's milk would dry up, but if this happened the twins were old enough to easily move onto diluted cows' milk.

I knocked gently on the door of her room and, hearing a weak voice call, "Come in," I entered. Antonia was curled up on the bed, her face nearly as white as the pillows on which she lay. My heart went out to her, but I simply behaved in the only way possible – namely, to be calm and considerate. I reassured her regarding her milk supply and took her pulse. I then asked when she'd last had anything to eat or drink, but her answer was vague.

"Antonia, the best thing you can do – for Ambrose and for your babies – is to keep on going. And that means having a regular intake of fluids, mainly milk if possible, and eating good nourishing meals," I said to her gently. "My mother has sent over some cakes and she and my father send their love and thoughts to you."

"Thank you, Ed. You're such a friend," she replied quietly and sank back onto the pillows.

I left the room, then located Clara Vivian and reported what I'd said to Antonia.

"Good advice, Ed," she replied. "I'll start with an eggnog – it's made from milk, eggs and honey and that'll do her a lot of good."

I took my leave of Clara, saying I'd phone her at The Manor each day to see how Antonia was getting on, and that she could call me at any time. Russell and I then drove back to Stanmore, where I spent the rest of the day feeling totally drained.

Mum&Dad were very understanding and Mum plied me with regular sustenance, much in the way I imagined Clara was doing for Antonia.

The days dragged by. I went to work, came home, ate, went to bed, got up . . . Slowly my mind and heart absorbed the fact of Ambrose's death and I began to return to some semblance of normalcy. I phoned Clara Vivian at The Manor every day and sent a message to Antonia that I was thinking of her.

Clara told me there would be a ceremony at the Crematorium during the week for family only, and that on the coming Sunday morning at ten a.m. a service would be held in The Manor chapel. All those who'd known and loved Ambrose were invited to attend.

"Please come, Ed, and bring your parents too," she said. "Antonia is wondering if you might be able to say a few words about your friendship with Ambrose."

"Tell Antonia I will be honoured to speak at the service," I replied.

I told Mum&Dad and we decided to ask Russell if we could go to the service at The Manor with him in his car.

"I can see it might be a good idea for *us* to acquire a vehicle in the not-too-distant future," Dad said, and this remark was typical of what we were like at that time – speaking of everyday matters in the midst of our grief.

The next Sunday morning, we arrived with Russell at The Manor a few minutes before ten o'clock. As I'd never been to a funeral or memorial service before, I didn't have much of an idea what to expect. Antonia had sent out word requesting everyone to wear bright colours in memory of Ambrose, which we all did. I suppose this may have made it a bit better, or at least maybe a fraction less awful – hard to know, really.

The Manor chapel was located down a flight of marble stairs leading from the ground floor. It was quite spacious, with seating on both sides of a wide central aisle. A large chandelier hung from the ceiling and hymn books lay ready for use on the wooden benches. When we arrived, the chapel was nearly full, but Clara Vivian had kept three places for us at the front so I could easily make my way to the stage when it was my turn to speak. In anticipation of a large crowd, folding wooden chairs had been placed in rows in the large vestibule outside the chapel's entrance, in which a man was playing soothing music on a small organ.

Presently, a little frisson passed through the assembled gathering and the organ-music took on a more stately tone. Bishop Leadbeater – resplendent in a magenta-coloured robe, with an enormous gold cross around his neck and a huge purple ring on one hand – had arrived to conduct the service. Ahead of six white-robed young attendants, he strode slowly along the aisle with measured steps. Reaching the stage, he gripped the lectern with both hands, cast a long slow look around at the assembled gathering and began to speak. His voice was slow and quiet at first then gradually gained in strength and resonance. The sonorous cadences flowing from his lips had a powerfully calming effect, I found, and while I didn't necessarily agree with all he had to say on life, death and the hereafter, I could see that his words would soothe many an aching heart.

Narne and Pappi both spoke, expressing their Theosophical viewpoint with total composure and certitude. Pappi looked very much aged, but managed to thank us all for being there and say how much Ambrose had loved Australia. Narne told us that she totally accepted how it was Ambrose's destiny to be born into their family and 'pass over' young, that he did not need to grow old and that his soul would live on in another incarnation.

She finished by saying, "We are thankful for having Ambrose in our lives, and we will give his beloved wife Antonia and his two tiny children all the help and love we can for the rest of our lives. Life works in mysterious ways. Amen." Everyone echoed the 'Amen' and then I was asked to speak.

I took my place at the lectern and simply told the gathering how I'd met Ambrose and Antonia, that I'd become friends with Ambrose and what an important figure he'd been in my life. I told how only two Sundays ago, Ambrose had driven my parents and me over to Balmoral to see the Star Amphitheatre and then to the wharf to take the ferry back to the city. I finished by saying how, as we'd steamed away from the wharf, Ambrose had waved his red kerchief until he was hardly visible on the shore. The unsaid words, 'and that was the last time we ever saw him,' seemed to hang in the air.

Then I just stood there, utterly unable to move. After a moment I heard Antonia say softly: "Thank you, Ed, that was beautiful," and suddenly I could move again and walk back to take my seat next to Mum&Dad.

Bishop Leadbeater stepped up to the lectern again and spoke for a while, after which the gathering sang a few songs from the hymn-books and went upstairs for 'refreshments'. I talked for about a minute with Antonia, who looked pale but calm, and reiterated to Clara that she could call me any time.

Then we left. To tell the truth, it all seemed to pass in a blur. I saw the TS people I knew and Max, and was conscious that the mood of calm acceptance among those gathered together was very different from the loud lamentations I'd observed when walking past funerals at the Catholic church at Stanmore.

On the way home in the car with Russell, Dad said reflectively, "Theosophists view death differently from Christians, and there's a good deal to be said for their way of dealing with the things in life that can't be changed."

CHAPTER 19

AFTERNOON TEA WITH NARNE AND PAPPI

During the next week, I kept in touch with Clara Vivian to see how things were going with Antonia and the twins. I wondered if they'd prefer to be left in peace but Clara assured me this was not the case, saying, "When I tell Antonia you've rung, she smiles a little and it's the only time she does so. She's caring for the babies beautifully and she said to me, 'I don't know how I'd keep on going if it weren't for these two little creatures.'"

"Sounds like she's coping pretty well under the circumstances," I replied. "How is she sleeping?" Clara replied that whenever the twins slept, Antonia slept too. This seemed very sensible. However, even before Ambrose's death I had felt she looked somewhat pale and I did wonder if she might be anaemic.

At work, I consulted my colleague Dr Joanna Short, specialist in maternal and infant health. I told her I was concerned about a recently-widowed family friend who was breastfeeding eight-month-old twins and who looked somewhat peaky.

"Well," said Dr Short, getting quickly to the heart of the matter as she always did, "of course the lass is in a maximum stress situation right now, more's the pity. She can't change the death of her husband, nor can she help having twins. She sounds like she's dedicated to the breast-feeding, and good for her.

"The main thing she *can* do something about is nutrition. She needs to keep up her calcium level and eat a lot of iron-rich foods. So, my advice is: lots of milk and other dairy products and some liver and a good hearty steak, as often as possible."

"That all sounds very reasonable, Joanna" I replied. "But she happens to be a vegetarian."

Dr Short frowned. "That makes it a little harder . . ." Then she announced: "Syrup Minadex – that'll do the trick," explaining that Syrup Minadex was an iron tonic with additional vitamins that was, according to its label, suitable for vegetarians. I noted down the name, then asked what her view was regarding weaning. "Every case is different, of course," she told me. "But babies from seven months onwards can very easily be given a bottle or cup if the mother so wishes or events dictate."

That evening on my way home from the surgery I stopped at a pharmacy and asked for a bottle of Syrup Minadex.

"Who's it for?" the sales assistant asked. "Yourself, your wife or your kiddies?"

I plumped for 'myself' and as she wrapped up the bottle she told me it was good for all age groups and that she herself took a spoonful every morning. "And do you know, I've not had a cold in five years," she told me proudly.

That Saturday morning, I phoned Clara Vivian and asked if Sunday afternoon might be a convenient time to call by. She said 'yes', and that Narne and Pappi would also like to meet up with me. I set off from Stanmore just after lunch and on the ferry to Mosman, I thought about what I really wanted to know but couldn't ask, at least not at this juncture. Top of my list was: 'Is Antonia going to stay in Australia or return to the States and live with Narne and Pappi?'

By now, I'd visited The Manor more than half a dozen times, and as the ferry chugged towards Athol Wharf my mind presented me with a series of images from each of my visits – starting with the Open House day I'd attended with Mum&Dad two years before through to the memorial service for Ambrose held exactly one week ago.

When I arrived at The Manor, the front door was opened by Clara. She told me Antonia was sleeping at the moment,

"But this will be a good time for you to talk with Narne and Pappi," she said. She asked one of the residents to call them, then led the way into the refectory.

"At his hour, the room's generally empty so we won't be disturbed," she told me, boiling a kettle and putting some slices of fruitcake on a plate ready for afternoon tea. Presently, Narne and Pappi came in, looking tired but otherwise in good shape considering what they were going through.

We sat ourselves down at one of the large wooden tables and Clara passed round cups of tea and offered slices of cake. Pretty soon, Pappi said, "Well, Ed, let's down to brass tacks – Narne and I will only be in Sydney for another week. Much as we'd like to stay longer, back in the States I've got a business to run."

I nodded and he went on, "Our first priority is the well-being of Antonia and the twins. She's still in shock, naturally, but she's a great girl and holding up well – helped of course by her good mother, Clara, whom we've come to love very much in the short time we've known her."

Here Clara smiled and said, "It's mutual, Pappi," and Narne leant across the table and squeezed her hand.

"So," continued Pappi, "we've had a round-table discussion with Antonia and Clara and heard that their preference is for Antonia and the babies to stay here in Sydney rather than return to the States with us. Of course, we'd love to have them with us over there, but we do understand that after this terrible experience Antonia will feel happier to be here in Sydney surrounded by family and friends. You can bet your bottom dollar we'll be over as often as possible to see her and our two little grandchildren, and later on they'll be coming over to the States on a regular basis."

This plan sounded excellent and I told him so.

"Then," Pappi continued, "Here's where you come in, Ed."

"Oh yes?" I queried.

In a wild moment, triggered no doubt by the tension of the situation and everything we'd been through, I had the craziest notion: that Pappi was going to ask me to marry Antonia! I banished this aberration the moment it surfaced, but felt a little shaken that my mind was so deranged as to even generate such a bizarre thought. I put it down to strain, and consciously tried to tune in to what Pappi was now saying.

"Antonia and the twins will never have any money worries – ever," he said firmly. "That being the case, I need to sort things out financially in a watertight way before we leave Sydney – establish a trust fund and arrange for Antonia to buy a house."

"That's very good of you," I murmured, still feeling a bit shaken by my thought.

"They are our kin," Pappi declared, and Narne beside him nodded emphatically.

"Now, Ed," he continued, "I always like to keep my personal life separate from my business life, meaning I have never mixed Theosophy with money, apart from some philanthropic gestures I've made from time to time. So this means – I'm in need of a legal advisor. I've met your father and he strikes me as a very sound man, so I'd like to meet with him as soon as possible and get a recommendation on who to entrust with the job of ensuring Antonia and her children will never be short of a dollar, or I suppose here in Australia I should say 'a pound'."

We all laughed heartily at this – mainly to break the tension. I looked across at Clara, and she seemed close to tears. I wondered if she was thinking back to when she'd found herself left with five young children, no husband and no money.

"I'm sure my father would be very happy to help in this matter," I said. "He'll easily be able to put you in contact with the best people. When would you like to meet with him? I could telephone him from here if you'd like me to."

Narne and Pappi settled on a day and time during the next week. I phoned Dad, put him in the picture and soon it was all arranged. Antonia was still sleeping, so I said I didn't want to disturb her and gave the bottle of Syrup Minadex to Clara.

"Syrup Minadex!" she cried when she saw it. "That old favourite! I used to give it to my children when they were small. I'll see that Antonia gets started on it right away."

Narne and Pappi hadn't heard of the tonic, and they eagerly focused on its medicinal qualities and suitability for vegetarians. I noted this attention as yet another instance of people seizing on trivial topics while under stress.

Now seemed like a good moment to leave, so I said I'd keep in touch and call in during the next weekend. Clara went with me to the front door of The Manor, thanked me again for all my help and hugged me.

I was just closing the heavy wrought-iron front gate when I heard Pappi call, "Wait, Ed, I'll walk part of the way to the tram-stop with you." I wondered if he might be wanting to have a private word with me, and this turned out to be the case.

As we walked up the hill together, he got straight to the point: "I'll be glad to see Antonia out of The Manor and under her own roof," he announced.

"Why's that?" I asked.

"Well, Ed," he said. "I don't know how involved you are with the TS here, but over in the States we have a few areas of difference with some of the Sydney folk."

"Is that so?" I thought I might know what these were, but wanted to hear it from Pappi himself.

"Yes *siree*," he replied. "And it so happens they concern a personage who resides at The Manor with a new private bathroom overlooking the Harbour."

"You mean – Bishop Leadbeater?"

Pappi nodded. "Yes, the Right Reverend Bishop Charles Webster Leadbeater," he replied, giving each word a clipped emphasis.

"Well, if Antonia needs any help in finding a suitable place to buy, I'll be ready to help her in any way I can," I told him. "She and Ambrose were wonderful to me when I was doing my dissertation."

At the sound of his son's name, Pappi sighed. "Yes," he said sadly. "We never expected all this to come about." Then he seemed to brighten. "But there's still young Ambrose III – my dream's not over yet, and hope lives on . . ."

I couldn't but admire Pappi's capacity to keep on keeping on. We parted at this point, with me saying I looked forward to seeing him and Narne when they returned to Sydney. "And don't leave it too long, either."

"We surely won't" said Pappi, giving me a bear-hug.

Thirty minutes later, sitting outside on the ferry as it chugged its way through the cool evening back towards Circular Quay, I engaged in a spot of introspection concerning the strange instant during afternoon tea when I momentarily thought Pappi was about to ask me to marry Antonia. Although I had quickly banished this totally unacceptable thought-form, I couldn't deny to myself that it had occurred, and I now needed to analyse it.

Had it been triggered earlier in the week when I bought the Syrup Minadex and the saleswoman asked me who it was for – 'yourself, your wife or your kiddies'? I also reflected on Sigmund Freud's revolutionary theory that the human psyche is structured into three distinct, yet interacting systems: the *Id*, which comes up with uncoordinated, instinctual trends; the *Super-Ego*, which plays a moralizing, critical role; and the *Ego*, the organized, realistic part that mediates between the Id and the Super-Ego.

How neatly that strange moment at The Manor fitted into this framework, each part playing its role: the Id, in generating this wild thought in the first place; the Ego, in quickly acting to smother it; and the Super-Ego in roundly condemning the crass opportunism displayed so soon after the death of my good friend.

Then another possibility assailed me – could the thought have also been in Pappi's mind? Did I 'catch' it via thought-transference? My common sense soon disposed of this idea – clearly the whole thing was merely a matter of wishful thinking and I needed to keep stronger control over my thoughts. (And was this my Super-Ego speaking again?)

By now, the ferry was docking at Circular quay and I'd had enough of this somewhat uncomfortable soul-searching. As I crossed the gangplank onto the wharf, I spotted Max Herbst waiting to board the ferry for its return trip to Mosman.

"Good evening, Max!" I exclaimed. "Where are you off to?"

"Just visiting friends," he replied pleasantly. "Are you free for dinner some night this week?"

We quickly arranged where and when to meet, then the ferry skipper rang the departure bell, the deckhand removed the gangplank and the ferry chugged its way across the Harbour to Mosman.

A few days later, Dad had lunch with Pappi and introduced him to an old and respected legal friend, Ian Green, a man of many years' experience in administering trusts, deceased estates and so on. Apparently all went well at the lunch and Dad said how impressed he was by Pappi's ability to get things moving, "Especially since he must be still reeling from the shock of losing his only son."

During the lunch Dad had asked Pappi, as a successful businessman, what he would say was the secret of success.

"Delegation," Pappi had replied promptly. "The ability to delegate – to the right person, of course."

"And how do you know who that right person might be?" Dad asked, to which Pappi had responded,

"Ah . . . now *that's* the secret of success, and a secret's not a secret if it's told."

Although pressed by Dad, Pappi would divulge no more. And as Dad said to Mum and me, he saw a distinctly 'mystical' look come into Pappi's eyes – which set me wondering if my very science-minded father might be growing a bit 'occult' himself!

When Saturday came around, I rang The Manor and asked Clara Vivian if she thought I could call in the next day.

"Oh yes," she replied. "That'd be very good. Antonia was disappointed she missed you last Sunday, and of course Narne and Pappi started on their journey back to The States this morning."

The next day, as I set off on public transport to Mosman and The Manor, involving as it did a train journey, two tram-rides, a ferry trip and a longish walk, not to mention the same on the return trip home, I couldn't help thinking how much quicker and easier the journey would be by car. I also knew Dad's car-buying process would be considerably speeded up if I went ahead and learned to drive. Suddenly an idea occurred to me: why not ask Russell Fletcher to teach me – in his car?

That evening after dinner, I told Dad what I planned to do and he said, "I think I'd better learn to drive, too. This way we'll both be able to drive Mum around when we get the car."

Mum, at this point, happened to be nearby in the kitchen and heard every word. Dropping what she was doing, she came in and joined us.

"Excuse me, Arthur," she said firmly. "I will have you know that *I* will be taking driving lessons too, and when we get the car, *I* may drive *you* around on occasion."

"Good for you, Mum!" I said and hugged her. Dad, looking a bit surprised, followed suit.

CHAPTER 20

DRIVING LESSONS

When I asked Russell Fletcher if he'd teach me to drive – in his car – he was only too happy to oblige. This was one of the good things about Russell. He was very generous-spirited, but it did come with a certain amount of heavy-handed chiacking,[47] such as:

"Oh my goodness, the Best family's really jumped head-first into the twentieth century, no doubt about you! First the telephone, now driving lessons, and its only 1924! Next thing, you'll be getting a wireless."

"We've had a wireless for years, as you very well know, Russell," I said through gritted teeth, reflecting that although I didn't have to pay for these driving lessons, they did come at a price.

"I know, I know," Russell replied equably. "But when you're driving, Ed, you have to get used to distractions on the road and annoying passengers – it's par for the course, old boy."

After a few more lessons, Russell suggested that as part of my training we could drive over to The Manor and say hello to the Manorites. This idea had a lot to recommend it, so I rang The Manor and spoke to Antonia. She said she'd love to see us and expressed admiration that I could now (under Russell's beady eye) navigate through the city, get the car onto the vehicular ferry that plied between Dawes Point on the south side of the Harbour and Blues Point on the north and then drive to Mosman.

---

[47] chiacking: good-humoured bantering

When we arrived at The Manor, Russell was borne off by a couple of friends to join a group comfortably ensconced on the front verandah. This left me alone with Antonia, a rare event since usually there was someone around, either her mother Clara or one of the various helpers with the twins.

In the kitchen, Antonia made a pot of tea and put it on a tray with two mugs and a plate of oatmeal biscuits. She led the way into the empty refectory where we sat down opposite each other at a table near the window. To my eyes, Antonia didn't look exactly robust, but she seemed much stronger and considerably more animated than in those first dark days after Ambrose's death. She told me that, thanks to Pappi and Ian Green, all the legal matters were now sorted out, and there was nothing to stop her from going ahead and buying a house.

"But do you know, Ed," she told me with a slightly worried look, "right now I simply have no energy to do anything. All I really want to do is – absolutely nothing! Looking after my babies is excellent 'therapy' – but as for thinking about the future and making plans, that's totally beyond me."

I said this was completely understandable, and there was absolutely no rush for any big decisions.

"That's true," she replied. "But Pappi has hinted rather strongly that he'll be happier when I'm under my own roof and not part of The Manor community."

"Oh? And why's that?" I asked.

"It's got to do with the position taken by some members of the American TS regarding Bishop Leadbeater," she explained. "According to Pappi, and I'll quote you his words: 'It is not ideal for you to be literally living under the same roof as *that man*.' "

"Hmm," I replied. "Quite a strong stance. But . . . do you see much of CWL?"

She shook her head, saying, "His rooms are here on the ground floor only about twenty yards away from where we're sitting now, but I hardly ever see him. He usually emerges in the late afternoon to take a walk with some of his young friends and when he sees me, we greet each other courteously and he always asks after the 'little ones', as he calls them. But let's face it Ed, as a breast-feeding widow with twins, I doubt I'm quite his type!"

We both laughed, and then Antonia said, "Naturally, I do have to consider Pappi and Narne's wishes, and I am wondering if . . . Do you mind my talking with you about this, Ed? I don't want to be a bore . . ."

"Antonia, never in a million years could you ever be a bore," I replied fervently, wishing I could say a lot more. "Tell me anything that's on your mind."

"Thank you, Ed," she said, and her voice sounded a bit husky. "At the moment, the most I feel up to is finding somewhere to rent for a while here in Mosman. Then when I feel stronger, I can look around slowly and buy a suitable house."

"That sounds very reasonable," I replied, "and I'm sure Narne and Pappi will understand."

"Oh Ed, I'm glad you think so," she said, reaching over and squeezing my hand. "It's just that since the start of 1922, my life's been a real whirlwind – very enjoyable of course, up until Ambrose's death. But frankly, what I really need is peace and quiet until I've come to terms with all that's happened. I want to live very simply, caring for the babies and seeing my family and a few friends like you. Then, when the one-year anniversary of Ambrose's death has passed I'll throw off my widow's weeds and re-enter normal life."

I must've looked a little puzzled at this because Antonia laughed and said, "Oh, so you haven't heard of 'widow's weeds'?"

"No, I can't say I have," I replied. "Are they actual 'weeds' that you wear, or what?"

"Widows in the olden days used to dress in black, and their clothes were called 'widows' weeds'," she told me. "But that's not me, Ed, I can assure you. Do you remember how I asked people to wear bright colours at Ambrose's memorial service?"

I nodded, the scene was etched in my memory.

I think we both felt at this point it was time to join Russell and the others on the verandah. For my part, I certainly didn't want to give any impression of monopolising Antonia's attention. We then passed a pleasant half-hour with the group, who were discussing how well the Communal Living project was working, with a few minor problems yet to be ironed out.

Presently, Clara Vivian joined us with the now quite mobile twins. I observed them with interest, noticing that little Ingrid seemed to resemble Antonia quite a lot, and Ambrose III (known to all as 'Three') looked a lot like – Pappi Mortimer!

Clara noticed me looking at the two of them, so I asked who she thought they took after.

"Oh," she replied, smiling, "Ingrid is practically identical with Antonia at this age; and as for Three – well, we all think he's just like his grandfather Pappi!" When she said this, we both couldn't help laughing, for the likeness was indeed strong.

We took our leave soon after this and on the drive back to Stanmore, Russell remarked,

"I don't know whether you've noticed this at all, Ed, but Antonia is one very attractive woman."

Keeping my eyes firmly on the road I replied neutrally, "Well, she and Ambrose used to be a striking couple."

"When she's finished doing this widow thing, I've half a mind to make a play for her myself," Russell confided.

"Well, why not?" I managed to say nonchalantly, steering my way through the evening traffic and not taking my eyes off the road.

By the time we arrived at Stanmore I'd regained my internal equilibrium, reasoning that if Russell was the type of man who appealed to Antonia, then so be it. I conjured up a few concepts like 'destiny', 'inshallah' and so on and thanked Russell for giving up his time to teach me to drive. Then I asked how many more lessons would be needed before I could drive on my own.

"Oh, you're nearly ready," he told me. "I'd say only a couple more hours."

"Wonderful," I replied. That day could not come soon enough.

A few weeks later, I had dinner with Max Herbst. By now, our meetings had broadened out to encompass various topics of mutual interest. This evening, Max had some interesting TS news: Mr T.H. Martyn, president of the recently-formed Independent Theosophical Society (ITS) [48] had died suddenly in Malaya, while on a business trip. He had made an enormous contribution to Theosophy in Sydney over the past thirty years in both leadership and financial support, and Max and I had a lot of respect for him.

Mr Martyn's decision after the TS Convention in 1922 to take his dossier on CWL to the police was certainly controversial and, to some TS members, a deed of utter treason towards the Society. We, however, saw his actions as those of a man who simply could not countenance seeing the ideals to which he'd devoted so much of his life now being trampled on by people he viewed as less than morally sound.

---

[48] The Independent Theosophical Society was the former Sydney Lodge of the TS, and home to its approximately 600 members following the split of the Sydney TS in 1922 into two lodges, Sydney Lodge (for the 'Dissidents') and Blavatsky Lodge (for the 'Loyalists').

"How will Mr Martyn's death affect the ITS, do you think?" I asked.

"It'll have a huge impact," Max replied. "Mr Martyn's widow will take over from him, as far as that's possible, and become president. But it's going to be hard because he was such a huge presence. To his followers, his death is indeed a great loss."

We then moved on to talk of Krishnamurti, now head of the Order of the Star in the East[49] founded by Dr Besant to prepare the world for the coming of the new World Teacher (also known as the Lord Maitreya). Max reported that Krishnamurti was taking an increasingly active role in the Order, despite still experiencing crippling episodes of pain due to his Process. He had recently been in Holland, first at Castle Eerde, Arnhem, for a TS Convention and the third International Star Conference, and then on to the first-ever Star Camp at Ommen, about a mile from Castle Eerde.[50]

In Krishnamurti's evening camp-fire talks to the nearly five hundred members of the Order of the Star in the East, he focused on the need to *feel,* rather than simply have an intellectual appreciation of a Divine Teacher. To progress along the Path towards Discipleship, true passion was necessary. He likened the intensity of this passion to falling in love, adding that he'd noticed a regrettable lack of passion in many people, particularly older ones.

Following the Star camp, Lady Emily Lutyens arranged for Krishnamurti, Nitya, her daughters Mary and Betty and a group of friends to stay for a time at Pergine, northern Italy, in order to help them along the Path to Discipleship. In the mornings, Krishnamurti would hold talks in the open air to clarify and expand on the qualities that his listeners needed to nurture in themselves, namely Unselfishness, Love and Sympathy. He advised the young

---

[49] From 1927 known as 'The Order of the Star'.
[50] See Glossary: Castle Eerde

single girls in the group that although they might aspire to marriage and family life, this was incompatible with serving the Masters. He was quite severe, saying that to play at having both would make them bourgeois, and there was nothing worse than mediocrity. However at the same time, he stressed that they must at all costs not deny emotion and grow hard, his definition of 'emotion' being 'the power to respond instantly'.[51]

"Hmm, quite a tall order, that," I observed.

"For some," Max replied enigmatically, adding, "Apparently Krishnamurti finds these young people rather unresponsive, likening them to sponges who simply suck in his words and seem to make no personal progress."

This prompted me to ask, as I had often done, "How do you know all this, Max?"

"I have my informants," he replied as he had done many times before, then gave out a little more. "There are usually quite a few individuals around Krishnamurti and they talk amongst themselves, write letters, speak on the telephone and so on. Word does get around, you know, and for obvious reasons many people take a very close interest in what Krishnamurti says and does."

He went on to tell me how one evening Krishnamurti had an intuition that something important was about to happen. The next morning, it transpired that the Lord Maitreya had visited him during the night and, after talking with him for a while, had left a message for the whole group to hear.

"Interesting stuff," I murmured. "And since you're privy to so much that goes on with Krishnamurti, I wonder if perchance you might also be acquainted with the content of that message."

"Well, strange that you should say that, or perhaps not so strange at all," Max replied. "It so happens that I

---

[51] Lutyens, Krishnamurti, 192.

do have a copy of the message – right here, as a matter of fact." He opened his briefcase and, after rummaging round inside it, produced a somewhat crumpled sheet of paper.

"Eureka!" he announced and started to read out the message:

" 'Learn to serve Me, for along that path alone will you find me.
Forget yourself, for only am I to be found.
Do not look for the Great Ones when they may be very near you.
You are like the blind man who seeks sunshine.
You are like the hungry man who is offered food and will not eat.
The happiness you seek is not far off; it lies in every common stone.
I am there if you will only see. I am the Helper if you will let Me help.' " [52]

"Intriguing . . ." I commented.

"Mmm," Max replied. "All that can be said with any certainty is that it is considerably different from previous messages that have been brought through."

"Different in *style* or in *content*?" I asked

"Both," Max answered and then, as if to distract me from this line of enquiry, told me that Nitya's tuberculosis had flared up again.

"I'm sorry to hear that," I replied. "TB's dashed hard to get rid of once it's taken hold. Are Krishnamurti and Nitya still in Europe?"

"No, the Pergine group is now on its way to Naples to travel by sea to India and spend some time at Adyar. After that, Krishnamurti, Nitya, Lady Emily Lutyens, her two daughters and several others will proceed on to Sydney for the Star Convention in April next year."

---

[52] Lutyens, 1984, 193-4.

CHAPTER 21

DEVELOPMENTS ON
SEVERAL FRONTS

By October 1924, the Star Amphitheatre, known simply as 'The Amphitheatre', was up-and-running. A formal opening was never held, due to Bishop Leadbeater's several bouts of ill-health and so, in the words of the Star organisers, 'we glided quietly into our usage, a play on Saturday afternoons and a lecture every Sunday evening.'[53] The first of these lectures was delivered by TS member Dr J. J. (Koos) van de Leeuw whose topic, 'The Message of the Star', was very well received by the audience.

For me, 1925 got off to a good start. Thanks to Russell Fletcher's selfless efforts with the driving lessons, I was now competent to be in sole charge of a motor vehicle. One evening when I arrived home from the surgery, a handsome maroon 1922 Packard Tourer was parked outside our house. I assumed it belonged to one of Dad's accountancy clients who'd come for some after-hours money advice. However, when I got inside and found no one else present apart from Mum&Dad who were grinning from ear to ear, I know something else was afoot.

"Who owns the Packard outside?" I asked.

Dad smiled modestly, "We do – it's ours."

I could hardly believe it! I hugged them both and, over a cup of tea in the kitchen, they told me how this

---

[53] *The Star in the East*. Editorial notes, Jan. 1925, 2.

momentous event had come about. Apparently one of Dad's colleagues was going overseas and wanted to sell his car. He put the word around and Dad made the best offer.

"So here you are, Son," he said, handing me the keys. "How about the three of us go for a spin – just around the block?"

Having only ever driven one car – namely, Russell's – I felt slightly unnerved by this request. However, I strode out to the Packard jangling the car-keys confidently and whistling a carefree tune. When I'd figured out how to get the vehicle started, I toot-tooted the horn and quick as a flash Mum&Dad came out of the house. Rather touchingly, they were both wearing their best 'going out' clothes. We drove down our street, watched by neighbours who waved to us cheerily, then ventured a little further afield, returning very chuffed at having made it back home without incident.

I offered to pay for half of the car but Dad said, "No, Ed – I'd rather you put your money away for later on, you'll need it then for a house. But how about you pay for petrol and any running repairs." Naturally, I agreed to this.

Once I'd got the hang of driving the Packard, I decided to put my expertise to the test by motoring over to The Manor one weekend. Accordingly, I phoned Antonia, who said they'd be delighted to see me.

The next Sunday afternoon, I arrived at The Manor without mishap and found Antonia and her mother in the front garden cutting flowers to fill the large vases inside. They expressed admiration at my driving prowess and the car, too, received a few accolades. It was indeed a vehicle to be proud of, and even Russell Fletcher said he was impressed.

Over afternoon tea on the verandah, Antonia told me she'd found a house to rent.

"It's a 'semi'[54] and it's fully furnished, which is lucky since I have no furniture to speak of. It has three bedrooms: one for me, one for the twins and one for Mother, who's coming to live with us. Oh, and it also has a big back garden which will be nice for the children."

"Sounds good," I said. "Whereabouts is it?"

"About a mile or so from here," she replied, "close to Mosman Junction. It's convenient for shopping and transport and, best of all, we can move in next weekend. It's a big step for me to take, Ed, but I feel up to it now, and thankfully with Mother there I won't be on my own.

"This might sound strange to you," she went on. "But for most of my life I've lived in a communal set-up – first here in Sydney as a schoolgirl boarding at Morven Garden School, then when I taught there and lived-in as a house mistress. And after that Ambrose and I were in the Ojai Valley California with other people, and next with Narne and Pappi in Connecticut. Then finally, here I am at The Manor in the middle of the Communal Living project. The idea of living in a house with only my immediate family feels rather strange, to tell the truth."

I said I thought she'd soon adjust to this new way of living, and maybe even come to like it. I spoke from a total lack of experience, of course, but thought it best to sound positive, since it was about to happen anyway.

"If you need a hand to move your possessions, I'll be very happy to help," I offered.

Antonia looked at me gratefully. "Oh Ed, that'd be marvellous! I haven't got a lot of stuff, one or two car trips should do it, I'd say. But it'll be much nicer if you're there rather than a strange removalist."

We talked a little more about the move, with Antonia saying she'd cabled Narne and Pappi with the news that

---

[54] 'Semi' is a commonly-used term for a semi-detached house, a dwelling that is built as one of a pair that share a common wall. Often, the layout of each house is a mirror-image of the other.

she was about to move into a rented semi in Mosman, and they'd replied saying they were very pleased.

"Poor, dear Pappi," she said. "Narne tells me he's channelling his grief into the business and his hopes for the future into Ambrose III, who in his mind will succeed him in the firm." We both smiled at this, it being so typical of Pappi, and I recalled how he'd expressed the same hopes to me in the weeks after Ambrose's death.

I glanced across at Three, who at this moment was lying on the carpet playing with a toy car while his sister Ingrid was busy tucking her doll into a small pram ready to go for a walk along The Manor verandah.

"How old are the twins now?" I asked.

"They'll be two in August, would you believe," Antonia told me. "And I'm thinking of holding a small party for them. Of course the guests will all be grown-ups, but it might be rather fun."

I said I thought it was a great idea. More than anything, I was very glad to hear her sounding much more like her old self again.

"Actually," she went on, "now is probably a good time to be moving out from The Manor. From next week onwards, streams of TS members will be arriving from interstate and overseas to stay here during the TS Convention in April."

"Any 'notables'?" I wondered, feeling sure there would be.

"Oh, yes," Antonia replied. "There's a contingent coming from Adyar that includes Lady Emily Lutyens, two of her daughters and several others. They're all very keen to work on their spiritual advancements under the guidance of Krishnamurti, who will be staying nearby with his brother Nitya."

I wondered out loud how Lady Emily Lutyens came to be involved in Theosophy, and Antonia told me that she was married to a famous English architect, Sir Edwin Lutyens, and the mother of five children. She'd first met

Krishnamurti in 1911 when he and Nitya came to London with Annie Besant, and, when Mrs Besant formed the Order of the Star in the East, she'd asked Lady Emily to become National Representative of the Order in England. Lady Emily threw herself wholeheartedly into this role, and in the process became totally engrossed in Krishnamurti and the cause of the new World Teacher.

"Lady Emily would follow Krishnamurti to the ends of the earth, if need be," Antonia finished.

The next weekend, I drove over to The Manor again and took Antonia's possessions to her new abode in Gouldsbury St, Mosman. The house was an attractive white-painted semi in a row of similar dwellings overlooking a park. All Antonia's family – Clara, her three sisters and her brother – were there to give a hand with the move and when the place looked fairly ship-shape we all sat round the kitchen table and had a cup of tea. I was glad that Clara was coming to live with Antonia, and I think all of us at that moment felt the absence of Ambrose particularly keenly.

As if she could intuit my thoughts, Antonia said, "Do you remember how Ambrose wanted us to move out from The Manor into a place of our own? Well, one day we drove along this very street and he said this was exactly where he'd like to live. And here we are! Isn't life strange?"

The next Wednesday evening I had dinner with Max and at some point the talk turned to Krishnamurti and his strange Process.

"It'll be interesting to see what Dr Mary Rocke has to say when she returns from visiting Ojai and spending some time with Krishnamurti and his support team," Max said. "The Process certainly has some strange features – intense pain in the lower spine and the nape of the neck, loss of consciousness, crying out, speaking in his first language which he normally doesn't remember, intense fatigue, inability to bear loud sounds, and so on. And yet there are times when he seems perfectly fine.

"Also, while he's in this strange state he says he can't have a married woman on duty in the room with him. Fortunately, Rosalind Williams is there a lot of the time so she's able help out Nitya, who really bears the brunt of the whole thing. During the Process, which in this episode has lasted more than a hundred nights, he may receive messages from the Masters which he copies out later. Leadbeater, I might add, is of the opinion that these messages are not in the style of the Masters."

"Hmm, interesting . . . " I commented, then said, "By the way, what's the medical consensus on the 'Process' over there in California?"

"There isn't any," replied Max, "due to the fact that Krishnamurti refuses to go see a doctor. Nitya says he and Krishnamurti have concluded that it's part of the awakening of his kundalini."

"*Kundalini*?" I queried. "Is that a medical term? If so, it's one I'm not familiar with."

"It's a Sanskrit word that refers to a form of primal energy said to be located at the base of the spine," Max explained. "The kundalini can only be awakened through a combination of high thinking, right living and unselfish activity. And with this awakening comes an enormous release of energy that can be quite transformational."

Hmm, interesting . . . " I said again. I didn't recall this phenomenon being addressed at all during my medical course at Sydney University.

Max went on to say that although Krishnamurti appeared to the outside world as serene, even somewhat detached, he in fact experienced many doubts regarding his capacity to fulfil the role mapped for him by Annie Besant, CWL and of course the Masters. He was also deeply sensitive to the rudeness and jeers he quite frequently met from the general public.

"Do you have any actual examples of this?" I wondered.

"I certainly do," he replied. "In 1922 in Sydney while walking in the streets, Krishnamurti might encounter comments like: 'There goes that chap printed in the papers, the Messiah!' and 'Hello! There goes that fellow with thirty lives'.[55] As well, he'd sometimes be subjected to instances of racial prejudice, such as the remark by an Australian fellow-passenger on the boat from Sydney to San Francisco who asked why 'a dark man' was allowed to travel first class." [56]

"Hmm," I responded. "Not nice at all."

We wound up the session with Max saying, "Regarding Krishnamurti, I think we've more or less arrived at the present time. This being the case, and bearing in mind that the man himself will arrive here in Sydney fairly soon, I suggest we put him to one side for a while and turn our attention to a couple of other TS identities.

"A lot of changes are coming in the Society, due partly to the fact that dear old Annie Besant and CWL are now getting on in years. They're both nearly eighty and can't go on forever, notwithstanding the fact that Dr Besant has just embarked on a thirty-lecture tour of India."

"She must have the stamina of an ox, especially in that heat!" I said admiringly.

"I'll say," agreed Max. "But the time is approaching for a 'changing of the guard' in the TS and I'd like to shift the focus onto a man who's going to play a major role in the coming years, if I'm not mistaken."

"Whose name is?"

Max smiled in an irritatingly mysterious way. "Tell you next time we meet . . ." was all he'd say.

---

[55] Lutyens, Krishnamurti, 145.
[56] Ibid., 147.

After Antonia had settled into her rented semi, she found she rather enjoyed it. Having her mother Clara there with her was a great help and towards the end of the year she decided to hold a 'house-warming' afternoon tea party for a small group: her siblings, Mum&Dad and me, Russell Fletcher, Dora van Gelder, Max Herbst, Joyce Housman and several others. It all went well, and I was pleased to see Dad and Max deep in discussion and Mum and Joyce earnestly talking together. Russell, I noticed, seemed to be paying Antonia's sister Helena quite a lot of attention.

Holding a tray of drinks to offer around, I passed him and a hummed a few bars of the song 'Clementine'.

Russell followed me out of the room.

"What's that supposed to mean?" he hissed.

"What?" I asked innocently.

"That reference to 'Clementine',".

"Oh that," I replied. "The last few lines just popped into my head:

'So I kissed her little sister,
And forgot my Clementine.' "

Russell laughed. "Helena *is* rather nice, you know," he said.

Mme. Helena Petrovna
Blavatsky

Mrs Annie Besant

Bishop Charles Webster Leadbeater (CWL)

*Dora van Gelder and
friends with Bishop
Leadbeater (Java, 1914)*

*Mrs Annie Besant, CWL,
and Krishnamurti (left to
right)*

*Krishnamurti, aged 17, arrives in London with brother Nitya
and Mrs Annie Besant.*

C.W. Leadbeater with Mrs Besant on her arrival in Sydney, May 1922.

The Star Amphitheatre, Mosman in 1924.

*Jiddu Krishnamurti (above). Bishop
George Arundale with wife Rukmini
(right).*

The Manor, Clifton Gardens, Mosman

The Garden School, Balmoral, Mosman

The Star Amphitheatre, Balmoral, Mosman
Painting by Ethel Carrick Fox, 1925

69 Hunter Street, Sydney

Mr. T.H. Martyn

Mr.s Alice Cleather

Mr. Basil Crump

PART 3

APRIL 1925 – 1929

CONTENTS

CHAPTER 22

A CHANCE MEETING

By March 1925, the party of TS 'notables' (Krishnamurti, Nitya, Lady Emily Lutyens and her two daughters, Raja[57] and several others) had left Colombo aboard the Orient Line RMS *Ormuz* and were steaming across the Indian Ocean towards Australia. Nitya, however, was in exceedingly poor health, only rarely emerging from the cabin he shared with Krishnamurti to get a breath of fresh air up on deck.

On reaching Australia, Krishnamurti, Lady Emily and Raja, spoke at packed OSE gatherings convened in their honour. In Fremantle, Perth, Adelaide and Melbourne, Krishnamurti was presented with deeds for parcels of land to be used for building meeting-places to aid in the work of the new World Teacher.[58] One such dream had already become reality – the monumental Star Amphitheatre at Balmoral Beach, Sydney.

The *Ormuz* was scheduled to arrive in Sydney Harbour on Friday April 3, 1925, which happened to be my rostered day off from the General Practice. On an impulse, I decided to join the band of Theosophists at the Walsh Bay wharf to welcome the party from Adyar.

As the time neared for the passengers to disembark, who should arrive on the wharf but Bishop Leadbeater, accompanied by a gaggle of youths and holding the arm of his current favourite, a good-looking boy of about

---

[57] Full name: Rajagopalachary or D.Rajagopal, friend to Krishnamurti and long-time worker for the Theosophical cause
[58] As was customary, Krishnamurti arranged for the sites to be held by trusts.

---

fifteen whose name I learned was Theodore St John. I hadn't seen CWL for quite a while, and was struck anew by the immense energy he radiated, despite his long white beard and silvery mane of hair. Attired in a purple full-length robe under a magenta cloak, with a large amethyst brooch resplendent on his chest, CWL looked theatrically perfect – that is, until he laughed, revealing two long, fang-like, somewhat yellow eye-teeth.

When the Adyar contingent descended the gangplank and set foot on dry land, they were practically mobbed by the waiting crowd. We had only a momentary glimpse of Krishnamurti and Nitya before they were whisked away to a house in David St, Mosman, guests of the prominent Theosophist Mr John Mackay. The rest of the party and their luggage were then transported in several vehicles to stay nearby at The Manor, now Bishop Leadbeater's permanent home in Sydney.

For the visitors from Adyar, and indeed for all the inhabitants of The Manor, living under the same roof as CWL was far from dull. During communal meals he expected conversation to be kept at a muted level, but often in the evening a select group would be invited to his living quarters on the ground floor. Here he would discourse on the Masters 'with a most infectious conviction of their reality'.[59]

To accompany CWL on one of his late afternoon walks in the bushland around The Manor was another memorable experience. Surrounded by a group of mostly young people, CWL would share with them his clairvoyant observations on the *devas,* or nature-spirits, who dwelt among the grasses and trees. The large sandstone boulders they passed on these early-evening strolls provided him with an opportunity to speak at length

---

[59] Lutyens, Krishnamurti, 203.

on the subject of rocks as sentient beings with human-like feelings, including the capacity to fall in love. [60]

On April 7th, two days before the start of TS Convention, Nitya received distressing medical news: the condition of his lungs had deteriorated considerably. On the advice of his specialist doctor, plans were made to relocate him away from the humid air of Mosman, where the sea breeze blew straight in from the Pacific Ocean. Without wasting any time, Dr Mary Rocke immediately travelled to the Blue Mountains west of Sydney and rented a house in the hamlet of Leura, 3,000 feet above sea level. Here, Nitya with his group of helpers stayed for a number of weeks. Krishnamurti visited him regularly, but the long train trip to and from Leura and his worry about Nitya's health took a toll of his energy.

Some other matters, too, were much on Krishnamurti's mind. In the three years since he'd last been at The Manor, the atmosphere in its community had changed markedly. Now, a distinctly 'hot-house', religious ambience prevailed. Given his dislike of religious trappings and ritual, it was not surprising that Krishnamurti did not feel comfortable when he dropped in to The Manor to visit Lady Emily and the rest of the of the group from Adyar.

He was not simply imagining things. Life at The Manor was becoming increasingly closely linked with the Liberal Catholic Church. Each morning, Mass was celebrated in the chapel, and Benediction every evening. On Sundays, Bishop Leadbeater conducted two services at the Liberal Catholic Church in Redfern and it was incumbent upon members of The Manor community to go to at least one of these. No one wanted to have their journey along the Spiritual Pathway impeded by slack

---

[60] Ibid., 203.

church attendance. Everyone seemed obsessed with their own development as well as that of others. Echoing through the corridors, a common question could be heard: 'How far on are you?'[61]

It was believed that steps along the Path were very likely to occur during the occult festival of Wesak, which in 1925 fell on the night of Friday 8th of May. The Manor community was keenly focused on this event, with members doing their utmost to nurture their moral development. This sense of expectancy was fueled by Bishop Leadbeater, who compiled lists of those who might advance, with his chief acolyte Theodore St John giving out hints as to who might be rewarded. When the results became available after Wesak, they were way beyond Leadbeater's expectations: worldwide, over seventy advancements occurred, including a number at The Manor.

One evening after dinner, Krishnamurti addressed the gathering on 'The importance of what you *are* and not of any labels.'[62] This message reinforced the theme he'd focused on earlier in the year: 'merely putting on a badge or calling oneself a member of the Star is like having in your possession a cheque without a banking account'.[63]

As the TS Convention reached its end, Nitya's medical specialists gave their verdict on his health: he was not fit enough yet to undertake the voyage from Sydney to San Francisco and then on to Ojai, California.

Krishnamurti, impatient to quit Australia, found this waiting period interminable. Growing increasingly bored, he engaged in some decidedly 'unholy' behavior, according to Marty Lutyens. One day, she was part of a group of young people sitting indoors in a circle holding

---

[61] Ibid., 206.
[62] Ibid., 207.
[63] Ibid., 207.

hands with eyes closed, and at one point she happened to open her eyes. To her surprise, she found Krichnamurti outside, grinning and winking at her through the window.[64]

For the first time ever, Krishnamurti was beginning to doubt whether Nitya was going to recover his health. Eventually, however, he was deemed well enough to undertake the voyage and on June 24, 1925 aboard the AMS *Sierra* bound for San Francisco, the two brothers with a small group including a doctor-friend, were finally able to leave Sydney.

As the year progressed, so did my friendship with Antonia and her family. Once past the anniversary of Ambrose's death, Antonia did indeed start to 'rejoin the world'. It was a big advantage having the Amphitheatre only about a mile away from where she now lived and easily accessible on foot or by tram. Volunteers were always needed for various tasks, so Antonia went down there several times a week to lend a hand while Clara cared for the twins back at the house.

Although Antonia always seemed pleased when we met, I had absolutely no idea if she entertained any special feelings for me. And naturally, I never gave her the slightest hint of how I felt about her. Nonetheless, this state of affairs (or non-affairs) could not go on indefinitely.

I knew that Russell Fletcher was on the horizon in regard to Antonia, though I couldn't really believe he'd appeal to her. When hearing of unlikely liaisons, Mum would often say: 'Well, there's no accounting for tastes', so I couldn't totally dismiss the possibility of an attraction blossoming there.

One day, I casually quizzed Russell regarding activity on this front.

---

[64] Ibid., 205.

"I've invited Antonia to a couple of concerts at the Amphitheatre," he replied, "but she always asks if she can bring her mother or one of her sisters. I don't know why she does this – in the good old days, Antonia used to go about everywhere with Ambrose without needing a chaperone. It's not as though she's never been married. "

"She's actually been married twice," I put in, feeling slightly caddish but needing to say something to avoid any suspicions on Russell's part concerning my own interest in the matter.

"As a matter of fact," Russell went on, "because of all this chaperoning, I've got to know her sister Helena more. And do you know Ed, this is one helluva sweet girl. In fact, if I don't watch out, I could easily fall for her – if you really want to know!"

This would definitely be a first for Russell, as hitherto his interest in girls had been, shall we say, more geared to 'expediency' than any higher sentiment.

"Well, you couldn't do better than Helena," I replied warmly. "She's very lovely."

Even if Russell was never real competition, it still didn't make a difference to my own situation. Something was needed to unblock this impasse. I remembered my father's words, 'Nature abhors a vacuum.'

Nature was not alone here – I definitely abhorred the vacuum I was in and longed to escape from its clutches. But if I muffed it, then all would be lost. And if I did nothing, all would be lost for this reason, too.

Fate, as they say, works in mysterious ways. One day after a busy morning seeing patients, I decided go to the local park and eat my lunch in the sun. I'd just sat down on a bench and opened up my packet of sandwiches when across the road I glimpsed – Joyce Housman, of all people!

I called her name and she waved and came over.

"Ed!" she exclaimed. "What are *you* doing here?" I explained how I worked nearby and often came to the park at lunchtime, and she told me she'd been visiting a friend in the area and was now on her way back to the train station.

"Do you have time for a cup of tea?" I suggested. "There's a café just around the corner." Joyce thought this sounded good so we headed off to the café and ordered tea and a couple of jam tarts.

After a bit of small-talk, Joyce looked at me searchingly then said,

"Ed, tell me to mind my own business, if you like . . . You know how I've been developing my clairvoyant powers recently . . ."

"I didn't know that, Joyce," I replied. "And I would never tell you to mind your own business. I've always enjoyed our chats. Now, tell me – what's on your mind?"

I felt I sounded rather doctor-like here, but Joyce soon put me straight.

"Well, it's really what's on *your* mind, Ed, as a matter of fact," she said. "Do you give me leave to continue?"

"Certainly, Joyce, please – go for it," I told her.

A mystical expression came over Joyce's face and she stared into the distance.

"All I can do is tell you what I see," she said slowly. "And what I see is . . . a lovely young woman who's very much in your thoughts. You'd like to tell her that you love her, but you don't want to spoil a beautiful friendship if it turns out she doesn't return your feelings . . ."

I stared at her. This was uncanny! I hardly knew what so say. Joyce came out of her semi-trance and, on seeing the look on my face, said, "Does this mean anything to you, Ed?"

"It certainly does," I managed to say. "It's absolutely spot-on!"

She smiled, a touch complacently. "Well, Ed, I've been doing a lot of work on my occult skills and I do feel I've come quite a long way on my psychic pathway. Now, is there anything more I can see . . ."

She gazed off into the distance again. This time I felt a bit apprehensive, not wanting her to see too much.

Suddenly, she snapped out of her reverie, looked at her watch and said briskly, "Well, Ed, this has been a lovely chance meeting, hasn't it. But now I must get on home. Do let me pay for our tea."

"Not on your life!" I replied. "I'm so glad I saw you and called out."

Picking up her basket, Joyce had one last piece of wisdom to impart: "Just remember, Ed, 'Faint heart never won fair lady!' " Then with a motherly kiss on my cheek, she was gone.

I found Joyce's sudden departure somewhat disconcerting. Had she 'read' my thoughts or seen an image of Antonia somehow projecting from my fevered brow? Was she making it all up, like a fairground fortuneteller? (Some of them *do* have psychic abilities, apparently). Had she and Antonia's mother, Clara, put their heads together?

All these thoughts went through my mind as I walked back to the surgery. And, arching over them was the glaring reality: tha no matter how Joyce had got there, she was absolutely right!

CHAPTER 23

CHANGES IN THE AIR

Although my chance meeting with Joyce Housman had given me enormous food for thought, I didn't want to plunge impetuously into anything I might come to regret. I questioned myself extensively on this reaction, wondering if I might be like Ibsen's Peer Gynt character who'd spent his life procrastinating and avoiding reality.

I soon disposed of this conceit by reminding myself that up until Ambrose's death, Antonia's existence had been totally bound up with his, and the possibility of my ever entertaining any romantic aspirations in that quarter had only arisen due to the tragic event that ended his life. To pounce on the girl as soon as she'd recovered from this shock would be the act of the most crass type of bounder, to my mind. And yet, did I not also enjoy the safety of worship from afar? This type of rumination would then be followed by 'He who hesitates is lost.' And of course, Joyce Housman's parting words that day in the cafe rang in my ears: 'Just remember, Ed, faint heart never won fair lady!'

I'd arranged to meet up with Max for dinner during the week and was curious to hear more about the person he'd hinted about at our last meeting, this 'new identity of interest' in the TS. Dinner and a discussion with Max would also have the advantage of taking my mind off Antonia, for the topic was becoming like a gramophone record with the needle stuck in one groove.

We went to a German café he rather liked, probably reminding him of the food he used to eat in his home country, not that we ever mentioned this time of his life. I quite liked German food once in a while, although it could be somewhat stodgy.

After we'd ordered, Max introduced the topic.

"Ever heard of Bishop George Sydney Arundale?" he asked.

"'Bishop' as in the Liberal Catholic Church?" I queried.

"Spot on," replied Max ironically. "How ever did you guess? George Arundale is an important character in the ongoing TS story, and his star is certainly on the rise now.

"Here's a thumbnail sketch of the fellow: George Arundale was born in England in 1878. His mother died in childbirth and he was adopted by his aunt, Miss Francesca Arundale, an early Theosophist and devotee of Madame Blavatsky. Through Theosophical connections, the young George became one of CWL's pupils and later studied at Cambridge.

"In 1902 he met Annie Besant, fell under her spell and went to India. He taught at the Central Hindu College in Benares and later became principal there. In 1910, Mrs Besant took Krishnamurti, Nitya and Hubert van Hook to Benares on a visit, and here the boys met George Arundale. Krishnamurti made a deep impression on Arundale, and the two became very close. Together with Arundale, Krishnamurti formed a 'Preparation for Initiation' group, focusing on the four required attributes: Discrimination, Desirelessness, Good Conduct and Love."

"Quite a package," I commented, hoping my words didn't sound at all flippant. Max simply ignored this remark, continuing:

"Following this experience," he continued, "Arundale founded an organisation for people in India who believed that the new World Teacher's arrival was imminent. He named it – "

"I know – the Order of the Star in the East!" I cut in.

"Nearly right, but not quite," replied Max in his best lecturing tone. "Its original name was 'the Order of the *Rising Sun*'.

"Mrs Besant was quick to spot the Order's potential and soon transformed it into an international organization. She changed its name to 'The Order of the Star in the East', made Krishnamurti its head, herself and CWL co-protectors and rewarded Arundale with the title of 'Private Secretary to the Head'.

"Administration was kept very simple – no subscriptions and no rules – with members receiving a certificate and the chance to wear an Order of the Star in the East badge. Now, today, the Order of the Star in the East has over 44,000 members in 40 countries." [65]

"Incredible!" I said, impressed yet again at Mrs Besant's talent for recognizing a good idea and building on it.

"But was the Order of the Star in the East universally welcomed?" I wondered. "Did all members of the TS come on board with it?"

"By and large, yes," Max replied. "However, some members did question Mrs Besant's right to create an 'organisation within an organistion', as it were.

"Her response was that since the TS had been formed expressly to prepare humanity for the new World Teacher, this was exactly what the Order was doing, and therefore no conflict at all existed.

"While this response placated some members," he continued, "it was quite a different story in Germany. Here, TS members reacted strongly against the promotion of the new Order. Their leader, one Rudolph Steiner, was outspoken in rejecting the claims of CWL and Mrs Besant that Krishnamurti was the vehicle for the new World Teacher, and in 1913 almost the whole of the German TS

---

[65] See Glossary: Order of the Star in the East: Declaration of Principles.

broke away. Under the leadership of Steiner they formed the Anthroposophical Society, which is still extant today.

"As for George Arundale, in the Theosophical world his reputation continued to rise and in 1916 he was appointed General Secretary of the TS in England and Wales. During the Great War, Mrs Besant and Arundale spent time in India vigorously campaigning for Self-Rule there, a cause that along with the TS they passionately espoused.

In 1917, they were arrested for their activities and interned for three months at Ootacamund in the Western Ghats. This event received wide publicity and simply increased their international renown."

"Annie Besant – what an amazing woman!"

Max nodded. "Agreed. But Dr Besant will be 80 years old next year, so time's running out for her and CWL. They're of an age, give or take a year.

"And now," he continued, "regarding George Arundale, we'll come right up to the present time because he and his friend and co-bishop, James Ingall Wedgwood [66] are likely to supplant Besant and CWL as leaders of the TS.

"In 1920, when he was aged 42, George Arundale married a beautiful Indian girl of 16 called Rukmini,[67] a classically-trained Indian dancer. Rukmini came from a Brahmin family who were also Theosophists. Initially, Rukmini's family vigorously opposed the match, for in marrying Arundale she would become the first Brahmin woman to marry a foreigner and so would break caste.

"Rukmini and George Arundale are devoted to the Theosophical cause in general and the Order of the Star in the East in particular. Arundale has recently become a priest in the Liberal Catholic Church and now I believe he's been ordained as a bishop. This rapid progress up the

---

[66] See Glossary: Wedgwood, James Ingall.
[67] Full name: Rukmini Devi Neelakandra Sastri.

ecclesiastic ladder is currently raising quite a few eyebrows in some Theosophical circles, I can tell you."

He glanced at his watch, then said, "There's a lot more to say relating to Arundale's work on the theory of education, but this is enough for one session, so let's call it a day." We parted on this note and I made my way back home to Stanmore.

During the night as I slept, my subconscious mind must have been working overtime, for I woke the next morning resolved to telephone Antonia and invite her and one of her sisters to a play at the Amphitheatre. This invitation in itself would mark a change, as hitherto I'd always met with her during the daytime, at weekends, in the company of others, and with some specific reason. I thought I'd include a sister in the invitation because it would mask the fact that this was a 'date'. Also, I wasn't sure what protocol, if any, existed regarding the dating of a widow.

Accordingly, feeling decidedly nervous, I telephoned her. Antonia accepted the invitation very pleasantly and went on to ask whether I'd mind terribly much if she didn't bring any of her sisters, as all three of them were going to a dance on the Saturday evening.

Inwardly delighted, I replied it was fine by me if it was fine by her. We arranged I'd motor over to Mosman, pick her up at her house then we'd drive on down to the Amphitheatre.

All went according to plan. The play, by a local playwright, was a repeat performance by popular request, it having been well received some months earlier. We couldn't have wished for a more beautiful evening: a full moon hung over the Bay of Balmoral, the sky was clear and a light north-easterly breeze gently ruffled the water. The play lived up to its reputation and the excellent acoustics of the auditorium meant every word uttered by the actors was crystal clear to the audience.

'So far, so good,' I thought as I helped Antonia into the car. We drove up the hill to Gouldsbury St and I stopped the car outside her house.

"Ed," she said. "Would you like to come in for a cup of tea? You've got quite a long drive ahead of you back to Stanmore and I'm sure we wouldn't disturb Mother and the twins."

"Why, that's a nice idea, Antonia," I replied smoothly. "I think I'll take you up on it. Thank you very much."

We walked up the path and Antonia opened the front door quietly. Turning on the hall light, she led the way into the kitchen where she boiled the kettle and placed two cups and saucers on a tray.

"And you'll have a slice of fruitcake, won't you?" she asked. "My sister Helena baked it last week. It's probably not as good as your mother makes, but it's pretty tasty for a beginner."

She carried the tray into the sitting room, poured the tea and handed me a slice of Helena's fruitcake. I pronounced it delicious and the tea very welcome, then wondered what to say next. Strangely, my customary capacity to make conversation seemed to have deserted me.

I hoped Antonia hadn't noticed this, and it seemed that she hadn't, for the next thing she had to say was:

"Ed, I have something to tell you." She was smiling as she said this, so I thought it must be something quite pleasant.

"Oh yes?" I said. "What is it?"

"As you know," she went on. "When Ambrose died, I was heart-broken and thought I'd never care for anyone ever again. But Ed, life works in mysterious ways – I think we both know this – and I now find there *is* someone I have come to care for rather deeply."

At this, my heart felt as though it was going to stop and an icy chill ran through me. I simply couldn't believe what I was hearing.

"Oh, yes?" I managed to say in an even, neutral tone. "Tell me about him."

Again, Antonia smiled. She was obviously very keen on this specimen, whoever he was.

"I've known him for a while now," she continued. "He's not actually a member of the TS but he knows a lot about it and understands us well."

I managed to muster one question,

"And what does he do for a living, pray?"

"He's a medical man, actually," she said, again with that smile.

That clinched it for me. Getting to my feet, I said stiffly, "Well, I wish you and Russell Fletcher the best of happiness." Then, picking up my car-keys from where they lay on the table, I added, "And now I must be off. I've a busy day ahead of me tomorrow."

At this, Antonia stood up too. Barring my way, and still with that smile on her face, she said, "You're not going anywhere, Ed, you idiot! The person I'm talking about is – *you!*"

At that moment, it seemed as though a million golden stars were cascading down upon me. I took a step towards Antonia and we fell into each other's arms . . . The rest of the night was spent talking and talking, and still there was so much more to say. I told Antonia I'd 'held a torch for her' since the very first time I saw her, that evening early in 1922 when I'd attended the TS meeting with Russell Fletcher. My idea that she might fancy Russell caused her much amusement.

At a certain point, the subject of Ambrose came up, as of course it had to. I said that in comparison with Ambrose, wasn't I rather un-flamboyant, and might this not be a problem to her?

After a moment's silence, she allayed my fears on this score, saying, "Ed, ever since the time we met, I have come to know you and observe your character. I have also met your parents and got to know and value them and the way they lead their lives.

"My father was a flamboyant character, in some ways rather like Ambrose. Even though this type of person can be wonderful company, there can also be some negative aspects – as my mother found out to her cost.

"And Ed, I will never again say this about Ambrose, who both of us loved so much in our own ways – but life with him was not exactly a bed of roses. Ambrose was someone who liked to get his own way. He was also, like his father Pappi, very good at getting things done. When we left Australia and were on the boat to Colombo, Ambrose was nearly driven mad by the fact that we were so carefully chaperoned by the married Theosophists on board, but at the same time he was very conscious of my good reputation. Being on board the ship with nothing much to do also inflamed our desire for each another.

"This was the background to his brilliant scheme – we would get married as soon as we reached Adyar. Then, the fact that I immediately fell pregnant and into the bargain had twins – well, this was totally beyond my control. But it all added up to a very less carefree life than Ambrose had envisaged for himself, and he rather chafed at this."

At this point she fell silent, then took a deep breath and continued,

"Who knows how it all would have ended. Suffice to say: your dependability, your thoughtfulness for others and your intrinsic stability – these are the qualities I love and value in you. And of course, you *are* extremely handsome too, did you know?" This was not something I myself was aware of, to tell the truth, but if Antonia thought so, then I wasn't going to dispute it, especially not right now!

As the night wore on, over many cups of tea, we moved forward swiftly though the stages that most young couples take months to traverse. Quite frankly, I could've done with a stiff whisky or two but that was not to be had in this Theosophical household where fate, destiny, karma (and let's not ignore genetics, which work in their own mysterious ways) had landed me at this point in my life.

We agreed it was different for us – and how I loved hearing Antonia say the word 'us' – because we'd been friends in our earlier era, and also because of her current situation as a widow with two children. I told her I had a dream to be married to her, and she said it would give her great happiness to make my dream come true.

With dawn approaching, I wanted to be out of the house before Clara or the twins awoke. We agreed there was no point in keeping our news a secret from our families. So then, in the same room, but under such vastly different circumstances, I stood up, picked up my car-keys from the table and got ready to leave. After embracing each other once more, we arranged to talk on the phone mid-morning and meet up later in the day.

CHAPTER 24

EVENTS HAVE A LIFE
OF THEIR OWN

I drove home from Antonia's house in a daze of astounded happiness. Luckily, there were very few cars on the road at that early hour of the morning because afterwards I had no memory of putting the Packard onto the car-punt to cross the Harbour or driving through the city back to Stanmore. On arriving home, I thought I'd creep into the house without waking Mum&Dad, but to my surprise they were both up and fully dressed. Mum spoke first.

"Oh, Ed!" she cried. "We've been *so* worried! We wondered what on earth had happened to you! Did you have an accident in the car? We were just about to leave for the hospital!" Dad looked a bit tired, I thought, as if he'd had a bad night's sleep.

"We *were* a bit worried, Son," he said. "Would have been good if you'd phoned to tell us you were staying out all night."

A wave of remorse swept over me and I felt deeply ashamed at my selfishness. Never before had I behaved like this. The only thing to do was to tell them exactly what had transpired.

"Mum, Dad," I said. "I have some exciting news. I am engaged to be married – to Antonia Mortimer!"

Mum&Dad simply couldn't believe their ears. They were absolutely stunned. Then they jumped up from their chairs and hugged me. Mum burst into tears and kept on saying, "I simply had no idea!" and, "She's such a lovely girl!"

Dad said, "It's certainly a surprise, but one I think we'll adjust to very happily. Antonia is indeed a beautiful young woman and she has a very caring nature, from my observations of her. Now, how about a drink to celebrate!" He went off to the cellar and returned a few moments later with two bottles of champagne and three glasses.

Never have I needed a drink more, so we toasted my happiness, and all our happiness, until there came a knock at the door.

"Oh, my goodness!" Mum exclaimed. "I'd totally forgotten! The Aunts are coming over this morning to make the soap!" (Soap-making was a yearly ritual that my mother and her two sisters had engaged in for as long as I could remember.)

She ushered Aunt and Auntikin into the kitchen. They looked at the bottles and champagne glasses and then at our flushed and happy faces.

"I see a celebration's in progress," said Aunt. "What's the happy occasion?"

"Ed has become engaged!" cried Mum, and burst into tears again. Dad looked a bit teary himself, I noticed, probably due to champagne at breakfast-time following his disturbed night.

The Aunts were thrilled and, although none of us would have mentioned it, we were all aware that my taking this step in life meant that, simultaneously and thereby, Mum was one tiny step closer to achieving a dream of her own . . .

I phoned Antonia, and Mum&Dad spoke to her and to her mother Clara, and said how happy they were. Antonia's sisters and brother also came on the phone and welcomed me into their family, which touched me greatly. Although I wanted to rush back over to Mosman and be with Antonia again, we were both exhausted after such a momentous night. We agreed to try and get a few hours' sleep and that around five o'clock I'd bring Mum&Dad over to meet Antonia's family in our new role as 'soon-to-be-inlaws.'

I went up to my room and fell asleep immediately. Occasionally I'd be aware of the telephone ringing downstairs and surmised that Mum had spread the word among her friends. When I emerged from my room in the mid-afternoon, she presented me with a list of people who'd rung to offer congratulations.

"I expect there'll be a few disappointed girls down at the tennis club," she remarked, a tad smugly, though in my view with no foundation for this supposition.

Everyone we knew was very surprised and happy for us, though I did notice a touch of incredulity in some quarters. The fact that Antonia was a widow and the mother of twins seemed to elevate me greatly in the eyes of Mum's friends, though some of them needed her assurance that her boy hadn't been ambushed by a predatory, older woman-of-the-world. (Mum explained we'd known each other 'for ages' and Antonia was only two years older than me.) Some, too, had heard she was heiress to a vast hardware fortune in the USA, which notion we were quick to quash.

The choicest comment I received came courtesy of Russell Fletcher, who phoned and said, "No offence, old boy, but quite frankly I'm amazed. I wouldn't have thought you had it in you to snaffle a prize like Antonia Mortimer." I ignored this, simply asking him:

"How are you going with her sister Helena?"

"Slow but steady progress on that front," Russell replied. "Though I think I've yet to convince her mother I'm worthy of her daughter's hand."

"Well, good luck to you, old friend" I replied charitably, safe in the knowledge I had no worries on this score. I could see why Clara might feel unsure about Russell, as he didn't work as a doctor in a regular way, preferring sessional work at a big hospital while setting up his medical equipment company.

When Mum&Dad and I arrived at Antonia's house there were congratulations all round and we celebrated the engagement over non-alcoholic punch and ginger ale. Word had travelled quickly and a whole stream of well-wishers, mainly Theosophists, dropped in to share in the happy event. Antonia had sent a cable to Narne and Pappi and during the evening she received a reply expressing their pleasure at our news.

One of the those who dropped in was Max Herbst. I was always pleased to see Max, of course, but a bit puzzled to have him appear now, as I wouldn't have thought this type of occasion was his natural territory.

Antonia must have noticed this, for she took me aside and whispered, "I don't know whether you know this, Ed, but Max and my mother are 'more than just good friends'."

For me, this news was just another strange moment in the strangest twenty-four hours in my life, and by now I was practically beyond absorbing any more input. I simply murmured how pleased I was and went on to greet a few more of the well-wishers who kept coming through the front door.

By around nine-thirty, the party was starting to thin out. As Max was leaving, he said,

"Ed, you're a dark horse, aren't you! How about we meet for dinner one evening next week?"

"Certainly, Max, love to," I replied, wondering which one of us was in fact the darker horse.

Naturally, over the next few days Antonia and I had a huge amount to discuss. Some decisions were reached quickly, others took longer:

When to get married? We felt a five-month engagement would suffice, as after all we weren't unknown to each other. This would mean our wedding would be early February.

What type of wedding? If we chose a church, the logical place would be the Liberal Catholic church in Redfern. However, given the events of the last few years this venue would not be congenial for a number of our TS guests. So, best to have it at a Registry Office (and as Antonia pointed out: 'This'll be my third trip down the aisle in four years, so I'm not exactly a wedding novice!')

Where to hold the wedding reception? Where better than The Amphitheatre, Balmoral, looking out over that huge expanse of water, surrounded by family and friends and introducing non-TS friends to this wonderful site and all it offered.

What about the honeymoon? We were thinking of maybe a week in New Zealand, where neither of us had been. Antonia was confident that Clara would be happy to look after the twins, helped by their three doting aunts, Antonia's younger sisters.

The biggest question facing us was – living arrangements. I'd never before had to think of anything like this but now that I did so, I found I had a very strong and instinctive wish not to inhabit a house that was financed by my wife's former parents-in-law, the Mortimers, two of the kindest and best-disposed people in the world. Antonia certainly understood my feelings on this matter, but what to do about it?

This was the vexed question that was on our minds the next Saturday afternoon. When we'd become engaged, Antonia had mentioned some of my better points, including how well I interacted with the twins. I really liked these two little children and, as with many an only child, the idea of a large family had a lot of appeal. To be starting married life with two children already was, in my view, a bonus. Now, when Clara asked us if we could take over the twins for a short time while she did some shopping, I could hardly look anything but keen.

A few minutes later, she produced the twin-stroller with Ingrid and Three, now called 'Tree', already sitting in it. This slight name-change had come about because Ingrid couldn't yet say 'th' and called her brother 'Tree'. The rest of us fell in with this, liking the sound of 'Tree' even more than 'Three'. So, off we went along the street pushing the stroller, looking for all the world like a regular married couple.

As we walked, we discussed our accommodation 'problem'. First, where to live? We both liked Mosman and Antonia valued being close to her TS friends, the Amphitheatre with all its activities, and The Manor. I liked Mosman, too, for its clean breezes off the Pacific Ocean and lovely beaches and bays. For me, the only negative aspects would be my journey to work across town, and the fact that Mum&Dad might feel left out on a limb at Stanmore with their only child living far away on the north side of Sydney Harbour.

After a while, we came to a children's playground and got the twins out of the stroller to ride on the swings. Eventually they were ready to go home and, on the way back, the same idea struck us: Why not buy a pair of semi-detached houses (otherwise known as 'semis')?

Each of us would own one of the houses and with a few alterations we could make them into one single dwelling. This way, Narne and Pappi could fulfill their wish to have their grandchildren suitably housed, and I would not feel in any way beholden to them. I'd need to arrange a mortgage to buy my semi, but this didn't pose a huge problem as I was earning a reasonable amount.

We were delighted with this plan and, in the part of Mosman where Antonia was now living there were quite a few semis. Surely, we'd be able to find a pair to buy. Before anything else, though, we needed to consult the people with an interest in the matter: Antonia's mother Clara, Narne and Pappi, and Mum&Dad. That evening, discussions were held in Mosman and Stanmore, and a long letter sent to Greenwich, Connecticut the next day.

Mum&Dad listened intently as I outlined our idea and said they'd been wondering how we'd deal with the living arrangements. Dad offered some financial assistance towards the cost, saying, "If we can't help our only son get a start in life, then we're not much good as parents!" With their injection of funds, I knew I'd be able to pay down the mortgage without too much trouble.

I told them I didn't feel too good about the idea of leaving them in Stanmore while I went to live in Mosman and they said they'd talked about this, too.

"Later on, when you have a family," Mum said delicately, "Dad and I would want to be involved as much as possible, and when that time comes we'll think of moving over to Mosman ourselves."

It seemed as though all my concerns were evaporating. I just had one more,

"What about The Aunts? Won't Aunt and Auntikin feel a bit stranded being the only ones in our family left at Stanmore?"

"Not at all," Mum replied firmly. "The way those two have been gallivanting round the world whenever their fancy took them – did they ever think they might be leaving *me* stranded at Stanmore? Not on your Nellie! And by the way, Ed, they told me just the other day they've nearly saved up for their next trip, so they'll be off again in a few months' time."

Dad then observed, "I don't think we need to worry about The Aunts. They're a pretty independent pair, and when they come back, if we're all living at Mosman, they might like to get a place there too."

Narne and Pappi saw a lot of merit in our plan to acquire a pair of semis. In his letter to Antonia, Pappi wrote:

I understand Ed's feelings on this matter, and it's to his credit. I know I've said this before, but I'll say it again: we're delighted that you and Ed have thrown in your lot together. He's a fine young man and we greatly esteem his parents too. They're our kind of folk, feet on the ground and salt of the earth.

True to form, Pappi was quick to come up with an action plan:

Go see the estate agent who handles the house you are renting. Ask him if the owner might be interested in selling. Find out who owns the house it's joined to, and see if they might also want to sell. If you have no luck with this, get the agent to canvass all the other semi-detached houses in the street, see if you can get hold of a pair.

And by the way, Antonia my dear, how would it be if Narne and I come to Sydney round New Year's Day?

Antonia telephoned me with Narne and Pappi's positive response and Pappi's action plan, finishing with, "First thing tomorrow morning I'll go to the estate agent and get things under way."

After the whirlwind events of the past days, Max Herbst and Theosophical matters were not exactly in the forefront of my mind. So when Max rang and suggested we meet for dinner during the week, it took me a moment to work out which night would be best. We settled for Thursday, and as I took a train into the city after work, I thought about Max and how the dynamic between us must now necessarily undergo at least some change. Max obviously hadn't had the faintest idea that I was in love with Antonia (from a distance), just as I had no inkling that he and Clara Vivian were 'more than just friends.'

'My God,' I thought with a start. 'Max Herbst is practically my father-in-law!' That is, in the absence of Antonia's father who now resided in Tibet as a Buddhist monk. On reflection, I was relieved that the father-in-law slot would be filled by Max rather than the monk, if only on the grounds of 'the devil you know . . .' , for after all, Antonia's father could well be a man of infinite wisdom and a joy to have around.

When I met up with Max at the restaurant, he got down to business straight away, saying, "Ed, I want to offer you my congratulations on your engagement and wish you and Antonia the best of happiness throughout your lives. She is a wonderful girl from a wonderful family." This speech was somewhat formal and old-fashioned, very different from the usual way Max spoke, and I got the impression that maybe this was how they did things back where Max hailed from.

Then he cleared his throat and continued in a bit of a rush, "And because we are now adding a kinship factor to our friendship, due to my relationship with Antonia's mother, Clara, I think I owe it to you to tell you more about my earlier life than I have hitherto shared with anyone, apart from Clara Vivian."

"Max," I replied. "Steady on, old man – don't feel you need to tell me anything at all. We're good friends and I'm very happy that you and Clara are together."

Max gave a small smile, I could tell he was feeling quite wound-up about something, and on second thoughts maybe it *might* be better if he got it off his chest.

"I want to tell you about my former life in Europe," he said. "And then I may never refer to it again. In 1918 when the War ended and all that hideous slaughter was over and, miraculously, I was still in one piece, I found my way back to my home-town in Germany and my wife and two young daughters. We'd only been back together again for six months when all three of them succumbed to the influenza epidemic – the Spanish Flu – that swept through Europe and spread throughout the world.

"Without my wife and children, my world collapsed. All that had sustained me during my years in the War was gone, and my one thought was to get as far away from Europe as I possibly could. Australia was the furthest and most sensible choice because I spoke English and hoped my academic record might help me get a teaching job in a university.

"After losing my wife, I never thought I'd become involved with another woman. But to my surprise I did find myself able to feel emotions again, and the one who brought those feelings alive was – Clara Vivian."

My eyes got a bit moist at this point, so I took a deep breath then replied to Max in a similar vein to how he'd spoken to me, saying what a wonderful woman Clara was and wishing them both every happiness.

"Thank you, Ed," Max responded, then in a matter-of-fact way said, "That's enough now. Let's get back to our subject. The good ship TS is entering uncharted waters and, if I'm not mistaken, dangerous reefs lie ahead."

CHAPTER 25

DEVELOPMENTS ON
EVERY FRONT

From the day of my engagement onwards, nearly every facet of my life was different in some way. One area that did remain largely the same, however, was my working life. I noticed, though, that my older colleagues treated me more as an equal now and didn't give me quite so much weekend work.

Antonia and I enjoyed regaling each other with comments people made on hearing of our news. The one we most enjoyed came from my colleague Dr Joanna Short.

"Well, Ed," she said in her brisk and direct way. "Too bad you're out of the marriage-market, my boy. I actually had you in mind for a niece of mine . . . lovely girl. I definitely saw you as MM."

"I never even knew I was *on* the marriage-market, Joanna," I said. "And what on earth does MM stand for?"

"Marriage Material," Joanna replied and we both had a good laugh.

When I next had dinner with Max Herbst, it was impossible to ignore the fact that we were now members of the same kinship group. Max alluded to this in his usual urbane and semi-sardonic way, saying, "Now that we've had a few 'changes in the group dynamics', maybe I'll have to get you to write another thesis."

"Maybe you will, Max," I replied robustly. "But you'd have to exempt yourself on family grounds from supervising it. And of course, I'd have to live through the whole experience before being able to draw any worthwhile conclusions."

"I have no doubt it'd be the making of you," Max commented drily.

During the meal, it occurred to me that Max would be a good person to ask regarding a question that had been in the back of my mind ever since Dad had asked me 'how religious' Antonia and her family were. I opened up the topic by first describing Mum&Dad, who by now Max knew quite well, as 'not religious themselves but respectful of other people's beliefs.'

"They sound like many Theosophists I know," Max observed.

I said I'd never noticed that Antonia was 'overtly' religious (in our present context this meant involved with the Liberal Catholic Church) but rather that her perspective on the world seemed imbued with a general 'Theosophical' outlook. And if this contributed to the person Antonia was, then it was something I greatly valued, both for myself and our future children. Like many people from unusual religious backgrounds, most Theosophists refrained from imposing their world-view on others.

Max listened, then said this was more or less how he saw the Vivian family. He told me he visualised their involvement as several concentric circles round a centre or bulls-eye occupied by Paul Vivian, Clara's ex-husband. In the first ring out from the centre was Clara, and in the next ring were Antonia and her siblings.

"You see, Ed – the salient factor here is that the family members did not come to Sydney of their own free will," he expounded. "Clara and the children accompanied Paul Vivian from Brisbane to Sydney because he wanted to be closer to the epicentre of Australian Theosophy.

"Being an adult, Clara of course understood what Theosophy was all about and was a member of the TS and a Co-Mason. But the children were different – they were *born* into Theosophy. And as newcomers to Sydney with no relatives here, Clara and the children found in the TS a ready-made friendship and quasi-kinship group. Then, when her husband Paul 'decamped to Perth with his paramour' – which, as you know, is how this matter is referred to in the Vivian family – the TS became even more important in their lives. At Morven Garden School, the TS fed, clothed, housed and educated the five children, under the care of the two very dedicated principals, the Misses Lily Arnold and Jessie MacDonald.

"As Theosophy has no dogma, no compulsory beliefs, members can focus on whichever aspects resonate with them at any given time," he finished. This all sounded eminently reasonable to me, and I resolved to say something along the same lines to Dad, if the topic cropped up again.

Max then turned his attention to the astonishing events in the world of Theosophy that were taking place at Huizen, Holland, the centre of the Liberal Catholic Church in Europe. Many observers were looking askance at the number of Initiations that were being announced, and the speed of advancements along the Path. An example of this was the progress of George Arundale over in England. One week after Bishop James Wedgwood ordained Arundale as a priest, he saw fit to consecrate him as a bishop within the Liberal Catholic Church.

For this event to come about, the agreement of CWL in distant Sydney was required. Arundale assured those around him that CWL had given his 'cordial consent, on the astral plane'.[68] Soon after, however, a cable arrived from CWL expressing his strong disapproval of the step. Throughout this time, Arundale claimed to be in frequent communication with the Masters, conveying various

---

[68] Lutyens, Krishnamurti, 211.

detailed messages to the initiates regarding appropriate attire, living arrangements and dietary regimens. As the days went by, psychic promotions proceeded at an ever-increasing pace. For Lady Emily and her party, as well as many others, Huizen was indeed a heady place to be.

On the night of August 9, Arundale 'brought through' the names of ten out of the twelve apostles who had been chosen by the 'Lord' to work with him though his 'vehicle' when the time would be ripe. The names on the list were: Dr Besant, Bishop Leadbeater, Raja (C. Jinarajadafa), Bishop Arundale and his wife Rukmini, Bishop Wedgwood, Krishnamurti's brother Nitya, Lady Emily, Rajagopol and Oscar Kollerstrom (a Liberal Catholic priest). And at the same time, yet more Advancements were being announced.

The next day, many of the Huizen contingent moved to Ommen, about 15 miles away, for the Star Camp and Congress. In a lengthy speech to the gathering, Dr Besant gave out the names of seven of the Apostles and went on to announce the founding of a World Religion, as well as a World University which would have three centres: Adyar, Sydney and Huizen.

Bishop Arundale explained that the Master he was particularly close to (known as 'the Mahachohan') had commanded him to commence this step, explaining that the new university would not seek external recognition. Rather, the plan was to award degrees and Initiations that would be recognized by the world, 'as no degrees conferred by human agency can ever be.' [69]

On hearing this, I was moved to comment: "Cripes, Max, this makes our degrees from Sydney University look a bit ordinary!"

"Certainly does," replied Max. "And in these fairly radical innovations, we can see a considerable power build-up occurring around Arundale and Wedgwood. As

---

[69] Ibid., 214.

well as awarding Initiations, ordaining priests and bishops and conferring degrees, they are as powerful as a Pope, albeit within the much more limited context of the Liberal Catholic Church.

"How does Krishnamurti feel about these developments?" I wondered, feeling fairly sure I knew the answer.

"Krishnamurti, who is presently over in California looking after the now very ill Nitya, and CWL in Sydney were both in their own ways extremely displeased by the news of these initiatives," Max told me. "Krishnamurti was totally sceptical about the events reported from Huizen, but he would find it unthinkable to speak out publicly against Dr Besant.

"When Dr Besant wrote to Krishnamurti asking him to corroborate the advancements that had come about at Huizen, he replied saying he did not remember (ie on the astral plane) any of the events at Huizen as he was extremely tired due to taking care of Nitya, and furthermore his Process was causing him a lot of pain in his head and spine.[70]

"Krishnamurti felt that many extremely spiritual and sacred things were now being utterly debased. He viewed claims that CWL, Raja, Arundale, Oscar Kollestrom and he, Krishnamurti, had all taken their fifth Initiation (ie were now Adepts) as simply ridiculous. As for Rukmini's meteoric rise to Adepthood following three Initiations in three days, it simply beggared belief. Adepthood equated to divinity, and CWL had never claimed anything more for Krishnamurti than that he was a *vehicle* for divinity.

"If things keep on like this," Max finished, "the TS may end up in an almighty conflict that will make the 1922 Sydney 'troubles' look like a storm in a teacup."

"I fear you may be right," I replied.

---

[70] Ibid., 217.

We parted on a cheerful note, both having other more immediate matters on our minds, pertaining to our now strangely 'parallel' personal lives.

Even though it was fairly late in the evening when I got home to Stanmore, I rang Antonia. She had some interesting news: the Mosman estate agent had made some progress with finding a pair of semis we could buy.

"He actually has two pairs in Gouldsbury St," she told me. "Both are good, but one pair is more favourable, I feel."

"Excellent!" I exclaimed. "Where exactly are they?"

"The first pair is numbers 38 and 40 Gouldsbury St," she replied, "and the other two are – the semi I'm living in now and the one it's joined to!"

I could hardly believe it. "And which pair do you prefer?" I asked.

"The one I'm in now," she said. "I really do like this house so much! If we can stay here it will be less of an upheaval, especially for the children. I'll cable Pappi and Narne and tell them where we've got to." We talked of other things for a while, then reluctantly concluded our call as by now it was very late indeed and the twins, like most small children, were extremely early risers.

At breakfast the next morning I filled Mum&Dad in on this development, and told them Antonia was contacting Pappi and Narne over in the States. That evening, Antonia phoned with more news. The estate agent had told her that the owner of the semi she was renting said he'd been toying with the idea of selling it but hadn't considered selling its pair.

When Pappi received this news, he immediately cabled the estate agent to get things moving, and a few hours later, Antonia received word from Pappi saying 'It's a done deal!'

The agent told us Pappi had made a preliminary offer at market price for Antonia's semi, then put in an extremely generous offer for the other one, conditional upon the owner selling both. Realising an offer like this might never come his way again, the owner agreed to sell the two semis. His only proviso was that the tenants in the other semi be allowed to stay until their lease expires in three months' time. Pappi was happy to agree to this.

"And then, Ed," Antonia said, laughing, "Pappi sent a second cable saying he'd like *you* to buy the first semi, (that is, the one I'm living in), and he'll buy the second one. He said, and these are his exact words: 'This way, when you and Ed have 'tied the knot', he'll be able to rest content that your marital bedroom will be under a roof that belongs entirely to him!"

"Pappi's a classic," I said, laughing. "He's really one of a kind!"

The fact that we wouldn't get possession of the second semi until probably March of the next year was fine with us. When we did gain possession, we'd still need arrange a builder to remove the wall between the two houses and strengthen the resulting wide hall and roof.

Having by now adapted to the concept of 'Clara and Max' as a couple, I wondered if they were likely to get married. When I raised this question with Antonia, she was amused, saying, "Why would they want to do that? They've both been married already, and there's not likely to be 'the patter of tiny feet' at their age. Also, Theosophists in general aren't great 'marry-ers' – myself excluded, of course!"

We then discussed a couple of other matters, the first being how Clara would feel about being part of Antonia's household when it would include me. I was pretty sure that Antonia would want Clara to stay, as she loved her mother dearly and also liked the idea of an extended-family-commune arrangement. This proved to be the case: Clara said she'd be very happy to stay, and would be 'elsewhere' for a certain amount of time (Max had a flat near the University). I was extremely pleased by this outcome as I got on well with Clara and she was already part of the household and greatly loved by the twins.

We also had a talk about the honeymoon. Although we'd initially decided on a week in New Zealand, Antonia was now having second thoughts.

"It's just a bit too far away from the children," she said, "and it's across a vast stretch of water. [71] If anything happened to us and we died, I'd never forgive myself – although of course I'd be dead – but it would be terrible for the twins."

After a pause, I said thoughtfully, "Hmm, to lose one parent may be regarded as a misfortune; to lose both looks like carelessness."

Antonia simply stared at me, probably wondering what sort of callous monster she'd got mixed up with. With a debonair shrug I told her: "Oscar Wilde, '*The Importance of Being Earnest*' – Act 1, if I remember rightly," whereupon she collapsed in a relieved fit of giggles.

Jokes aside, I didn't care where we went for the honeymoon. My friends often pointedly reminded me that I'd never been out of Australia, so I reasoned that a short extension to this state was neither here nor there. We still had a few months left before the wedding and no doubt we'd work something out.

---

[71] The Tasman Sea.

CHAPTER 26

NOVEMBER – DECEMBER
1925

On the home-front at Stanmore a lot was happening, and in quite unexpected ways. There's no way but to call it what it was: Mum had embarked on a personal 'renaissance', a rebirth of her 'essence' that manifested in several very different areas. The first evidence of this change came when she asked if she could borrow my car keys for the day. This was fine by me as I never took the car to work, but I did wonder why she wanted them.

"I've decided to learn to drive," she announced. "I've contacted a driving school and said that I wish to learn to drive a Packard, no other brand of car, only a Packard. They told me that until I'm fairly proficient, I'd have to learn on one of their cars, but after five or six lessons I can move on to driving the Packard. And for this I'll need my own set of keys. So if I can borrow your set I'll get them copied right away."

Dad and I were very surprised. Dad said, "Well, I take my hat off to you, Isobel. And I don't mind saying this – you're a good deal gamer than I am, that's for certain." After a few moments' thought, he went on: "This plan of yours has a lot to recommend it – I won't need to learn to drive now, and as a matter of fact I wasn't looking forward to it. But what's going to happen when Ed gets married next year and takes the Packard to Mosman – what'll you do then?"

Mum had an answer ready, "Well, Arthur, we'll jolly well buy another car – a smaller one but big enough for a few additional passengers one day, I hope."

This was not the only innovation concerning Mum. One day, Clara Vivian told me that Joyce Housman was wanting to speak to my mother and wondered if I could check with Mum and, if she agreed, then maybe I could pass our phone number on to Joyce and she would take it from there. This was how the women of Mum's generation behaved about phone-numbers. They didn't just pass them around willy-nilly, there was a certain protocol and rigmarole involved. In a way, it was an updated version of leaving one's calling card, I surmised.

A few days later, Joyce telephoned Mum and put an interesting and flattering suggestion to her. When Mum had visited The Manor on several occasions during the last couple of years, she'd found common ground with a group of Theosophical women on a topic very close to her heart – nutrition and cooking. Notwithstanding that the other women were vegetarian and Mum wasn't, she found she could join in the discussion and make some useful contributions, including sharing several recipes which the others wrote down.

Apparently, these recipes had been very well received by their families (which didn't surprise Dad and me) and now Joyce wanted to know if Mum might be interested in presenting a 'food' session for a TS group that met once a month in the city. She envisaged it might take the form of a one-week set of meals that made use of vegetables in season and other non-meat ingredients in imaginative and tasty dishes.

Mum was rather overwhelmed by this idea, but extremely chuffed to be asked. Although she was a robust member of her women's friendship group and never hesitant about airing her views, she found Joyce's suggestion quite 'something else again'. After telling Joyce she'd need to think about it, she went through a short phase of feeling she couldn't possibly do it as she'd never done anything of that nature before.

Dad and I encouraged her, Dad saying: "You're such a wonderful cook, it's a great opportunity to share your skills with others. Only problem is, I think a lot of husbands will have to watch their waistlines!" I told her how all through my childhood she'd urged me to try new things and, now that it was her turn, I found it odd that she wasn't keen to take her own advice. This 'psychology' worked, for she took a deep breath and said, "Alright, I'll do it! I'll phone Joyce right away."

Max, who was over in New York at a conference, sent postcards to Clara from time to time. Then one day Clara received a letter from Narne and Pappi saying Max had visited them at their home in Greenwich Connecticut recently on a free day from the conference.

'We *did* enjoy Max's visit,' Narne wrote. 'Such an interesting man. And it was lovely seeing the photographs of you lot.' She recounted how Max had produced from his wallet a photo of Clara and several of Antonia with the twins and me. Narne finished her letter with the words: 'You-all mean so much to Max. You know that, don't you.'

I couldn't help but muse, 'How strange life is: that cynical, totally unsentimental Max Herbst, the former Herr Doktor Maximilian von Herbenstein, would sit in a drawing-room in Greenwich Connecticut USA showing family photos of Antonia, the twins and me to Ambrose Mortimer's parents, Narne and Pappi.' Of course, I knew what Joyce Housman would say: 'Ed, it was simply meant to be.'

Narne and Pappi would be coming to Sydney in a few weeks' time and they asked Antonia to book a hotel nearby. I suggested they could stay at The Manor but Antonia said, "Oh no, Ed, that would never do. Don't you remember? Pappi has quite an aversion to CWL." Now that she mentioned it, of course I did recall how Pappi, along with many others in the American TS, had certain strong reservations about CWL or, as some in the Sydney TS put it 'questions about his moral probity', a phrase I knew that Ambrose would've relished.

Naturally enough, I thought about Ambrose often, and when I did so it was always followed in a rush by the uncomfortable recognition that the happiness I presently enjoyed had only come about through his death. This was extremely discomforting, so much so that to regain my equilibrium I often needed to take a long walk through the quiet streets of Mosman.

I wondered if Antonia ever felt the same way. So, believing it preferable to air a possibly 'thorny' matter rather than brush it under the carpet, one evening I raised the topic.

I told Antonia how happy I was with her, but how bad I felt knowing that this could have only come about though Ambrose's death. It sounded somewhat bald when I said it, but that was the crux of it. I had no idea how Antonia would react. For a moment she was silent and although she was smiling at me, her eyes were full of tears.

"Dear Ed," she said. "Thank you for speaking about this, for it's something I, too, am conscious of. You may not feel as strongly about fate and destiny as I do, but just looking at the way Ambrose died, I see that those events unfolded according to how they were meant to." After a pause, she went on, "You might have noticed that Narne and Pappi Mortimer seemed to come to terms with Ambrose's death relatively quickly and this may have seemed strange to you as a non-Theosophist, and maybe somewhat callous. Although they of course suffered deeply at the loss of Ambrose, their Theosophical beliefs sustained them and enabled them to bear it with acceptance. As they see it, and as I do too, it was Ambrose's destiny to die young, and to leave behind two children to be brought up in the care of a loving and sensible mother.

"As I've mentioned before," she continued, "Ambrose was not cut out for domesticity, whereas I certainly am. By and large, we had a wonderful time together and I wouldn't have missed it for the world. But while we were in the States, I came to realize we were two very different people and we really wanted different things in life.

"I was quite young when I met Ambrose and I was swept off my feet by him – you remember us then, of course. But as time went on, I started to do a lot of soul-searching regarding my values. Of course, the birth of the twins speeded up the end of our carefree time together, and made our essential differences starker. And now here with you, Ed, I feel I can look forward to having the kind of life I want, with a person whose ideals and way of life are similar to my own in all the important ways."

I felt a great sense of relief at Antonia's words and the thoughtful way she expressed them. If it were possible to love her even more, then I did so after what she said. As well, Antonia's response reminded me of how Max had reassured a concerned man whose wife had joined the TS, telling him that Theosophy could enrich their marriage rather than be a source of friction within it. Even though I myself wasn't a member of the TS, I could nonetheless see that Theosophy offered a very humane and enlightened window through which to view life, one that enabled a calm acceptance of the things we cannot change rather than suffering needless anguish over matters beyond our control. I recalled Dad saying the same thing after Ambrose's memorial service at The Manor . . .

Meanwhile, in the TS world, following on from the Star Camp and Congress in Holland during August, the next important event on the calendar was the Golden

Jubilee Convention. This would take place at Adyar, near Madras. at the end of December to commemorate the fiftieth anniversary of the founding of the TS in New York in 1875 by Madame Helena Blavatsky, Colonel Henry Steel Olcott and others at one with them.

Max Herbst was still over in the USA, which I found personally inconvenient, having become accustomed to our regular meetings and the updates he provided on TS events. In his absence, I'd have to rely on eyewitness accounts and personal observations for any news on the Golden Jubilee.

In November, Theosophists from all over the world started converging on Adyar. Dr Besant, Krishnamurti, Lady Emily Lutyens and several others travelled from England to Rome and thence to Naples where they boarded a ship bound for Colombo, Ceylon. While in Rome, they met up with Bishop Arundale, his wife Rukmini and Bishop Wedgwood. Word reached us in Australia via the Theosophical grapevine that the two bishops' attitude towards Krishnamurti was distinctly condescending. Rumour also had it that Arundale even went so far as to intimate to Krishnamurti that the Master Mahachohan deplored his attitude towards some cherished aspects of Theosophy. Further, we heard that Arundale and Wedgwood had even told Krishnamurti that 'if he would acknowledge them as his disciples and confirm that they were Adepts, then Nitya's life would be spared.'[72]

Krishnamurti, although at times deeply worried about Nitya's health, had always believed his brother would pull through his tubercular crises. He unquestioningly assumed that, as part of the plan devised from on high for his life's mission, Nitya would always be at his side. But on the morning of November 14, as their ship passed through the Suez Canal, Dr Besant came

---

[72] Lutyens, Krishnamurti, 219.

to him with news from Ojai, California: Nitya had died the day before.

On hearing this shocking information, Krishnamurti was struck down by almost insuperable grief. According to Shiva Rao, who shared a cabin with him, the news 'broke him completely; it did more – his entire philosophy of life – the implicit faith in the future as outlined by Mrs Besant and Mr Leadbeater, Nitya's vital part in it, all appeared shattered at that moment.' [73]

After ten days of agony, Krishnamurti came through his paroxysm of sorrow and emerged looking positively refreshed, saying, '. . . An old dream is dead and a new one is being born . . . A new vision is coming into being and a new consciousness is being unfolded . . . On the physical plane we could be separated and now we are inseparable . . . for my brother and I are one . . .' [74] As word spread throughout the TS world, the shock was scarcely less, with members rocked to their very core by the unthinkable event that had come to pass.

At the same time, CWL, accompanied by a party of seventy Theosophists including Theodore St John and Dr Mary Rocke, was also *en route* to India from Australia to attend the Golden Jubilee at Adyar. When their ship berthed at Colombo, the group was met by Krishnamurti, Dr Besant, Bishop Wedgwood, Lady Emily and Raja, who'd arrived there some days earlier.

After the group expressed their condolences to Krishnamurti on the death of Nitya, CWL took him aside and murmured, "Well at least *you* are an Arhat," [75] thus conveying his belief that Krishnamurti had passed the fourth Initiation, whilst not saying the same for any of the others.

---

[73] Ibid., 220.
[74] Krishnamurti: editorial notes, *Herald of the Star*, Jan.1926.
[75] Lutyens, Krishnamurti, 221.

(Here, Max explained that CWL hoped that he and Dr Besant might achieve their fifth Initiation in their next lifetime but did not expect to attain this status in their present time on earth.)

The contingent, which by now had now grown to arround eighty people, travelled to Madras in a specially chartered train, and at each stop the Jubilee delegates were met with garlands of flowers, mass prostrations by well-wishers and sumptuous vegetarian dishes. All in all, it was a wonderful experience, especially for those who'd never been out of Australia.

Three days before the Convention opened, Krishnamurti, attired in a white *dhoti,* conducted the consecration ceremony of a Hindu Temple within the Adyar Compound. As a Brahmin, he was entitled to undertake this role. The spirit of tolerance and respect for other faiths that was embodied in the TS's first Object could be seen in the Zoroastrian and Buddhist shrines, the synagogue, the mosque and the Liberal Catholic chapel that co-existed at Adyar.

Despite the erection of a temporary village of grass huts, the physical conditions at Adyar were not at all comfortable for the four thousand Convention delegates. Apart from being seriously overcrowded, the visitors had the misfortune to encounter cold and rainy conditions for almost the whole time. To make matters even worse, many had been hoping to experience some remarkable event during the Jubilee, but at the end of the four days at Adyar they were left empty-handed in this respect.

Those who stayed on to attend the Star Congress the next day (December 28th), however, were a good deal more fortunate. They were present when Krishnamurti, speaking to a large crowd, underwent a profound change in the delivery and content of his message.

Referring to the coming World Teacher, he said: "He comes only to those who want, who desire, who long ... and *I* come for those who want sympathy, who want happiness, who are longing to be released, who are longing to find happiness in all things, I come to reform and not to tear down, I come not to destroy but to build."[76]

At the moment when Krishnamurti stopped speaking of *he* and began using *I*, many of those present noticed a profound change in the timbre and power of his voice. As Dr Besant reported, 'There was no excitement, no flurry, even on the 28th of December when, as our brother Krishnaji (ie Krishnamurti) was concluding his 'speech', his sentence was broken into by our Lord the World Teacher, who took possession of his body and spoke a couple of sentences.'[77]

Dr Besant had no doubt whatsoever: the Coming had begun. Krishnamurti did not doubt it either, saying to the crowd at the end of the Star Congress, "You have drunk at the fountain of wisdom and knowledge. The memory of December 28th should be to you as if you were guarding a precious jewel . . . then when He comes again, and I am sure that He will come again very soon, it will be for us a nobler and far more beautiful occasion than even last time.'[78] CWL shared in this certainty, reporting there was not 'a shadow of doubt' that 'He' had used 'the Vehicle' more than once' at the gathering . . .'[79]

But not everyone present at Krishnamurti's speech was so affected by it. Sitting in the audience were Bishop Wedgwood, Bishop Arundale and Rukmini. They said they weren't aware of any change, and that they thought Krishnamurti was simply 'quoting scripture'.[80]

---

[76] Herald of the Star, Feb. 1926.
[77] Besant, *Theosophist*, Jan. 1926.
[78] Krishnamurti's speech to National Representatives, *Herald of the Star*, Mar. 1926.
[79] Bishop C.W.Leadbeater's response to a question on the World Teacher, *Herald of the Star*, June 1926.
[80] Lutyens, Krishnamurti, 224.

CHAPTER 27

DECEMBER 1925

From November onwards, life in our family started to speed up. Dad and I went to the bank and organized the mortgage for 'my' semi. I had a certain amount of money saved up but Dad advised me to keep some in reserve for the expenses that would surely crop up in the coming months. Plans were progressing with the builder to get the house alterations underway after the tenant left, and Mum was having extensive pow-wows with Joyce Housman on the nutrition and recipes session she was going to present.

Joyce was an excellent organizer and jollied Mum along through the process, also briefing her on the venue. The session would be held at the Co-Masonic Temple, which was in Redfern next door to the Liberal Catholic church, and it would be advertised there and also at the two TS lodges and the Amphitheatre.

Mum was not familiar with Co-masonry,[81] but Joyce soon filled her in on it, saying, "It's very like Freemasonry, except that it's open to both sexes. Dr Besant is a great supporter of Co-Masonry as an excellent way to prepare women for participating in public life." A moment's thought made it abundantly clear to me that no male Theosophist worth his salt could in all conscience belong to Fremasonry, a movement that excluded women and thus stood at odds with the TS regarding discrimination on the grounds of gnder. When Mum

---

[81] Co-Masonry originated in France in the 1890s.The first Australian Co-Masonic lodges began in Melbourne in 1911 and Sydney in 1912. Worldwide, hundreds of lodges were formed.

learned that Joyce, Clara Vivian, Narne and Pappi and now even Krishnamurti were Co-Masons, she settled into the idea.

Her session would start at 5.30pm, a convenient time for working people, and Mum could expect to see female lodge-members attired in full-length white robes, as this was their customary garb at Co-Masonic meetings. In answer to Mum's question regarding numbers, Joyce told her: "I think we'll get around twenty people. And if you write out, say, seven or eight recipes, I'll have them mimeographed at TS head office. All you'll need to do is make a schedule of the week's meals and then tell the audience how to make each one and what its nutritional benefits are." Put like this, it sounded quite simple.

When Antonia suggested we do a trial run with an audience comprised of Clara, Joyce, herself and me, Mum jumped at the idea. I was there to represent any male Co-Masons who might attend, and as Antonia rather cheekily said, "To ask the sort of questions that men would ask."

The weeks hurtled by. Max finally returned from New York and told us interesting tales of life in America. He mentioned his visit to Narne and Pappi and said how welcoming they were. I longed to ask if, as a social anthropologist, he'd brought any cultural artifacts from Australia to show them, "Like ah . . . coloured beads, a throwing stick and . . . um . . . any *photographs*?" but knew if I did so our friendship might never be quite the same.

I confined myself, therefore, to artlessly wondering out loud how Max had ever managed to find his way from New York City to Greenwich. He shot me one of his withering looks I knew so well and replied, "I took a *train* from Grand Central Station, that's how, Ed. And you really need to get out of Australia before you *totally* stagnate down here on this antipodean island that pretends to be a continent. There's a big wide world out there, you know." I agreed with him meekly and we settled back into our usual pattern of interaction.

Having been away in America for some months, Max had little TS news to tell me that I didn't already know. He observed that the rift between Krishnamurti and the Arundale-Wedgwood faction seemed to be widening, and mentioned how relieved he was that Krishnamurti had reached a state of personal acceptance regarding the death of his beloved Nitya.

I'd heard that Dr Besant was finding herself in a very awkward position regarding Krishnamurti and his views on the proliferation of Initiations, bearing in mind she herself was a beneficiary of recent promotions and was also on good terms with Wedgwood and Arundale. However, I hadn't yet heard about the steps she'd taken to try to resolve the situation.

Max told me that while Dr Besant was at Adyar, she'd called a meeting of CWL, Arundale, Wedgwood and Raja in her drawing-room. Then, leading Krishnamurti by the hand, she'd brought him into the assembled gathering, seated him on a sofa between herself and CWL and asked him directly if he would accept them all as his disciples. Krishnamurti's response was clear and to the point – he would not accept any of them, 'except perhaps Dr Besant herself.'[82]

Naturally, concerted efforts were made to prevent this serious discord at the heart of the TS from becoming public knowledge, but as Max observed, "A dispute so central to the TS could scarcely stay secret for long."

Soon, the day of Mum's recipes and nutrition session at the Co-Masonic Temple arrived and thankfully, all went well. So well, in fact, that she was even asked to do a repeat session in the New Year, this time at The Manor, for those who couldn't attend the first one.

---

[82] Lutyens, Krishnamurti, 223.

Narne and Pappi arrived from the States the next week in a flurry of outrageously extravagant gifts for us all. They were delighted to be with us and absolutely thrilled to see their two little grandchildren, Ingrid and Tree, again. We put on a big party to welcome them and celebrate the twins' second birthday, which had become engulfed in Antonia's and my engagement and not been properly marked.

The twins adored their American grandparents, and it was fascinating to see how Tree instantly bonded with Pappi. He followed his grandfather everywhere like a shadow and looked just like him, having inherited Pappi's square build and fair colouring. Narne confided to us that Tree's devotion was leading Pappi to think about setting up a subsidiary of Mortimer's Hardware right here in Sydney.

"Pappi always needs a project and a goal," she said. "And of course he's never lost his hope of one day having an heir for Mortimer's Hardware. I always felt in my bones that our darling Ambrose was not cut out to be a hardware merchant, and this is what came to pass, tho' in a way we could never have foreseen."

Pappi was certainly busy. He was very pleased with the two semis, soon to become one, and spent a whole afternoon ensconced with Ian Green, who was overseeing the trust he'd established for Antonia and the twins. Antonia attended part of this meeting too, and emerged from it with her head spinning from the sheer amount of data and money involved. Briefly, she'd have access to ample funds to cover all the twins' needs, and a huge endowment would come to her as Ambrose's widow. Antonia and I had discussed this matter and were in complete accord: we wanted to make our own way financially, apart from using the trust to cover the twins' expenses

Regarding her inheritance, Antonia had a dream. As a trained teacher, she very much wanted to start up a preschool based on Theosophical educational principles and open to low-income families who couldn't afford private school fees. She put it to Pappi and Ian Green that her money be invested until such time as she was ready to commence the school, which she hoped would be the first of a number of others.

Pappi responded positively this idea. He was very familiar with Theosophical theories on education and had sent his own children to Theosophical schools in the States. These schools embodied an educational philosophy articulated a number of years earlier by George Arundale, an educator with some years' experience. As well, they also incorporated many of the features of the three-fold program devised by CWL and Annie Besant in 1916 in which, alongside traditional educational subjects, considerable attention was devoted to religion and ritual. Morven Garden School at Gore Hill in Sydney was based on these principles, and it was here that Antonia had gained first-hand experience of this educational approach.

Several years earlier, the Morven Garden School had been forced to close due to financial constraints. The two much-loved and dedicated principals, Miss Lily Arnold and Miss Jessie MacDonald, had then established the Garden School in Stanton Rd, Mosman. Although The Garden School was privately supported by endowments and not formally affiliated with the TS, many Theosophists sent their children there and I knew this was where Antonia wanted the twins to go.

When Narne and Pappi were nearing the end of their stay in Sydney, Pappi decided he'd like to make a visit to The Garden School, saying:

"I want to see where my little grandchildren will spend their schooldays. I can then visualize them there when we're back in the States." With this in mind, it was therefore arranged that on the next Saturday, Narne, Pappi and Antonia would take afternoon tea at The Garden School with Miss Arnold and Miss MacDonald.

A few days before the visit, Antonia said, "I'd really like you to come too, Ed. I remember when you were researching your dissertation you said you were very interested in the Theosophical approach to education, and yet we've never really got around to discussing it." I remembered this too, but now I could say, "I was really more interested in spending some time with *you*, truth be known. And if it wouldn't be too much of a crowd for the two principals, then I'd very much like to come with you."

Several days before the visit, Antonia gave me some reading matter on the Theosophical approach to education. Briefly, I learned that Theosophical schools are based on the premise that:

'Every child has its own unique temperament, character and abilities, and these must be studied and developed individually; that kindness and love must dominate in the treatment of the child, punishment and fear being eliminated, if the best results are to be obtained; that religion must be made a personal practical thing to each child – something which will link her or him with the great unseen inner world of reality. To secure these results the teachers in turn must pursue their work with love for it, and the motto ... is the motive of its staff – 'Education as Service'.[83]

Cramming for examinations and overstrain did not have a place in this approach, and:

'Each child is encouraged to have its own garden to facilitate Nature Study, and make it more interesting . . . all pupils are encouraged to play tennis daily and spend a large portion of their

---

[83] *Theosophy in Australasia* Supplement, Mar. 1, 1918.

time in the open air. School classes are held
whenever possible out of doors . . . Art
eurythmics[84], the drama, handicrafts, open-air
life with tuition in games are important features
. . . The school is non-sectarian in character, and
children may attend any Church selected by their
parents.'[85]

To me, the sentiments thus expressed sounded very
humane. Antonia, speaking first as a pupil and then as a
teacher within this educational approach, vouched that
she'd never witnessed any untoward behaviour, and
indeed a general sense of harmony and wellbeing was to
be found throughout Morven Garden School.

The next Saturday afternoon saw me, together with
Antonia, Narne and Pappi, walking down the steep hill to
The Garden School, which was located in a large three-
storeyed stone house at 30 Stanton Rd Mosman, just
above the Amphitheatre and Edwards Beach. On one of
the imposing stone gateposts a sign announced 'The
Garden School'[86] and from the wrought iron gates, a dark
asphalt drive swept around the big house and swung into
a huge circular area surrounded by gardens and trees. The
school stood in four acres of gardens and commanded a
spectacular water view stretching through the Sydney
Harbour Heads and out to the horizon.

Miss Arnold and Miss MacDonald, two rather large
elderly women dressed entirely in white, conducted us
into a high-ceilinged ante-room. Here, presiding over a
tasty array of cakes and biscuits, they spoke of their

---

[84] Eurythmics: harmonious bodily movement as a form of artistic
expression
[85] *Theosophy in Australasia* Supplement, Mar 1, 1918.
[86] In 1928 the words 'THWENG – Co-educational School' were
added to the other gatepost. 'THWENG' stood for Truth,
Harmony, Wisdom, Education, Natural Grace.

educational philosophy and answered our questions. Although it was school holidays, we noticed a few children playing in the gardens, and were told they were pupils who lived all year round at the school due to problems of various kinds in their home-lives. These children were supported financially and in all other ways by the school and were never caused to feel any different from other pupils. Antonia, who herself had been one such child at Morven Garden School, could vouch that this was so.

When we'd finished afternoon tea Miss Arnold, who'd been deep in discussion with Pappi Mortimer said, "Miss MacDonald, I wonder if you'd mind showing our visitors over the school while Mr Mortimer and I discuss some educational interests we have in common."

At this hint, Miss MacDonald led Narne, Antonia and me out of the room for a tour of the school and grounds. From the outside, the building was not outstanding except for its size, the interior with its high ceilings, curving front stairway and great number of rooms did possess a certain grandeur.

We were shown over 'The Boys' House', which contained their dormitory and the 'Old House' facing the sea where the girls slept in a glassed-in verandah above the other floors of kitchens, dining-rooms, classrooms and assembly hall. We were all impressed by the high standard of the establishment and the delightful 'garden schoolroom' where many of the lessons were held. When we rejoined Pappi and Miss Arnold, I observed that Pappi had made notes on a sheet of paper which he now folded and put in his coat pocket.

Just before we left the school, Miss MacDonald produced a large ledger in which to enter the twins' names on the waiting list for the kindergarten group.

When Antonia gave their names as 'Ingrid and Tree Mortimer,' the two headmistresses did not miss a beat. Miss Arnold smiled and said, "'Tree' – what a lovely name! Do you know, we have a Flora, a Rosa and a Daisy in our school, and next year we'll be acquiring a boy called Peter[87], whose name comes from the Greek word for 'stone', but we haven't yet had a 'Tree'."

Miss Arnold's reaction to his name was so different from the puzzled looks we often received from strangers when we said Tree's name that I felt an immediate rush of warmth towards her. I surmised that as a 'traditional' Theosophist, Miss Arnold would be of the view that all inanimate objects were sentient beings. And therefore, or so I reasoned, she'd find it quite natural for a child to be named 'Tree'.

As we walked up the hill back to Gouldsbury St, we all agreed that the afternoon had been very worthwhile, with Narne, Pappi and Antonia all saying how happy they were to think of the twins being in such good hands next year when they'd start at The Garden School.

---

[87] This boy was Peter Finch (1916-1977), who became a famous actor and film-star.
See also Appendix 2: The Theosophical childhood of Peter Finch, actor and film-star 1916-1977..

CHAPTER 28

1926

After Narne and Pappi returned to the States, we had three weeks in which to prepare for our wedding. Not that there was much to do: we'd already booked the Registry Office for 2 pm on Saturday 6th February 1926 and the Amphitheatre, Balmoral for a mid-afternoon celebration with a group of around thirty friends and family.

Following some discussion, we'd arrived at what for us would be the perfect honeymoon but we wondered if others would view it in the same light.

"Why don't we just keep it to ourselves," Antonia suggested. "Only tell Mother and your parents."

"Good idea," I replied. This way, we'd avoid any possible scornful reactions from friends such as Russell Fletcher.

On the day of the wedding, Antonia, wearing a lovely silken dress with a pattern of flowers and looking even more beautiful than ever, arrived by taxicab from Mosman at the Central Registry Office in the city, accompanied by Clara and the twins. From Stanmore Mum&Dad, The Aunts and I appeared, also by taxi. The no-nonsense ceremony started at 2pm sharp and by 2.30 Antonia and I were lawful-wedded man and wife. We than hailed two taxis and set off to the Amphitheatre for the reception. Antonia, the new Mrs Best, and I travelled in one with The Aunts, because they would depart on their third trip to England while we'd be away on our honeymoon.

The Amphitheatre was a perfect choice for the reception, with room for everyone to move around, delicious food and drink laid on, and of course the breathtaking view straight out the Sydney Harbour Heads. My friends from work and the tennis club and a few others unconnected with Theosophy were amazed by the size, outlook and elegant design of the building, and after a few speeches (short) and general expressions of goodwill, at 5pm we were ready to start on our honeymoon.

One tiny irritation emerged when I went to get the car from where I'd parked it around the corner from the Amphitheatre earlier in the day. Now, the entire vehicle was swathed in white ribbons, with a large JUST MARRIED placard attached to the rear. Inwardly cursing, but maintaining a sociable façade for the benefit of the assembled guests, I helped Antonia into the car. As I did so, I scanned the crowd, looking for one particular face. Then I spotted him – Russell Fletcher, chortling away in the background. Graciously waving to the throng, we drove away accompanied by a scattering of confetti and much goodwill.

Once round the corner, I stopped the car abruptly and tore off all the signs that advertised our status to the world, then off we drove to start our married life at a secret location very close to Sydney that enabled Antonia to phone her mother every evening and hear how the household was managing.

As an only child who'd hitherto lived with my parents in the one house since birth, I found my new life in Gouldsbury St Mosman with a wife, two step-children and a mother-in-law under the same roof 'novel', to say the least. Added to this was the constant noise of the builders from early morning as the two semis were converted into one dwelling, and my daily cross-city journey to work and back. With all this, it was not surprising that I had little spare time to sit around speculating on Krishnamurti and how he might be faring in his life, wherever he was in the world. But lest I sound like a whinger, let me say very clearly that I thoroughly enjoyed my new life and could still scarcely credit it was real.

After a few months, things settled down to the extent I was now able to meet up with Max for dinner. I knew there'd be a number of TS events to catch up on, and I wasn't wrong. After some generalities, Max said: "While I was in the States, Pappi Mortimer introduced me to a Theosophical friend of his, a retired 'captain of industry' who shared my interest in Krishnamurti. After a very pleasant lunch, this fellow asked me if I'd be interested in writing a book about Krishmaurti and his life in the TS.

"The idea had a certain appeal," Max finished, typically concealing any emotions such as jubilation and/or excitement.

I responded in like manner, simply remarking, "Just up your alley, Max, I'd imagine," followed by, "Sounds like you won't have much time for dinner anymore."

Max responded to this with: "Oh no, Ed. I'll need you more than ever to bounce ideas off."

I acquiesced in a suitably pleasant but restrained manner, while noting that in this exchange Max had opened up more than he usually did. Maybe his new life, as well as the passage of time, was healing some of the scars from the past.

I had one question, of a practical nature, "Will you need to take time off from lecturing at the university?"

"You must be kidding!" he replied, using one of the Americanisms he'd picked up on his recent trip. "There's ample time for both." Which was probably true, I reflected, given that he wasn't living in a household like mine.

Becoming more matter-of-fact, he continued:

"This guy, 'my contact', has friends in various parts of the TS, worldwide – so I should soon be able to get a much closer picture of what's going on, all in confidence, of course."

To this, I nodded discreetly.

"When the whole thing blows up, it'll be headlines world-wide," he finished.

"So – you really think it's all going to erupt, do you?"

He nodded, saying, "It's now become an impossibility for anyone to believe in Arundale and Wedgwood and also in Krishnamurti. Their viewpoints have become irreconcilable and it looks like we're heading for a complete split."

"What's your evidence?" I asked. "Or is this simply a hunch?"

"A bit of both," Max replied. "But how's this for something I heard recently – it may give you a glimpse into where things are going." He then proceeded to regale me with an event that had occurred during the last year but which, even now, very few people knew about.

In summary, it was this:

During July (1925) Bishop Arundale wrote to Dr Besant telling her that, as well as the great number of Initiations occurring at Huizen, the possibility had arisen 'of a visit on the physical plane to the castle of the Master the Count, somewhere in Hungary.'[88]

This news was sensational – such a visit would prove the existence of the Masters beyond all doubt. While the location of the Count's castle was not known, Arundale intimated that he had been instructed (astrally) to open a well-known European guidebook (the *Continental Bradshaw*) at random and escort a select group to the location on which his finger landed.

A band of dedicated TS members including Dr Besant, Arundale, his wife Rukmini and Wedgwood had set off on their secret expedition to wait at Amsterdam for

---

[88] Lutyens, *Krishnamurti*, 210.

their next instructions. At the same time, Lady Emily Lutyens and her friend Miss Esther Bright left London to do the same at Innsbruk, Austria. But although they all remained at their posts for some days, no further instructions were ever received.

When several weeks later the whole group met up again back in London, the fruitless journey was simply not alluded to, with a stern-looking Dr Besant attributing the expedition's failure to the superior powers of the 'black forces'[89].

"I can see why they weren't anxious to rush around publicising this experience," I commented.

"Agree – they wouldn't want to shout it from the rooftops," was Max's reply.

We then had an interesting discussion on the role of Faith and Credulity in human behaviour. We agreed that whereas Credulity does not demand reason, evidence or argument, but only simple belief, Faith implies that you are persuaded for a reason, by arguments, with evidence. However, at a certain point, 'a leap of faith', may occur in which the holder of this position becomes convinced that their position is correct and impregnable. Here, we concurred, things tend to get a bit blurred.

From this theoretical exploration, we then moved back to analyzing the real-life situation in front of us. Did Arundale actually believe that the Master the Count was about to manifest on the material plane? From the evidence before us, it seemed that he did. Why else, except through total certitude, would he lead these senior and dedicated members of the TS on what turned out to be a wild goose chase? Max said that there seemed to be no evidence of insincerity on Arundale's part, so it may have been a case of mass hysteria or delusion, of which there are many recorded instances in the history of the human race.

---

[89] Ibid., 215.

The whole episode was quite puzzling and, together with the incredible numbers of Initiations, and the speed of progression through the Stages, it was obvious that a radical change was taking place within the structure of the TS under the direction of the two Liberal Catholic bishops and their followers.

According to Max, Krishnamurti was extremely unhappy about the widespread Initiations. He had tried to talk with Dr Besant, but found she seemed almost 'hypnotised' by Arundale.

On March 26, 1926 Krishnamurti, in a letter to CWL, wrote:

> '. . . I have woken up so often with feelings of revolt and distrust that my impressions and intuitions are growing stronger and stronger and I feel that the events of the last ten months aren't clean and wholesome. Of course there's nothing to be done but wait for events to develop . . . this apostles business is the limit. I don't believe in it all and this is *not* based on prejudice. With that we shall have difficulty and I am *not* going to give in over that. I think it's wrong and purely George's (ie., Arundale's) imagination . . .' [90]

After taking a short break for a smoke, Max continued updating me on TS doings in recent months.

"The idea had been in Krishnamurti's mind for a while to hold a gathering for special friends three weeks prior to the Star Camp at Ommen, Holland. So, on July 3, 1926 thirty-five people from all over the world converged on Castle Eerde. Lady Emily Lutyens with her daughters Mary and Betty were there, as well as other old and new friends. A one- hour meeting each morning would be held in the large drawing-room. Max had come by several

---

[90] Ibid., 228.

accounts of these meetings and read out excerpts from one of these:

> " 'Krishna (ie Krishnamurti) spoke as never before and one feels now that his consciousness and that of the Lord are so completely blended that there is no distinction any more. He said, 'Follow me and I will show you the way into the Kingdom of Happiness. I will give each of you the key with which you can unlock the gate into the garden,' and it was no effort to him to use the personal pronoun . . . the face of the Lord shone through the face of Krishna and His glorious aura encompassed us in an almost blinding light . . .' " [91]

Max had one more item of interest to impart: "The TS Convention at Ommen (Holland) commenced on July 24th and among the 2,000 participants were Dr Besant and Bishop Wedgwood. On the 27th, they attended Krishnamurti's talk, and at the end of it, Wedgwood leaned over and whispered something to Dr Besant. Afterwards, back at the Castle, Dr Besant went to Krishnamurti's room and told him that 'a powerful black magician' who was well-known to her was 'speaking through him'.[92]

"Krishnamurti, naturally, was aghast at hearing this, and vowed never again to speak in public if Dr Besant believed this. Upset. she took back what she'd said. However, 'influence of the blacks' came to be used by Wedgwood and his cohort more and more frequently as Krishnamurti's path diverged yet further from theirs.

---

[91] Ibid., 231. Excerpt from letter, Lady Emily Lutyens to Raja.
[92] Ibid., 234.

Although Max and I saw each other at various family gatherings, we didn't get the chance for another real talk until round Christmas, and then it was more or less a quick bulletin.

Max told me Krishnamurti was under strain and pain from his 'Process'. Dr Besant was feeling the tension of her divided loyalties and longed to give up her public duties and simply follow Krishnamurti as his disciple. CWL however, counselled her against taking this step on the grounds that it would contravene her Master's orders. She then decided to accompany Krishnamurti to America and immediately booked a passage on the same ocean liner bound for New York.

When their ship arrived there on August 26th, a posse of reporters came on board to interview them. The next day, newspaper headlines trumpeted: *'Cult of Star Awaits Glory of Coming Lord', 'New Gospel Told by Annie Besant, 'A new Messiah in Tennis flannels', 'New Deity Comes in Plus-Fours',* and so on. [93]

In the following days, Krishnamurti gave interviews to more than forty journalists, generally making a favourable impression and handling some tricky questions well. One reporter, however, was not so impressed, writing: 'Here's what I think of that Oriental. I wouldn't give him a job in a third-rate Chu Chin Chow company'. [94]

After attending a TS Convention in Chicago Krishnamurti was at last able to show Dr Besant to a place very dear to his heart – the Ojai Valley, California. Together with other friends including Lady Emily and her daughter Mary, they spent five months there enjoying a good rest, despite Krishnamurti periodically suffering debilitating episodes of his 'Process'.

---

[93] Ibid., 236.
[94] Ibid., 237.

CHAPTER 29

END OF 1926 – END OF 1927

One Sunday morning at the end of September, we were sitting at the table having breakfast with the twins when Antonia suddenly jumped to her feet.

"Oh, Ed! I feel really sick. Please keep an eye on the children!" she announced, making a dash for the bathroom. Several minutes later, she emerged looking wan and rather shaken.

"What's up?" I asked.

"I just felt very nauseous all of a sudden . . . maybe it's a tummy bug."

"Maybe it is," I replied, but wondered if it wasn't.

A couple of weeks later after another bout of morning nausea and a few more symptoms, we knew. Antonia was pregnant and, all being well, our baby would be born next year in June. We waited a few more weeks to tell close family members, who were delighted at hearing our news.

One day when Mum&Dad were visiting us, MMum said to Dad, "Right – now, Arthur, let's put our house up for sale and move over to Mosman."

"Hold your horses, Isobel," Dad replied. "There's no need to rush it. I'd rather take our time and find a place that suits us both – one with a large kitchen for you and a nice sunny back yard for my botanical projects."

As a long-time observer of Mum&Dad, I gave Dad full marks for this response, catering as it did to interests close to both their hearts, with Mum's mentioned first. Also, Dad had recently started on a new experiment that involved grafting different coloured flowering fruit trees onto each other. This project took up a lot of space in our backyard so he certainly wouldn't want to move anywhere smaller.

By now, Mum was a competent and confident driver. She and Dad were also the proud owners of a 1923 Ford Model T centre-door sedan, and were able to drive over to Mosman to see us at weekends. With The Aunts now living in England, it seemed there was more drawing my parents towards Mosman than was keeping them at Stanmore. Mum acknowledged that she'd miss her old Stanmore friends, but said she could always drive over to see them once in a while.

Although I was quite busy at this stage, it was impossible to ignore Mum's ongoing personal blossoming. Following her successful nutrition and recipes session at the Co-Masonic temple in Redfern, she'd been asked to give more of these talks, and the venue for some of them would be The Manor, Mosman.

Always a focal point for TS activity, The Manor had recently acquired a whole new dimension. From an out-building in the grounds, a radio aerial now rose high into the sky and from this site the TS's radio station, 2GB, [95] had begun to broadcast. Each week, a steady stream of personnel involved in the programs made their way to the 'studio' and often called in at the 'big house'.

One day while Mum was at The Manor presenting a nutrition talk to a group of women from nearby suburbs, one of the 2GB program managers asked if he might sit in on the session. Mum, by now a seasoned public speaker, was not at all fazed by his request.

She started off in her usual way, saying, "My name is Mrs Isobel Best. I am not a Theosophist myself, nor do I have any specific qualifications in nutrition. But what I *do* have is an abiding respect for healthy, wholesome food

---

[95] See Glossary: 2GB radio station

as the foundation for a strong constitution and good health. The other two essential components for this, in my view, are regular exercise and a good night's sleep. I can't help with these, they are up to you, but what I *can* provide is some guidance on nutrition from my many years of interest in healthy cooking and wholesome eating."

A smattering of applause followed this statement and then off she went into her talk. After a question and answer session at the end, everyone departed, except for the 2GB man. Thinking he might have a query about one of the recipes, Mum asked if she could help him.

"Yes, Mrs Best, I very much hope you can," he replied, then introduced himself and asked if she'd be interested in doing a regular half-hour nutrition-and-recipes session on radio 2GB. Mum nearly fell over in shock at hearing this, but quickly composed herself and said she'd have to talk it over with her husband. The manager presented his card and said he'd look forward to hearing from her.

As soon as she arrived back home, Mum rang Dad at his office. He was as stunned as she was, and urged her to take up the offer.

"I'm glad you feel I should do it," she told him. "Because I'd very much like to. And you know, Arthur, I think we'd both better lose some weight."

"For heaven's sake why?" Dad demanded. "It's a *radio* program. No one will see how you look."

"That's not the point," she said firmly. "If I'm going to speak publicly about good nutrition, then I have to be an advertisement for it – and that means you, too."

"I don't see the logic of that," Dad grumbled, though very delighted and proud of her.

Mum enjoyed learning the ropes of broadcasting and a few months later when I went to the studio and watched her in action, the program-manager told me what a success she was.

"Your mother is so . . . so *genuine*, so full of integrity," he marvelled.

"She certainly is. That's always been her trademark," I replied, proud to have a commercial commodity for a mother.

While Mum and Dad had now started losing weight, Antonia was gaining it at quite a rapid rate. Not surprisingly, I wondered if she might be expecting twins, but she didn't think so, saying, "Probably my stomach got stretched during the first pregnancy."

We were starting to think about names, but found it harder than we'd imagined. We wanted to honour our parents, or rather Mum&Dad and Clara (no-one rushing to honour Antonia's father, still living the life of a Buddhist monk in the mountains of Tibet). Mum&Dad, however, were adamant they did not want their names perpetuated. Dad told us he'd always disliked 'Arthur' and Mum said she felt the name 'Isabel Best' had an unfortunate ring to it, sounding like the start of a question: 'Is a bell best for the front door or would a buzzer or door-knocker be better?'

The name game became a bit of an after-dinner pastime – we even went through a mercifully brief moment of thinking 'Theo' for a boy and 'Sophy' for a girl (ie 'Theo-sophy'). Eventually, Antonia came up with two real possibilities – 'James' (after one of Mum's brothers who'd died in the War, and also to honour the psychologist William James), and 'Clarisa' (a near-compound of 'Clara' and 'Isobel') for a girl.

The months passed, and it became clearer and clearer that Antonia was indeed expecting twins. As things transpired, however, we had a rather dreadful time of it. The twins (a boy and a girl) arrived safely on June 28th, 1927 but immediately after the delivery, Antonia suffered excessive bleeding. She was rushed into the operating theatre and in order to save her life, her doctor had to perform an emergency hysterectomy.

It was an extremely worrying time. Antonia was desperately ill, and as well as two newborn babies we had two very young children to look after. Fortunately, Clara, Mum&Dad and Antonia's siblings were there to assist. Max contributed in a thoughtful way and completely off his own bat: by arranging for a local laundry to deal with all our washing and ironing.

Gradually, Antonia regained her strength. Although shocked by what had happened, she was resilient and realistic, saying, "Look, let's just be glad I'm alive. And we have two bonny babies and two beautiful children."

Everyone we knew helped out. Miss Arnold and Miss MacDonald at The Garden School sent word that Ingrid and Tree, now nearly four, could start kindergarten a little earlier than planned. Narne and Pappi over in the States cabled us saying, 'Can we be grandparents of the new twins, too?' and we assured them they already were.

With all our domestic travails, a number of months passed before I was able to meet up with Max for an extended discussion of TS matters. By December, things had settled down considerably and Max took me out to dinner to celebrate the return to a semblance of domestic normality and brief me on developments within the TS.

Over a meal at a little Russian restaurant in a nearby suburb, he filled me in on recent events. Some of these I'd already heard about, others were completely new. I simply let him run, very much enjoying having a civilized meal that wasn't interrupted by babies and/or small children.

"Slowly but surely, we're moving towards a showdown within the TS," he said, "as you'll soon see. Back in April, you'll recall, Dr Besant made a statement to the Associated Press of America that started with the words: 'The Divine spirit has descended once more on a man, Krishnamurti . . .' and ended with '. . . The World Teacher is here.'[96]

"Naturally, this excited a great deal of interest in the press. Then, only a few weeks later, Krishnamurti spoke at a meeting of the Esoteric Section of the TS in Paris at which he referred to the Masters as *only incidents.*'" [97]

"Hmm, quite provocative, I'd have thought," I said, "Since the Masters are at the very core of the Esoteric Section."

"Exactly. His words unleashed an enormous furore," Max replied. "And Ed, it's good to see your brain's not completely softened by domesticity."

"Not yet, anyway," I answered. "Now tell me the rest of the news, like a good fellow, but without the personal observations."

"Let me see now," Max said, appearing to look through some notes, "Oh, yes – at a Star meeting in London, Bishop Arundale declared he differed from Dr Besant in that he did not believe that Krishnamurti's consciousness had now blended with the Lord's. However, notwithstanding this, he stressed the importance of maintaining a united public front on such matters."

"Easier said than done, I'd say." I remarked.

Max nodded. "This year," he went on, "in June another gathering in Holland was held at Castle Eerde prior to the Camp at Ommen. Whereas the year before, Krishnamurti's theme had been 'The Kingdom of Happiness', this year he spoke on 'Liberation', stressing the need to be free and uncompromising, facing oneself and weeding out any elements that are unworthy of the self that one wants to be.

---

[96] *Theosophist*, April 1927, cited in M. Lutyens, Krishnamurti, 241.
[97] Lutyens, Krishnamurti 242, reporting a communication from Krishnaurti to Lady Emily Lutyens.

"As he told the gathering . . ." Here Max paused, then, taking a slightly crumpled newspaper clipping from his coat pocket, continued,

> " 'You must not make me an authority . . . I can be the door but you must pass through and find the liberation that is beyond it . . . No-one can give you liberation, you have to find it within, but because I have found [it], I would show you the way . . .' [98]

"Obviously, Kriahnamurti was saying here that all gurus, including the Masters, are not necessary – individuals can find the way to the truth by themselves. To many who'd assembled at Castle Eerde to hear him speak, these words were revolutionary and extremely shocking, even blasphemous."

"I can understand that," I replied. "A large part of his audience would have been used to being told exactly what they must do, with their progress along the Spiritual Path very clearly mapped out."

Max nodded. "Precisely – and yet more changes were coming. Now that the new World Teacher has actually appeared, it follows that the aims of the Order of the Star in the East have now been fulfilled, and therefore a thorough overhaul of the organization is required. Accordingly, the name of the Order has been changed to 'The Order of the Star' and new Objects drawn up, which are: 'Firstly: to draw together all those who believe in the presence in the world of the World Teacher; and secondly, to work for Him in all ways for His realisation of His ideal for humanity' ".

After reciting the new Objects, Max continued, "And then comes a statement that 'The Order has no dogmas, creeds or systems of beliefs. Its inspiration is the Teacher, its purpose to embody His universal life,'"

---

[98] Ibid. 244.

I was curious to know how Krishnamurti might have been feeling at this time.

"I'm told he very much wanted to become a *sannyasa*," Max told me, "which, in the Hindu philosophy of the four stages of life, refers to someone who has renounced worldly attachments.[99] Apparently, he first expressed this longing at the start of the year, while at the same time recognising that the time for this change was not yet come, and he must wait for it 'with eager patience,'[100] as he put it.

"Meanwhile, the popularity of the Eerde Camp was growing like wildfire," he continued, "with almost three thousand attendees, many staying in hotels in nearby villages. Following Krishnamurti's earlier comments that the Masters were 'only incidents' there was general concern as to whether or not he believed in them. People were also confused about his use of an unfamiliar term, 'The Beloved'.

"On August 2nd he spoke publicly on this matter, telling the gathering that from childhood he had seen Sri Krishna, Master K.H (Kuthumi), the Buddha – all in the form that was put before him – and that when he talked about 'The Beloved', to him it was *all* of them, and yet it was *beyond* all these forms. Further, it did not matter what name was given. He finished by saying:

" '. . . It's no good asking me who is the Beloved. Of what use is explanation? For you will not understand the Beloved until you are able to see Him in every animal, in every blade of grass, in every person that is suffering, in every individual.' "[101]

---

[99] See Glossary: *Sannyasa*
[100] Lutyens, 1984, 245, letter from Krishnamurti to Raja, Feb.9, 1927.
[101] Ibid., 250, quoting from a speech by Krishnamurti.

When Max had finished speaking I observed that I could well understand the widespread confusion among those who heard him speak.

Max agreed. "That would have been a common reaction. But for some of those present, Krishnamurti's words came like shafts of enlightenment. Overall, however, the feeling was one of deep bewilderment. Dr Besant, among others, was becoming alarmed at what she saw as a divisive and destructive atmosphere currently prevailing, and she voiced her concerns to a number of people.

"As we all know, Dr Besant has never been one to sit around moping about events" he continued. "And soon, she and Krishnamurti set off on the long voyage to Bombay, *en route* for the TS convention at Adyar in December. When their ship berthed at Bombay, she took the opportunity to make an announcement to the waiting crowd of reporters, saying,

" 'I bear witness that he (Krishnamurti) has been accounted worthy of that for which he had been chosen, worthy to blend his consciousness with that of a fragment, an *amsa*, of the omnipresent consciousness of the World Teacher . . .' " [102]

This utterance, of course, received huge publicity and prompted Bishop Arundale to write an article saying he 'had doubts about even that fragment being with Krishnamurti always.'[103] Arundale then went on to observe that, as Dr Besant was always right, so in this instance, too, she must be right. And at the TS Convention at Adyar in December, Dr Besant again made it clear that Krishnamurti was 'The Teacher', and declared herself his 'devoted disciple.'[104]

---

[102] Ibid., 254.
[103] Theosophy in India, Oct.1927.
[104] Lutyens, Krishnamurti,, 303, chronology entry for Dec. 1927.

Straight after the Convention came the Star Camp, attended by more than a thousand people and judged by Krishnamurti as 'a fair success' [105] but very draining of his energy.

"He can certainly draw a crowd," I remarked.

At this point, Max looked at his watch and suggested it was time we concluded our discussion and went to our respective homes.

"I've really enjoyed the evening," I told him, "and I'll be all ears to hear what comes next in the saga of the TS."

"I don't think you'll need to wait long," Max replied.

---

[105] Ibid., 256, letter, Krishnamurti to Lady Emily Lutyens, Jan. 17, 1928.

CHAPTER 30

1928

On the home-front, things were now progressing in a satisfactory manner. Antonia's health was now good and we'd grown used to the fact that our two babies, James and Clarisa, would be the only children we'd ever produce.

Dad took a scientific approach, saying, "My studies in Animal Husbandry tell me that once a multiple birth has occurred, the chances of it recurring and indeed yielding more offspring increase markedly with each pregnancy."

My witty riposte to this was: "Although I'm a husband, Dad, I am not an animal," then adding: "And there *are* ways and means for avoiding pregnancy, you know."

"I do know, Son," Dad replied sagely. "But I also know there's many a slip twixt the cup and the lip."

"Very true," I agreed. "But why are we having this conversation, I wonder? For Antonia and me, the stable door is firmly shut."

During the next few months, Mum&Dad arranged the sale of their Stanmore house and bought a cottage several streets away from us with all the attributes Dad wanted – big kitchen for Mum, sunny backyard for his botanical experiments and a garage for their car.

It was excellent having so many helpers close by. Dad was a great storyteller, and when I'd arrive home from the surgery I could tell from the gales of laughter coming from the playroom that he was telling Ingrid and Tree another tall tale. Mum's major contribution was through her cooking. She provided a steady stream of nourishing and tasty meals for all the age-groups in our household. As well, she shared her repertoire of recipes with her radio audience on 2GB by including meals for 'fussy eater' children, as Ingrid and Tree tended to be. Clara emerged as a world-class knitter of children's jumpers, cardigans, hats, socks and mittens – all without needing a pattern!

And finally, Max. True to type, he contributed intellectual stimulus. Acting on his belief that Australians were grossly ignorant of the outside world, he took it upon himself to teach Ingrid and Tree the names of all the countries and capital cities of Europe and the Middle East. To this end, he made a map of out of cardboard with the various countries and their capitals clearly marked and then cut it up to make a jigsaw. The twins enjoyed his teaching sessions greatly, and when they'd mastered the jigsaw, he moved on to teaching them basic arithmetic – in German.

The next time I saw Max in a social context was at the engagement party for Antonia's sister Helena. My old friend Russell Fletcher had finally succeeded in persuading Helena, and also Clara, that he was a steady and reliable marriage prospect for Helena. Interestingly, in the process of demonstrating that he was indeed a suitable swain, Russell had actually undergone an internal transformation and ended up genuinely eligible for her hand.

Just before the engagement party, a parcel arrived addressed to Clara and plastered all over with Indian postage stamps. She obviously recognized the handwriting and, with a meaningful glance at Antonia, proceeded to open the package. Inside were a number of small packets, which Clara unwrapped one by one to reveal a collection of Tibetan handcrafts and artifacts –

brightly embroidered leather bags, scarves, necklaces and small carved statues.

"From Father," Antonia told me. "He does this from time to time – just the gifts, never a letter or return address."

"I'll put them on the coffee table in the corner, some of you children may like to have them," Clara said.

Antonia made no move to claim any of the pieces and I wondered if any of her siblings would, either. During the party, I kept an eye on the handcrafts sitting on the coffee table, but none of Clara's children went anywhere near them. The only people who took any interest were Mum, Dad and Max, and at the end of the party when we were cleaning up, the items were still sitting there.

"Take them along to the next TS meeting, Mother," Antonia advised. "Someone will certainly appreciate them. After all, they *are* Tibetan." I never saw the items again, so assume they found a happy home.

The next few months saw a great deal of activity in the TS, with May being particularly busy. Outwardly at least, Krishnamurti was going from strength to strength, making his first public appearance in America speaking at the famous Hollywood Bowl to an audience of 16,000.

"Then," Max told me, "in the same month, Dr Besant over in Adyar launched a new divine identity – the 'World Mother' (her preferred name for the Virgin Mary). And this entity was embodied by – I wonder if you can guess . . . ?"

"Surely not – herself?" I hazarded.

"No, that might be going a bit far, even for Dr Besant," Max replied, then added in a portentous voice: "The World Mother is none other than . . . Mrs Rukmini Arundale, Bishop Arundale's wife!"

"Well – I'll be blowed!" I exclaimed. "How extraordinary!"

Max smiled. "Yes," he replied, "And apparently Krishnamurti thought so too, for he wrote to CWL a long letter in which he said . . . ." Here he paused, rummaged in his briefcase and produced a couple of sheets of paper. Clearing his throat for effect, he read out:

" 'I hear Amma (his name for Dr Besant) has proclaimed Mrs Arundale (Rukmini) as the representative of the World Mother etc. I hear also that I am dragged into it all. It is the work of George (Arundale), with his messages, the outcome of his fertile brain. His machinations are innumerable. I do not want to be mixed up in any of these things. . I know definitely what I want to do here, this time, and in this world, and I am going to do it. So few understand, hence it is going to be difficult and even now some of the so-called Apostles are creating trouble and derision . . .More and more, I am certain of my union with my Beloved, with the Teacher, with the life eternal. As Krishna, I do not exist and that is the truth. George (Arundale) and Wedgwood have begun to deny this but fortunately there is great space and open fields of understanding. I am *not* going to convert anyone to my way of thinking but I am going to assert the fact, when it is necessary . . .' " [106]

"Thank you, Max," I said when he'd finished. "That is most illuminating. It must be very helpful to have access to Krishnamurti's own correspondence so soon after he's written it. No need to wait around for years and delve in musty old libraries, eh?"

During 1928, as Krishnamurti's worldwide renown grew, he was constantly quizzed by reporters on TS

---

[106] Lutyens, Krishnamurti, 257-8, letter, Krishnamurti to Bishop C.W. Leadbeater, May,, 1928.

matters. When asked by the press what his views were on the World Mother, he said he could make no comment, as he knew nothing about it. On June 23, he spoke at the Salle Playel, Paris, the city's largest concert hall, and several days later gave a broadcast in French from the Eiffel Tower Radio Station on 'The Search for Happiness'.

At the Eerde Camp at the start of July he was somewhat dismayed to encounter considerable antagonism from those who found his words disturbing to their own world-view. But as time went on, although he met this reaction more and more frequently, he was also attracting the attention of a new, younger group who were deeply intrigued by what he currently had to say. During the Eerde Camp, his answers to the questions put to him generated such intense interest that they were collected in a booklet[107] and published even before the conclusion of the Camp.

When I saw these questions and answers in print, I could see how controversial many of Krishnamurti's utterances were. For example:

'I refuse to be your crutch. I am not going to be brought into a cage for your worship . . .'

and

'Is it not much simpler to make Life itself the goal – Life itself the guide, the Master and the God – than to have mediators, gurus, who must inevitably step down the Truth, and hence betray it?'

He also told a Reuters journalist that 'neither Buddha nor Christ had claimed divinity or wished to found a religion; it was their *followers* who had done so after they were dead.'[108] Small wonder there was confusion and anger in the ranks.

---

[107] Jiddue Krishnamurti, *Let Understanding be the Law* (Ommen, The Netherlands, Star Publishing Trust, 1928).

[108] Lutyens, Krishnamurti, 262.

Dr Besant, too, was in a profound state of turmoil. Although she had loved, supported and promoted Krishnamurti for many years, the fact that he'd taken on the mantle of the World Teacher in such a radically different way from how she'd envisaged it left her full of anguish.

It was inevitable that people everywhere would be confused by his pronouncements, and in Sydney it was no different. Antonia and Clara mixed with Theosophists constantly through their various activities, including taking Ingrid and Tree to The Garden School each day. To find out about the prevailing mood in TS circles, I asked them for their impressions.

"There's a lot of bewilderment around," Antonia told me, "especially among the older members. After having been so closely focused on their personal spiritual progress along the Path, they are completely thrown at learning that Krishnamurti says, for example, 'The only manner of attaining Truth is to become disciples of the Truth itself without a mediator,' and '. . . liberation can be attained at any stage of evolution by a man who understands, and that to worship stages as you do, is not essential . . .' " [109]

In late October, when Max and I caught up for a meal one evening, he had some very fresh and interesting news to impart: "Dr Besant has just closed down the Esoteric Section of the TS throughout the world."

I was astounded – in fact, almost lost for words. "That's a pretty drastic step," was my eventual response.

"It is indeed," Max agreed. "Considering that the Esoteric Section was founded by Madame Blavatsky way back in 1889 in order to bring TS members into direct contact with the Masters., Up until now, the ES has been intrinsic to the TS. But now, it is no more."

_____

[109] Ibid., 262.

"What was her rationale for this?" I wondered, and Max explained that Dr Besant held that, as Krishnamurti was the World Teacher, so he should be the only one to teach.

"I can see her reasoning, now," I commented, "And how did *he* react to Dr Besant's action?"

Being so well-informed on this profoundly significant decision, Max had no hesitation in telling me that Krishnamurti was very pleased and relieved that she had taken this step, and particularly that she'd done it independently of certain others.

Given where he'd arrived at personally and what he was publicly expressing, Krishnamurti saw the closure of the Esoteric Section as inevitable. He also knew that although many would be upset, those TS members who really listened to what he was saying would feel a sense of relief at the news.

Between Christmas and New Year, we held a party for family and friends, and during the evening I had a chance to ask Max for a TS update. He told me that Krishnamurti had just finished presiding over a gathering at Benares in India modeled on the Eerde Conventions. Dr Besant and CWL were not able to attend but several other senior TS members were there including Bishop Arundale.

Dr Besant had sent word decreeing that no religious ceremonies were to be held in the course of the Convention. However Bishop Arundale, as a Bishop of the Liberal Catholic Church, had conducted a Mass just outside the Convention Compound. This act was either lauded or condemned, depending on where members stood in the ever-widening schism within the Society

On the last day of the year, Ingrid and Tree were playing in the garden with a friend when I walked past.

They said, "Hello Daddy-Ed," which is what they called me, and I heard their friend say, "Why do you call him Daddy-Ed? Why don't you just call him Daddy?"

"Because he isn't our Daddy," Tree said. "Our Daddy's name is Daddy-Ambrose."

"Well, where's *he* then?" the friend asked.

"He's in another life now," Ingrid replied matter-of-factly. "That's why we've got Daddy-Ed."

"Oh," said their friend and they went on with their game.

CHAPTER 31

1929

Early in 1929, Narne and Pappi Mortimer sent word they planned to visit us mid-year. They'd like to come sooner, Narne told us, but Pappi had to sort out some important business matters before leaving the States.

When I mentioned this to Max, he responded,

"Shrewd man, Pappi. I'd put my money on him to ride out any economic storm."

"You mean over in there in USA?"

"I mean *everywhere*," Max replied. "You're so focused on your home life, Ed, you wouldn't know what's going on. But even *you* must be aware that in the past few years Australia's economic growth has stagnated, the price of wool has dropped and unemployment's rising. I won't bore you with some of the other indicators of tough times ahead."

"Such as? If you might be so kind."

"Such as the decline in Australia's terms of trade and our ability to borrow money abroad; and our rapidly increasing foreign debt, caused by government borrowings to finance large infrastructure projects," he informed me.

"Thank you for that, Max, you can stop right there," I said. "In fact, my father alluded to these warning signs only a few weeks ago, so they don't come as a complete surprise, if you really want to know. But does your economic prescience illuminate your own particular circumstances, I wonder, or is it all purely abstract?"

"Not by any means," Max answered without missing a beat. "Actually, I had been thinking of taking three months' leave from the university to finalise some legal matters in Germany and attend the TS Convention at Eerde in August. While it would be worthwhile for my treatise on Krishnamurti, I have reached the conclusion it would be more prudent to conserve my financial resources by remaining here."

"What are things like in Germany now?" I wondered.

"Unstable – politically and economically," Max replied.

At this point I moved on to another topic. Ever since the Great War, discretion was generally the more prudent strategy when conversing with a person from that country on possibly touchy matters.

Things at home were going along without any major incidents. Ingrid and Tree, now aged five and a half, trouped off to The Garden School each day with Antonia pushing James (known as 'Jimmy') and Clarisa ('Isa') in the stroller. Sometimes she left the little twins at home with Clara and stayed at the school until lunchtime giving a hand in the kindergarten room.

Following my talk with Max, I thought I'd ask Antonia how The Garden School was faring financially these days, as I knew that some years earlier the Morven Garden School had been forced to close due to money problems.

"The school's doing quite well," she told me. "But Miss Arnold was saying recently that enrolments are down this year, and some of the donations the school depends on aren't as large as before. You do know that Pappi's one of the major donors, don't you."

"I surmised as much," I replied.

"Dear Pappi – he keeps his philanthropy anonymous in all the causes he supports," Antonia said. "No-one at The Garden School knows – it's all done through one of his companies. I just hope the school will survive for a few more years so the little twins can get the benefit of it. And also, I want to teach there for a while before I start up my own project."

When the children were a bit older, Antonia was going to use her very sizable legacy from Ambrose to establish a string of schools for disadvantaged children, and we discussed it often. This much was certain: the schools would be named 'The Mortimer Schools', and be run on the educational approach of the schools in Germany pioneered by Rudolph Steiner (an erstwhile member of the TS) and more recently articulated by George Arundale, Miss Lily Arnold and others within the TS in various publications and now broadcasts through radio station 2GB.

"What do you hear about where things are moving in the TS?" I asked Antonia.

"Oh," she replied. "Whenever a group of Theosophists gets together, the talk is of nothing else but Krishnamurti. And of course, down at The Garden School many of the teachers and parents are closely watching developments."

"How's Joyce Housman coping with what she hears?" I wondered.

"Poor Joyce," Antonia replied. "When Mother and Joyce get talking on it, Joyce is hard to stop – she's really obsessed by it all."

This didn't surprise me. For someone like Joyce whose commitment to her beliefs and spiritual pathway ran very deep, the current controversies and contradictions being aired by authority figures within the Theosophical movement must be quite alarming, even discombobulating!

"What aspect is Joyce most concerned about?" I asked.

"Oh, the closing down of the Esoteric Section last year,"[110] Antonia replied. "She simply cannot come to terms with it. You know what Joyce is like – she feels that without the ES, she'll be quite adrift.

"And some of Krishnamurti's pronouncements, like his reference to the Masters as 'only incidents'[111] are extremely shocking to her. She feels very let down by someone whose word she's hitherto trusted implicitly.

"Regarding the Masters," she went on, "I can sympathise with Joyce. Having heard about their central role in Theosophy all my life, I'm amazed to find them 'incidental' all of a sudden."

We agreed that with the 'genie of change' now well and truly out of the bottle, there was no way on earth the TS could revert to how it was.

In March, Krishnamurti was back in the USA, staying in California at his beloved Ojai. According to Max, he was very surprised at the amount of anger he encountered from a number of TS members there, but he reasoned that at least this showed that his words were having some impression on his listeners.

Soon after this, Narne let us know that she and Pappi would arrive in Sydney at the end of July and stay for about a month. She asked Antonia to book their usual hotel around the corner from us in Mosman and said they could hardly wait to be here.

Although Narne and Pappi could charter flights for various legs of their journey, the trip was still long and arduous. Eventually they reached Sydney, looking not too worse for wear, and we were extremely happy to see them. Ingrid and Tree were smothered with love and presents and so were Jimmy and Clarisa.

---

[110] In late October 1928, Dr Besant closed the Esoteric Section of the TS throughout the world.

[111] Krishnamurti's Paris speech, May 25, 1927.

Over in Holland at the Ommen Camp on August 3, Krishnamurti opened proceedings by making a declaration that shocked many of his followers but did not come as a total surprise to others. With Dr Besant by his side and a face-to-face audience of three thousand with thousands more listening at home on their radios, Krishnamurti made what became known as his 'Truth is a Pathless Land' speech, beginning:

> "We are going to discuss this morning the dissolution of the Order of the Star. Many will be delighted, and others will be rather sad. It is a question neither for rejoicing nor for sadness, because it is inevitable, as I am going to explain . . .
>
> "I maintain that Truth is a pathless land, and you cannot approach it by any path whatsoever, by any religion, by any sect. That is my point of view, and I adhere to that absolutely and unconditionally. Truth, being limitless, unconditional, unapproachable by any path whatsoever, cannot be organized; nor should any organization be formed to lead or coerce people along any particular path . . . If you do, it becomes dead, crystalised; it becomes a creed, a sect, a religion, to be imposed on others . . ."

A further reason for closing the Order of the Star was:

> "If an organization is formed to search for truth, it becomes a crutch, a weakness, a bondage, and must cripple the individual and prevent him from growing, from establishing his uniqueness, which lies in the discovery for himself of that absolute, unconditional Truth. So that is another reason why I have decided, as I happen to be the Head of the Order, to dissolve it . . .

"You are all depending for your spirituality on someone else, for your happiness on someone else, for your enlightenment on someone else . . . when I say look within yourselves for the enlightenment, for the glory, for the purification, and for the incorruptibility of the self, not one of you is willing to do it. There may be a few, but very, very few. So why have an organization? . . ."

In conclusion, he told his audience:

"So those are some of the reasons why, after careful consideration for two years, I have made this decision . . . You can form other organisations and expect someone else. With that I am not concerned, nor with creating new cages, new decorations for those cages. My only concern is to set men absolutely, unconditionally free."[112]

The instant Krishnamurti finished speaking, journalists at the Camp sent cables flying through the airwaves all around the world to the desks of their newspaper editors. But they could only convey the bare outline of the momentous events. Fuller news reports appearing several days later were eagerly devoured by TS members and the wider public alike.

The ongoing 'pageant' of Theosophy – with its cast of colourful characters, progressive stances on many social questions and occasional brushes with scandal – meant that anything 'Theosophical' made good newspaper copy. Krishnamurti's address at Ommen was so radical it could not be ignored, and this naturally led to a number of TS identities making public statements justifying their own or Krishnamurti's stand on the matter.

---

[112] Lutyens, Krishnamurti, 272-5

The *Sydney Evening News* on August 6th, 1929 quoted Dr Besant as saying: 'Considering Krishnamurti's viewpoint, the dissolution of the Order appears to be a logical step. Various trusts will carry out the publication of Krishnamurti's writings and bring his message to the world. That message is only partly understood at present, but it contains profound truths. It will be more fully appreciated as humanity evolves.'

This was a measured and tactically canny response by Dr Besant, offering a plan of action and a way forward. With its reference to things becoming clearer in the future, it played for time, which was sorely needed, and also hinted at the need for the populace to put in some heavy work on its own spiritual development. Even in her old age and beset by many worries, Dr Besant could present this most daunting event in its most positive light.

Dr Besant, the Bishops Leadbeater, Arundale and Wedgwood, and other leading lights of the TS were now in a very awkward position, and Wedgwood was even reputed to have said that Dr Besant had become senile.

Mr John Mackay, President of the Australian TS, was currently at the Star Camp in Ommen and sent valuable eye-witness accounts of the unfolding drama to those in Sydney who were trying their best to keep up with the events as they occurred. These accounts, couched in measured language and coming from a trusted leader, did a lot to keep members calm during this confusing time.

Among Sydney Theosophists, a range of reactions prevailed. Joyce Housman embodied the shock and bewilderment of many, telling me a few days later:

"I see it like this, Ed – let's imagine you're living in a house with a group of friends and you decide that their way of living is not your way. Then, you may choose to leave this house. But do you demolish it? Bring it down? Utterly destroy it? No – you simply walk away from it and let the inhabitants of that house continue with their chosen way of life."

While Joyce's views reflected the sentiments of many Theosophists, others took the changes in their stride and even welcomed them. Typical of this cohort was the Reverend Harold Morton, General Secretary of the TS in Australia and a priest of the Liberal Catholic Church, who said: 'Krishnamurti is only broadening his field. The edict of dissolution is not at all unexpected here; in fact, we have known of it for some time and have been receiving bulletins from Mr Mackay . . . The dissolution really means a great change in method has been decided upon. Krishnamurti's ideas are international. He thinks in world terms and he must give expression to those thoughts. He is, paradoxically, an individualist and an internationalist. In Australia, all members of the order were heart and soul with Krishnamurti.' [113]

Another commentator described Krishnamurti's abolition of the Order of the Star as just what he expected: 'Krishnamurti represents the new thought of our time. He refuses to organize either mental or moral crutches for mankind. I rejoice that Krishnamurti has broken the bondage of mere organization, and is relying solely on the truth of his teaching to appeal to mankind.' [114]

While these statements may have contained a certain element of 'wishful thinking', they do show how keen many TS members were to show a strong and united face to a world that was not always sympathetic in its reporting of Theosophical affairs.

Then, on the 29th of August 1929, came the crash of the US Stock Market – an event that pushed everything else off the front pages of newspapers throughout the world. It also had a direct and immediate impact on Narne

---

[113] '*The Daily Guardian*' newspaper 7.8.1929

[114] Said by a 'Mr Landbury', who was described in *The Sydney Evening News* of 6.8.1929 as having paid a private visit to the camp of the Star in the East in Holland.

and Pappi, who were right here in Mosman just around the corner from us.

Although Pappi bore the news with fortitude, it was devastating for him. Not only did Mortimer's Hardware lose an immense amount of money, but a number of Pappi's business friends went under completely, some even jumping to their death from the skyscrapers of New York.

Narne told me how relieved she was that Pappi had acted on his hunch regarding the stock-market and quarantined some of his money. Regarding his losses, Pappi was philosophical, saying, "No matter. We'll make it up in coming years. It's only money. And hey – you know what? I'm going to start up a branch of Mortimer's Hardware here in Sydney and put young Tree in charge when he's a bit older."

From the look on Tree's face I could see he'd love this. Every Saturday morning, the two of them liked nothing more than visiting hardware shops together, with Tree just like a miniature Pappi. Scientists have only just started to decode the laws of genetic inheritance but if ever they'd like to see traits jumping a generation, I could put them in contact with Pappi and Tree!

For the TS, the latter part of 1929 grew even more tumultuous. Two months after Krishnamurti closed the Order of the Star,[115] Dr Besant took a most unexpected step: re-opening the Esoteric Section of the TS. She had done this, she explained, because in her view the Esoteric Section had a valuable role to play within the organization. Many people, she believed, were in need of

---

[115] After dissolving the Order of the Star, Krishnamurti resigned from the various Trusts connected with it, opened up the camps at Ommen and Ojai to non-members and subsequently returned Castle Eerde and its estates to Philip, Baron van Pallandt.

a 'crutch' to assist them through life, and she and the Esoteric Section were there to provide that support. Dr Besant's action in re-opening the Esoteric Section made Krishnamurti's subsequent resignation from the TS an inevitable consequence of the position he'd articulated at the 1929 camp. As for CWL, at the TS Convention at Adyar in December he kept his distance from Krishnamurti, reportedly saying that 'the Coming has gone wrong'.[116]

These events led to intense soul-searching amongst TS members, who came to terms with the new reality in ways that were compatable with their various life experiences and beliefs. While some drifted away, feeling the movement had lost its direction and indeed its entire *raison d'etre*, others saw Theosophy as wholly beneficial and of continuing relevance both to them personally and, even more importantly, to the whole world.

In the ensuing months Clara, Antonia, Joyce and I had long talks about the current state of affairs, with Narne and Pappi contributing a useful American perspective to these discussions. The overall feeling was that although the TS and the Liberal Catholic Church would get heavily battered in the process, they would survive the current convulsion.

---

[116] Lutyens, Krishnamurti, 277, 305

CHAPTER 32

AND WHERE TO
FROM HERE?

Meanwhile, the economic devastation of the Great Depression continued inexorably in many parts of the world. Although we in Australia were not as hard-hit as the Americans, the Crash impacted upon all aspects of our daily lives and a great number of people lost their jobs or had to work shorter hours. As a doctor, I came face to face every day with poverty, deprivation, malnutrition and chronic untreated illness.

As the little twins got a bit older and attended The Garden School along with their older brother and sister, Antonia would spend several days a week there teaching and generally assisting. And as time went by, the effects of the economic downturn became more and more apparent at the School. Enrolments fell as many parents could no longer afford the fees, and financial support of the donors fell away sharply. Pappi Mortimer, to his great credit, not only maintained but even increased the amount of his contribution, saying, "Make no mistake, I'm doin' it tough, but not as bad as some folks!"

Over the next several years, Antonia saw with sadness how the school declined, with increasing shortages of text-books and teaching materials, cut-backs in staff numbers and reductions in the quality of school meals. Eventually, in 1936, and with great sadness, the two principals were forced to close the doors of their unique and wonderful school. Their retirement years were spent living at The Manor where I would visit them regularly in my capacity as their personal physician..

Some people, however, did very well out of the Great Depression, one being Russell Fletcher. Although he had a medical degree, his talents were more suited to the business world and his medical equipment company flourished during the hard times. People who couldn't afford operations now resorted to crutches, splints, wheelchairs, ointments and trusses, all of which could be purchased from Russell Fletcher & Co.

Within a very short time, Russell was able to buy a large house in Musgrave St Mosman overlooking Mosman Bay, with terraced gardens sloping down to a harbour swimming pool made from sandstone blocks. Interestingly, Russell and Helena's house was next door to the very house Antonia and her siblings had lived in as children, before their father, Paul Vivian, had departed the scene.

The two houses were in fact identical, and Russell took great pride in telling me how he could now keep Helena 'in the manner to which she was accustomed'. I forbore to point out that Helena had only very briefly lived in her family's Musgrave St house as a small child, and the state to which she was much more accustomed was her life at the Morven Garden School totally dependent on the benevolence of the Theosophical Society. I doubted Russell would want to replicate that state of affairs.

Russell laboured under a conviction that Clara Vivian preferred me to him as a son-in-law, a sentiment of which I'd never seen a shred of evidence. However, it spurred him on to further business innovations which kept him and Helena and their two daughters in a very comfortable state. For our part, Antonia and I, with our children and Clara, were very happy living in our 'double-semi' in the more plebeian Gouldsbury Street, handy to

Mum&Dad several streets away and close to the library and shops.

As for the TS, although it maintained a continuing steady presence in Sydney and elsewhere, the dizzying buzz of the 1920s was never recaptured. The Amphitheatre at Balmoral continued to provide a program of lectures, music and theatrical events but, like The Garden School nearby, it succumbed to the financial hard times of the 1930s and was bought by the Catholic Church and eventually demolished to make way for a large apartment block.

Dr Annie Besant and Bishop Charles Webster Leadbeater, 'passed over' within months of each other in 1933 and 1934 respectively, thereby ringing down the curtain on a drama that began in New York in 1875 when Madame Helena Blavatsky and Henry Steel Olcott launched the Theosophical Society on an unsuspecting world. In 1934, George Arundale succeeded Dr Besant as President of the TS.[117] Over the years, his wife Rukmini made a great contribution in India to classical dance, animal welfare and the promotion of vegetarianism. From 1931 onwards, Bishop James Wedgwood lived in seclusion in England as a result of mental illness.

After resigning from the TS, Krishnamurti continued to address large audiences throughout the world and engage in debate with philosophical, religious and political leaders. Dora van Gelder, living in the USA with her husband Dr Fritz Kunz and son, went on to have a long career as an alternative healer and leader in the Theosophical Society in America, serving as President from 1975 to 1987.

---

[117] Bishop George Arundale remained in this role until his death in 1945.

And finally, on the family front:

Antonia fulfilled her dream of starting a chain of pre-schools for children in need of additional educational input. The Mortimer Schools, in both city and country locations, provided a sound and humane context for these children at the start of their learning pathway and were a force for good wherever they opened their doors.

Our four children grew up without too much incident, doted on by all their grandparents as well as 'Uncle Max' in his own reserved way. Antonia's siblings married and produced children, so our extended family group became quite large.

Among family and close friends, there existed clusters of shared interests. My father, Max and I gravitated towards one other; Mum, Clara and Joyce Housman always had a lot to share; and Uncle Russell found a role for himself as 'business mentor' to young Tree who, like his grandfather Pappi (but so unlike his father, Ambrose) was totally commerce-minded.

When Russell and Tree got together with Pappi, the three of them would talk business for hours, something I could never do. My son Jimmy often tuned in for a short while, and they graciously included him in their grand plans. In Jimmy, I saw a lot of my father – sensible, with a head for figures – in other words, a born accountant. And I might note here, he had inherited a dominant gene from Dad and me – hair that stood straight up like a hairbrush.

Russell took his mentoring role with Tree very seriously, telling me: "It's lucky I'm around for young Tree because quite frankly, Ed, you haven't got a commercial bone in your body."

To this I replied mildly, "No, I don't believe I have. And I'm happy to delegate that role to you, Russell," meanwhile enjoying a moment of internal merriment at having used the word 'delegate'.

My old friend Ambrose used to tell me how his father, Pappi, was fond of saying that the secret to success in business was due to one thing only – the ability to delegate. Through his death, Ambrose had avoided being delegated to by Pappi. However, the thought sometimes crossed my mind that Ambrose had delegated to *me* the job of raising his children. And if this were so, maybe somewhere in the cosmos, Ambrose might be having a bit of a chuckle at my now delegating to Russell Fletcher the job of mentoring his son Tree (or Ambrose III) in the ways of the world of business.

As time went on, Narne and Pappi spent more and more time with us in Sydney, Pappi pursuing his dream of extending Mortimer's Hardware to Australia, with young Tree heavily involved in the process. A new slogan for the firm had even been devised: 'East and West, Mortimer is Best', thus signifying a place in their enterprise for Jimmy and/or Clarisa to come aboard if they so wished.

The two girls, Ingrid and Clarisa, had a lot of Antonia's physical characteristics and her kind and considerate nature. Antonia was especially keen for her daughters to access some of the educational opportunities that she'd missed out on at the Morven Garden School, which, while very strong on the arts, did not focus on mathematics and the sciences, When the Garden School closed in 1936, we moved the children into the mainstream education system, where they settled in well. This we attributed to the sound start they'd received at under the benevolent eye of those two dedicated Theosophical educators, the Misses Lily Arnold and Jessie MacDonald.

Mum&Dad enjoyed their older years greatly, with Dad continuing his botanical experiments and Mum maintaining her nutrition career, even producing a cook book 'Granny Best's Best Recipes', sold at the Adyar bookshop in Sydney and available through radio station 2GB.

After a time, I noticed that Mum didn't visit her old friends in Stanmore so often and I asked her why this was. She told me that although she was still fond of them, their paths had rather diverged after she'd got to know the Theosophists, developed her nutrition interests and moved to Mosman.

There was one other thing, too, she said. Her old Stanmore friends often trotted out an enduring but totally baseless myth about Theosophists, namely that they'd built the Amphitheatre at Balmoral for Krishnamurti, the new Messiah, to walk on water through the Sydney Harbour Heads and preach there to the multitudes. No matter how many times Mum tried to disabuse them of this story, they never seemed convinced and this diminished her enjoyment of their company, while at the same time she was finding her new life a breath of fresh air.

And lastly, what became of The Aunts? Several days after Antonia and I got married, Aunt and Auntikin sailed away on their third trip to England – and never came back. This was not a conscious decision, rather more 'one thing leading to another'. A friend gave them life-use of a cottage near Cambridge and they simply settled into comfortable old age over there, keeping in contact with us via letters and, later on, phone calls at Christmas.

And so we journeyed on through life, enriched and strengthened through the contact we had with that strange, forward-thinking, imaginative, fearless, enriching and at times controversial entity known to the world as – Theosophy.

APPENDIX 1

LIVING AT THE MANOR, 1923 – 33

An interview with Esme (White) Farmer (1909 – 2002)

Author's note: I met Esme Farmer while doing preliminary research for this book. Esme, then in her late seventies, lived at The Manor, Mosman for ten years (1923– 33) from the age of 14 to 24. Below are excerpts from an interview conducted in 1987.

Background
Esme migrated to Australia with her parents and elder sister in 1913, settling in Perth, Western Australia. Her legal accountant father was disenchanted with orthodox Christianity and joined the Theosophical Society, becoming president there for several years. After attending the famous Sydney TS Convention in 1922, he decided to move his family to Sydney and came east with Esme, then aged thirteen. The rest of the family arrived soon after and they rented a flat at Cremorne

First Impressions of Sydney (1923). Esme attends a Liberal Catholic Church service with her sister.
"I seemed to be overwhelmed with love. The Theosophists opened their arms to me and I thought, 'This is for me!' There was wonderful organ music and the whole thing seemed absolutely to embrace me. I used to go to the Monday night meetings at The Manor, which

wasn't far from where we lived. The young people and the old people would be there and CWL (Bishop Charles Webster Leadbeater) used to talk and people would ask questions, and so I becamet involved and gradually got to know them all.

Coming to live at The Manor

"To get to live at The Manor, you had to be invited. CWL was interested in young people, of course, because they're fresher, more easily impressed and more open. CWL lived at the Manor himself.

"In April 1923, CWL was up in Brisbane and he wrote and said 'Esme must come to the Manor because she is going to take a Step (along the Spiritual Path). It was said that up in the Himalayas where the Masters – that is, the Master Khutumi and the Master Morea – had a cave, and the Master Khutumi put your image, your astral body, in there and they sort of watch you, watch your development. Not everyone was chosen like this, you had to be ready.

"I was delighted with this news. It was all very exciting and now I could get to know the young people who lived at The Manor. There was a nucleus of families, in those days, about forty or fifty people – it was absolutely bulging! Several families were the backbone of the Manor – they helped to pay the rent and all that. There was a Dutch family called the van Gelders – they were all clairvoyant. And then there were the Kollerstroms – Norna, Edith and Oscar, who was one of CWL's boys.

"So late one afternoon, Norna Kollerstrom came to see my father – she could twist him round her little finger – to say that I was to come to The Manor because it was imminent that I was to take this Step.

"And so I just bundled up my few belongings and went to The Manor without turning a hair – I didn't even look back. And instead of staying for three weeks, as planned, I stayed for ten years. I was fourteen years old and I never went home again.

"For the first three weeks at The Manor I shared large room with Norna and Edith Kollerstrom. I had a bed in the middle of the room and they had their beds along the walls. There was a cat that used to leap up onto my bed, but we weren't allowed to disturb this cat because CWL had 'individualised' it. Animals have a group soul, a number of animals to one soul, and when you become a human you then have a soul to yourself – you become individualised. Domestic animals have a very good chance because they are close to humans and the vibrations of humans are supposed to be higher or more intense than an animal's – they bask in this atmosphere and it brings on their development

"That first year at The Manor was quite magical, I just opened up like a flower to the marvellous spiritual atmosphere there, and I had this feeling that one was very safe. There was supposed to be an Angel over The Manor guarding us. My life seemed so dull before that. Nothing was happening, my family didn't entertain at all, I was just going to school, the public school at Mosman and then North Sydney Girls High. I left North Sydney High during my first year because I went to The Manor to live. School life finished then.

"There were quite a lot of rich Theosophists around, in England, and they contributed a lot financially. A Mrs McKay paid for me to live at the Manor for the first year (my father wouldn't have paid for me, no way!).

"All the young people were so interesting and the life of The Manor was very dynamic; there were lectures and people from all parts of the world that came and stayed for a little while, so there was a lot going on. We used to go the Liberal Catholic church in town on Sunday and on Thursday morning, and every day a morning Mass and an evening service was held in the little chapel at The Manor.

"Being so young, I soaked up the atmosphere with every pore of my being. I was no good at studying books intellectually, I was so busy absorbing the whole lot that I couldn't study . . . I was absorbing through the lectures and the people who lived there and the atmosphere and CWL.

"I recall one incident from that time – an English family, the Roberts, living at The Manor had a son, Erling, who was an artist and always scribbling and drawing things. Several of us were in the hall, sitting in chairs which were in the middle part, outside CWL's office and one of us said to Erling, 'Draw the Devil . . . with horns', and another said, 'Think of CWL'. So there we were, all concentrating on the Devil, and Erling was drawing away.

"Then out from CWL's office opposite flew Theodore (St John), CWL's boy at the time.

'What are all these thought-forms of the Devil coming into the room?' he demanded. There was absolutely no way he could have heard what we were saying, and we dispersed very rapidly. He was really clairvoyant!

"We were just a little afraid of CWL – he was very imposing. If he smiled at you, you felt that the day was made. There was always an inner group of young people – I was not absolutely inner.

1925 – Lady Emily Lutyens, her daughters and Krishnamurti

"In 1925 an English family, Lady Emily Lutyens and her daughters Mary and Betty came to stay at The Manor. I became friendly with Betty and this was when I also had my first glimpse of Krishnamurti, who was in Sydney with his brother Nitya who at this time was very ill.

"Krishnamurti was a very shy young man – a beautiful looking man. I came out onto a verandah, not knowing there was anybody else out there and I was a bit embarrassed when I saw all the others there. One of the group came over to me and said 'Krishnamurti would like you to come over.' I was so shy that I rushed back inside – and I've regretted it ever since (I would have been about 16 at the time and he would have been in his late twenties).

"After their time in Sydney, Krishnamurti and Lady Emily, who was like his mother in a way, went off to America (with Nitya and some others) where they spent some time in the Ojai Valley, California with other Theosophists.

"Towards the end of 1925, a large group went off to India – to the Fifty-Year Jubilee Convention in Adyar. My father wouldn't pay for me to go so I didn't go. I would have loved to have gone – half the ship were Theosophists.

"On the group's return from India, Mrs Mackay said in a loud and clear voice that she was 'not going to keep Esme White there any longer' and I quite agreed with her. For the next three months or so, I did some voluntary work – working in the bookshop we had in Adyar House in Bligh St.

"Mrs Mackay did not take any personal interest in me, her act of providing for me financially was to do good works, for good *karma*. I didn't have to relate to her. Mrs MacKay, a rather plump lady, was a wonderful cook and she gave cooking lessons – always vegetarian, of course, and we ate whatever we cooked.

"After Mrs Mackay said she wasn't going to support me any longer, everyone wondered what was going to happen to me. My father wasn't going to keep me there and I remember my sister saying, 'Esme hasn't got any qualifications – what is she going to do?'. Everybody around me was saying, 'Well, you mustn't go home to live, you must stay on,' and I myself said that I must stay there. Everyone was worrying except me.

"Several of us young people at The Manor were on the breadline, including an American girl whose money had run out and who thought she'd have to go back to America. Then one of my friends had this absolute inspiration! She said, 'The servants aren't all that satisfactory – why not let the young people manage the running of The Manor, the housework and the meals?'

"Two young men then took over the preparation of the vegetables and the washing down of all the tile-work, and two of us girls did the dining-room – laying the tables and washing up and going to the servery to check if the trays of food were ready to come through. That was more or less constant, three times a day. The next week we'd alternate with another pair of girls and do the rooms, finishing about lunchtime. This worked well and was the pattern for the rest of the time that I lived there – almost 10 years.

"After a while, CWL left the Manor. He was getting bad rheumatism by the sea, and they thought he'd be better off living in India. When CWL left, Bishop Arundale and his wife Rukmini came out to manage The Manor and I became great friends with Rukmini.

"One day, Bishop Arundale said to me, 'Look Esme, I think you've done enough housework, you'd better decide to learn something – shorthand and typewriting or something-or-other. For three days I was madly excited to think of shorthand and typewriting, then I grew more and more depressed about it.

"The idea of studying art appealed to me much more and my father paid for me to attend East Sydney Tech. for three years (it didn't cost very much). I still lived at The Manor, though, and they very kindly gave me a room which I occasionally shared when there was a convention on and girls came from Brisbane and other places. I ate all my meals at home, as my parents now had a flat nearby. I started my art course in 1929

1930 – A trip to India

"In 1930 came my chance to go to India. Bishop Arundale and Rukmini were going to India as part of a world tour with a group of Theosophists, financed by a very wealthy American woman, Mrs Gardiner, who was going with them. The Arundales always wanted the best.

"Mrs Gardiner also paid for Heather Kellett, a girl of around my age who was very close to CWL. My father, who was agreeable to the whole idea, paid for my fare. We went over on a P & O line ship, the 'Mooltan', and it took about three weeks to get to India and a hundred days to England. I had my 21st birthday on board ship on the way over – the Captain had a cake baked for me.

"My first touch of India was Ceylon. Of course I'd met a number of Indians at The Manor. We spent two and a half days in Colombo and went to Kandi. When we arrived in India we had VIP treatment because we were with the Arundales.

"To reach Adyar, we had to go by train to Madras, something like a 12-hour journey, and we had the most wonderful treatment on the train – the wife of a prominent Theosophist in the railways brought all her servants to a certain town that the train was passing through. The train stopped and they brought in a most marvellous Indian meal to us because there wasn't anything to eat on the train. The train was very comfortable – we were travelling first class so we had the very best treatment.

"When we were about two hours outside of Madras, Bishop Arundale disappeared and suddenly reappeared in Indian dress! Adyar was a lovely spot full of gard"ns and trees and many buildings. Along one side was the Adyar River and at the end of it was the sea.

"We were shown to a two-storey house – we slept upstairs under mosquito nets. It was very hot and we used to have a siesta after lunch and we had a servant who brought our meals – our breakfast chiefly. Luncheon in the middle of the day was our main meal and we used to go over to CWL's chambers for that. The Indians used to decorate the table with flower petals of all different kinds which they made into patterns, every day a different one. At lunch, we would meet all the other residents – English people and Indians. Of course, when there was a convention on, there were crowds and crowds of people.

"We also met Rukmini's family – her mother was a wonderful white-haired woman and she had a beautiful sister who was a doctor. This sister had found a discarded baby under a bridge and brought it home and her mother was looking after the little child who was about two years old at this time.

"At this stage Adyar was very well kept with gardeners to maintain the grounds – it was a beautiful compound. We went swimming in the river – it could be treacherous. The food was wonderful – we had some marvellous Indian meals – we could hardly stand up after them!

"Only three of our party came back to Australia – the others proceeded on with their world tour and we had the same treatment on the train – they brought us a lovely meal. We came back on the same ship – the 'Mooltan', and Heather and I had a slight flirtation with a couple of the officers. Shipboard life in those days was really wonderful – dances at night, evening dress – we took trunks of clothes!

1929 and onwards – Life beyond The Manor
"When I started my Art course in 1929, I suddenly found this world of culture! Up until then it had been this world of Theosophy, with its emphasis on spiritual striving – and suddenly I realized that there was this world of culture as well. When I returned from the trip to India I continued with my course and graduated in 1933.

"By this time, we were in the middle of the Depression- I didn't feel the Depression much – my father was a legal accountant and in that field they didn't feel it so much as in some others. Of course, I think that money was hard to come by. Then I said to my father that I felt I should go to England. At the end of my Art course I had won a prize for figure painting and Mrs Kollerstrom, who was always there at high moments of my life, came to the presentation of the prizes. She spoke to my teacher, Mr Lees, and he told her, 'Esme has soaked up art in every pore!' just as I had done with Theosophy . . . That was my way – I was not an intellectual."

Other observations

Attitude of the general public towards Theosophists

"In those days the attitude of the general newspapers was rather critical towards the TS – they made a bit of fun of it. They used to tell stories that we went around naked, which was absolutely untrue, all we did was that the young ones would go barefooted – after all, they were only fourteen and sixteen and in the summer we often went round barefooted in The Manor grounds. Raine Vreede, who was the son of Bishop Adriaan Vreede, lived at The Manor with his mother and sister and brother and used to bicycle through Sydney to the church sometimes barefooted. The papers were all the time looking for things of that nature to comment on.

"At school (in Sydney) I had a friend whose family was sympathetic to the idea of Theosophy. They were interested because so many people from different parts of the world came to The Manor. My friend's family were Christian Scientists and were sympathetic to many of the same ideas. Of course, when I lived at The Manor to live, my friends were totally there..

The Star Amphitheatre, Balmoral
"Dr Mary Rocke[118] became very enthusiastic about

---

[118] See Glossary entry: Dr Mary Rocke

building an amphitheatre at Balmoral for Krishnamurti to speak from. And of course the newspapers said 'Krishnamurti's coming across the water through the Sydney Harbour heads to Balmoral Beach to speak.' All those stories were cooked up by the press.

Madame Blavatsky and Colonel Alcott
    "CWL had known Madame Blavatsky and he used to tell some stories about her, so she was real to us in that sense. Madame Blavatsky was a very controversial figure – she was Russian, but she absolutely discarded all Russian tradition, she was a very unusual woman.

    "She absolutely led her own life and did all sorts of extraordinary feats – she went off alone, which was unheard of in those days, and travelled a great deal on horseback for long distances. She was a seeker, there's no doubt. When she was in India, she did contact her Master. She gradually found that they (the Masters) wanted her to bring about Theosophy. Madame Blavatsky eventually met Colonel Alcott, who was a very practical man who'd been an engineer. They were a very, very good team.

    "I once met a man in Cornwall who had met Madame Blavatsky and he was <u>not</u> impressed. He thought she was dirty, had dirty fingernails and was a bit of an imposter. He was, of course, a total outsider. This was when she was an older woman, in her time she was a very powerful character indeed. In the latter part of her life she had quite a few illnesses but the Masters seemed to revitalize her on these occasions because she had work to do,

Annie Besant
    "Annie Besant was first and foremost a wonderful orator. I only ever saw her when I went to India in 1930 and she was beginning to show little signs of senility and forgetfulness. We went to a concert at Adyar where some visiting boy choristers from England sang and she spoke

then … but I thought she was repeating herself quite a lot, it was rather like a record going round and round. She had the orator's note, though, and the words flowed on … she was past her prime and only a year or two later she died.

"Years before, she had been married to a parson. He asked her to marry him and apparently she didn't even answer him, but he took this for assent and the marriage went ahead . . . In those days . . . but of course the marriage wasn't a success. She had two children and she finally left him, which was very brave in those days because women didn't have any chance of a job or anything, except perhaps a governess or something. And then she became interested in the suffragettes

Note: Esme Farmer continued her career as an artist, exhibiting with the Macquarie Galleries, Sydney and having several portraits hung in the annual Archibald Prize.

APPENDIX 2

A Theosophical childhood - actor and film-star Peter Finch (1916 – 1977)

Peter Finch was born in London to parents who separated when he was two years old. He was brought up by his paternal grandmother in France. In 1925, his grandmother, a keen Theosophist, took the boy with her to Adyar, India, to attend the Theosophical Society's 50-year Jubilee.

Peter and his grandmother stayed there for a number of months and while she was occupied with Theosophical matters, the young boy went missing. After about three days, a search was made for him and he was discovered in the care of a Buddhist monk, wearing saffron robes, with his head shaved and holding a begging bowl.

He was returned to the Theosophical compound at Adyar, where Annie Besant was extremely unimpressed with his grandmother's care and arranged for him to be sent to Australia to live with his great-uncle Edward Finch at Greenwich Point, Sydney. For several years, Peter attended The Garden School at Mosman as a boarder.

In an interview for *Australian Women's Weekly* (27.2.37), Peter Finch gave this account of the incident (Note: it differs in some aspects from the version above):

RADIO ACTOR MIGHT HAVE BECOME MONK:
Strange Story of Peter Finch

Ask any radio personality for his most unusual experience and he would probably have to hesitate and think a while. Not so Peter Finch, talented juvenile lead now playing in B.S.A. productions from 2GB. For him the big adventure of his life was when he nearly became a Buddhist monk! It is a story that might have provided a plot for Rudyard Kipling to write a new kind of 'Kim'.

"I was living in India in the charge of a guardian, as my father was on out-post duty," explained Finch. "My guardian was intensely interested in Buddhism and, under the influence of a travelling Buddhist monk, he had my head shaved, put me in a long yellow robe, and sent me off in company with the monk to beg my way to Tibet, the land of mystery and monks.

"" do not remember much of the journey, except that we travelled in a filthy state, never cut our nails, slept on mats on the earthen floor at nights, and, having arrived at a village, we sat down with our begging bowls before us, and waited for the villagers to bring us food.

"Fortunately for my career as a radio actor, an Indian officer, a friend of my father's, recognised me, put me in a rickshaw and sent me home.

"My most vivid recollection of the adventure," added Peter Finch, "was my first glimpse of myself, bald-pated and filthy, in the mirror. I got such a surprise that I nearly fainted, and if I had any desire to be a Buddhist monk before that, I certainly had none after."

APPENDIX 3

Two Sisters Remember: Life at The Garden School

1. Helen (Ure) Maguire, a pupil at The Garden
    School from 1927 to 1934, wrote in 1966:

Background

My parents separated forever when I was seven years old, and within days of the event my brother and I and our three elder sisters were packed off to boarding school at The Garden School, Mosman. If our hearts broke, it was quietly, and little by little – my brother and I agreed later in life about this.

It was either luck, or my father's foresight, that placed us in an atmosphere of healing. Our aching need for our parents was gently overcome by the principals of the school – two loving, wise women (Miss Lily Arnold and Miss Jessie Macdonald).

In a spiritual sense, we were offered standards to live by. Physically, we had the routines of life with other children, and the freedom to wander in acres of garden. In contrast to our former life of background tensions, and the constant presence of financial anxiety, the new life must have felt like floating in a warm sea. Only our inner feelings of confusion at the loss of out parental anchors lingered on, but finally lessened. We adjusted, even to living at school during the school holidays.

My brother and I lived separately, he in the 'Boys' House'. The girls' dormitories were high up in the 'Old House' facing the sea – above other floors of kitchens, dining rooms, classrooms, library and the assembly hall. During the daytime and evening there was no segregation.

I am not sure how long it took me to begin communicating with the other children; to make a best friend, to join a skipping group, or those playing jacks or marbles. Boys and girls mixed freely in all these pursuits. I recall a long time of wandering off by myself after classes – 'standing and staring', and smooth shiny leaves, the curve of rose petals, or one or other of a number of statues in white marble beside the paths. These were my friends before I turned to make human ones. What great, good fortune it was for us not to have been lost in a harsher environment. I am still grateful. I still benefit from that second beginning.

Recollections of schooldays

The Garden School was situated on the hill between the headlands and above Edwards Beach, Balmoral in Sydney. From the three-storied side of the building an expanse of water could be seen – to the north, Middle Harbour and to the east stretching away through Sydney Heads to the horizon.

Many acres of garden surrounded the house with broad lawns, palm trees, camphor-laurel and gum trees. White marble steps led down from one side classroom to a rose garden guarded by a bust of Apollo. A number of Moreton Bay fig trees stood at the lower edge of the grounds and were wonderful to climb. I remember, too, a tall monkey-puzzle tree near where a marble Clytie stood.

On the top terrace a huge fig tree grew at one end, holding a rope ladder and swing for our amusement. At the other end was a cricket pitch and room for football. At the south end of this terrace was a horizontal bar and then steps leading down to a summer-house fitted with desks and forms for outdoor lessons in summer. So strange it was to sit, writing in books with shadows of vines and leaves thrown on them. The lower terrace, beside the drive, was more formally kept by the Latvian gardener and had a fishpond, small palms and gardens and seats in the shade, also used for lessons.

I remember English and Embroidery here, and a long talk from Miss Lily Arnold on The Facts of Life, given in such spiritual terms that we felt soothed and secure but gained no information. The theme was that God was love and that Love was good because God was good and that unselfish love bore fruit. Men, women and children did not come into it at all, which worried nobody. So we sat in a harmonious group, peaceful in the sun and shade, dreamy-eyed among the palms and listened.

Just below this terrace, garden seats were placed and each morning for 'Morning milk' time with Miss Jessie MacDonald. She sat in an armchair facing us and we discussed the (unwritten) rules of the school, the reasons for making them and sometimes the fact that some may have been broken the day before and by whom. This was an open discussion including the child involved and it was generally decided that the breach had not been worth the possible direct outcome, as most rules were made for our own protection. Any punishment was always mild – usually the child at fault had their freedom limited by half an hour and was sent to think about the incident sitting on their locker in the dormitory. This was a pleasure, as most of the dormitories faced the east and the thinking could be done while gazing at the expanses of sea and sky. Character-building began at these Talks and we were urged to examine ourselves honestly and try every day to eradicate some faults. If this is said to you every day, you do it, and I believe that at a very early age, without becoming priggish, we were trying to earn our own respect.

From these Talks, we would file into breakfast: long tables with white cloths, rows of table napkins and pieces of fruit. After Grace ('May this food build pure and strong bodies for use in the Masters' service') the routine ceremony was the spreading of napkins on knees and the balancing of fruit on napkin rings. Talk at table was not limited except in pitch, and breakfast was always porridge, brown bread and honey or syrup.

A teacher sat at the head of each table and was usually regarded in friendly fashion – except when it was Matron Walkdon, who was regarded with a great deal of amusement. She treated us for everything with one remedy – equal parts of olive oil, honey and lemon juice. This mixture was swallowed for anything from colds to constipation and applied externally for sunburn or hives. Oddly enough, it was effective!

I cannot recall looking forward to meals or thinking much about food at all – an often-repeated maxim (for the self-indulgent) was 'Eat to live, do not live to eat'. Food was not discussed, was never limited in amount but nothing must be left and 'eat what is put before you'. My stumbling-block here was the fairly frequent lemon sago and tapioca pudding which refused to be swallowed and could take me up to an hour to finish, while I listened to the voices of the successful sago-eaters playing outside. At the age of ten I left vegetarianism behind after asking for sausages and gravy one dinner-time. I was converted.

The vegetarian diet fitted in with Theosophy – the great belief of the two principals. They did not force these beliefs upon us, however. We were offered the theory of the Ladder of Evolution and Reincarnation as well as the Darwinian theory of Evolution together with the Life of Christ and stories from the Bible.

The principals' characters were as large as their physical proportions. The exceptional devotion they gave to the children was remarkably constant and consistent with their wish to develop good character and thinking individuality in their charges. In their opinion, competition was destructive to individuality – so no child was asked to cram for a test. Studying at night was discouraged and lights were out early. Early in the morning, if you wished to attend, a prep period was held.

I can remember being fascinated by grammatical parsing and analysis for about a week and doing it for fun after school! But when there was tennis or a part in the current play to be learned, interest in study started to diminish.

During the summer we often went to the beach, accompanied by a teacher. After school hours we proceeded, barefoot and in our swimming costumes, down Stanton Road about half a mile (1 kilometre) to the sands of Balmoral Beach. There was no great surf and it was ideal for swimming and this was what we did, even far out without thought of sharks. Mild breakers could be caught back to the beach and the rare 'dumpers' only happened with the Christmas tides – when there was less warm sand and more excitement. At the northern end of the beach, beyond the rock pool, where the water was still enough for under-water swimming, we spent hours diving and exploring among the rocks, almost syrupy-green shallows, mysterious brown crevices and the eurythmics of seaweed and anemones.

Then we'd hurry across the hot sand and up the hill in twos and threes (no 'crocodiles' for us!) to wash ready for tea – soup, brown bread, butter, honey or syrup.

Sometimes in the evening we stayed up to listen to music. An amateur string quartet played Bach and Mozart, while our salty eyelids drooped. Then the evening hymn – 'When sunset comes, all sweet and calm and tender...' and the evening prayer, 'The labours of the day are over, the time has come to rest. We resign to Thy hands, Oh Lord, our sleeping bodies. Give us to wake with smiles, give us to wake with smiling ...'

More wakeful up the stairs and tongues loosened in the dormitories with Matron Walkdon shushing us in her pale indignation, frizzy pale hair popping out from her limp veil. But she had a warm heart; she helped the kindergarten teacher make me a dress for dancing class, as I had none. Bright red georgette trimmed at the neck with bright green swans-down! A very long-lasting dress in fact, and in memory it seemed to have an endless hem for letting down.

In the morning, waking early, time to look from the dormitory windows away to the horizon and study the fantastic, changing dark grey clouds at dawn. Indeed, there seems to have been plenty of time 'to stand and stare' during my years at the school. Then Matron's voice and Manchester accent saying, 'Now, tease your ticks (ie shake your mattresses) and turn up your counterpanes.' And another day had begun. Exercises and races down on the side driveway followed, and we were joined in these by the boys. I find I do not often think of the school as co-educational and conclude that I must have always regarded boys as people.

By the time I was in first year (year 7), I think the school must have abandoned any idea of following a curriculum, having by then no money, no textbooks and very few trained teachers.[119] However, the bell rang regularly and lessons were given. Miss Arnold took us for English and History and left the textbooks as often as possible to read to us from Shakespeare, Tennyson, Goethe, Thoreau, Thackeray, Dickens, G.B. Shaw and many more. We limped along with various teachers in Maths and Geography.

Our Art teacher, Miss Needham, came to the school two afternoons per week and her lectures were a great influence on us. She brought with her a wonderful collection of slides of classical paintings and sculpture, interiors of cathedrals and general architectural marvels of the world. We sat in rows in the darkened assembly room, the huge lantern behind us and Miss Needham out front, seeming about seven feet tall, steel grey hair (rumoured to be a wig) and a long stick for pointing out

---

[119] Due to the onset of the Great Depression, many parents could no longer afford to pay school fees and a number of benefactors had to cease their financial support.

the features of the pictures on the screen. She told us much of the Greek myths and history and with the religious paintings, the life of Christ, but more from the standpoint of His influence on art than on humanity. She tapped peremptorily with her stick either for a change of slide or to curb any unruly spirits in her audience. But there were few interruptions of any kind. We loved these afternoons.

We had a great number of real French mistresses who came and went according to their tolerance regarding missing pages in the textbooks. We were, I remember, very willing and eager to learn French, but treated the interruptions and new beginnings with rather mature calm.

My most-loved interest was acting, and this was encouraged by the arrival of a young master. Mr Clarke, who adapted numerous stories for the end of term plays: Sabatini (to include the fencing class), Milne and Shaw. Shakespeare was a constant diet.

Mr Clarke I remember as sweaty and aesthetic, devoted to tennis as well as drama. He was against alcohol, war, and too much spiritual guidance. By second year (year 8) there were five in our class and we would drift up to his classroom from 'prayers', where we may have been listening to a record of Wagner, having been instructed to think uplifting thoughts. At the classroom door, we'd be met by Mr Clarke, who would say:

'Now, listen to me. You'll get nowhere in this world without money.' He'd then proceed to teach us Pitman's shorthand and had our group writing 30 words per minute by the end of the year. He also gave us a crammed course in physiology and to our own surprise, we were very interested and studied hard. He was endeavouring in some degree to fit us for the world we were shortly to meet – outside our garden and our high stone wall.

During my school years I was never bored; each day held some extreme interest for me. Nor do I remember ever being tense or anxious. We spent our days in a kind of lively contentment. Being a 'total' product of the school, I find it difficult to measure for success. I shared with the two principals as they intended: no ambition towards social or monetary goals, and I am grateful for the abiding love of books and people they instilled in me.

The school made us conscientious – later on, we learned to be practical. They taught us to be tolerant, gave us the ability to communicate with people and fired us with a burning ambition to contribute something to the world. Without a formal education and its proof in certificate form, it has been difficult to use these qualities in a wide sense – but there have always been people to communicate with, much use for tolerance and even after thirty years, ambition burns bright.

'An unqualified and unsolicited contribution', written in 1966

> 2. By Bette (Ure) Hamilton, a pupil at The Garden School from 1924 to 1930.

If I may, I should like to make a few comments regarding the education provided by The Garden School.

The first observation I would like to make is that in assessing its value it is necessary to compare it not with the excellent syllabus offered today but with what alternatives were available 30 to 40 years ago.

My memory of State schools (in Sydney) for the three years preceding 1924, and granting that it is a long time ago and I was very young, all I recall is ugly asphalt playgrounds, herding of crowds of children, strict teachers of whom I was rather nervous and the joy each day when school was over.

At the age of 8 or 9 years, when with my siblings I started at The Garden School, my early impressions were of friendliness, beautiful surroundings and interest.

It is true that the lack of textbooks and competitive examinations, both within the school and on a State-wide scale, were ideas thought up well before the Depression made job-hunting such a competitive proposition. At the same time, I recall Mis MacDonald telling me in about 1936 that an Educational Survey had been carried out by some authority in the USA who had sent a questionnaire to her which she had filled out and returned. The purpose of the questionnaire was to see what kind of education made people employable during the Depression. As The Garden School was a small school, Miss MacDonald said she had been able to get in touch with almost 100% of the pupils who had left school during this time and all had been employed. Some had been rationed, perhaps one week off in three, but in the great majority of cases all had been fully employed. This was no doubt true, but all these people would have been juniors in whatever field they had applied for, and it should be remembered that no one from The Garden School would have qualified to take a university course for LLB (law), medicine or science – or anything else requiring maths or subjects other than the humanities.

In regard to Arts subjects, if this were the aim, I would say that most of The Garden School pupils left school with a more mature appreciation and knowledge of drama, literature, schools of painting, architecture drawing acting, ballet, ballroom dancing, deportment, public speaking and conversational ability than their counterparts in any State school and possibly private school of that time.

Lacking a sound knowledge of maths, it is doubtful whether any of us would have succeeded in qualifying to enter a university for an Arts degree. On the credit side, however, I think it is true that those ex-pupils of The Garden School whose children have benefited from the best of education and taken Arts degrees at universities are not left out in discussions of topics studied, nor have our children felt that their higher education lessened the close communication of ideas that exists between us all. I have heard that in England, for instance, the high education level of the present generation in many cases makes them bored with their parents, and their parents find it difficult to talk with their children. This, fortunately, has not been the case for us.

Clara and her children on arrival in Sydney
from Brisbane

GLOSSARY

Castle Eerde, Holland: In 1924, Count Philip van Pallandt van Eerde deeded his ancestral home, the eighteenth-century Castle Eerde (pronounced Airder) at Ommen in Holland, together with 5,000acres of land to the Order of the Star. Van Pallandt was an ardent admirer of Krishnamurti, and that Eerde became the international Headquarters of Order of the Star in the East (from 1927 named The Order of the Star) and a number of large camps were held there. Krishnamurti, as his practice with gifts of property, made the gift into a Trust and, on disbanding the Order of the Star, arranged for the castle and its lands to be returned to van Pallandt, who refunded all that had been spent on improvements to the property.

Christian Science: a set of beliefs and practices belonging to the family of new religious movements. It was developed in 19th-century USA by Mary Baker Eddy, who argued in her 1875 book *Science and Health* that sickness was an illusion that could be corrected by prayer alone.

Coo-ee: an Australian Aboriginal word that has now passed into general Australian usage. It is uttered as a short, piercing call, useful when trying to gain a person's attention at a distance

Esoteric Section (ES) of the Theosophical Society (TS):
After founding the Theosophical Society (TS) in New York in 1975, Madame Helena Blavatsky in 1888 established the Eastern Section or, as it came to be known, the Esoteric Section (ES). The ES was devoted to the TS's third Object, namely: 'To investigate unexplored laws of

nature and the psychic powers latent in man'. TS members could apply to join the ES after two years, on condition they had done some work for the Society. If accepted, they began a course of training that that enabled them to progress along the Spiritual Path under an oath of secrecy and loyalty to the Head, Dr Besant or, in Australia, to her representative.

Central to the ES was the belief in evolution through a number of lives until perfection is arrived at and the soul is freed from *karma*, the inexorable law of consequence of actions, good and bad through different lifetimes. At a certain point, the soul is ready to embark on the Path of Discipleship, thence to Adepthood and finally to membership of a group of select beings who direct the world. Some of these Adepts, or Masters, choose to maintain human forms, and two of these, the Master Morya and the Master Kuthumi were closely involved with the TS and lived in Tibet. Madame Blavatsky, who had lived in Nepal prior to founding the TS, claimed to have met these two Masters. With the benefit of astral travel, their pupils could visit them, and they could also materialise at earthly locations.

Above these Masters were even higher beings, including the Lord Maitreya, who could take on a human body in order to guide the world though extremely difficult times. In one such manifestation Lord Maitreya came as Jesus Christ, and Madame Blavatsky and others believed the time was approaching when a great teacher would come again to show the world the way. In October, 1928, Annie Besant closed the ES throughout the world, and 12 months later, on October 1, 1929 she reopened it.

Finch, Peter. See Appendix 2: The Theosophical childhood of Peter Finch, actor and film-star (1916 – 1977)

Initiation: a rite of passage, or ceremony, marking entrance, or acceptance into a group or society. In the Theosophical tradition it has a specialised meaning which has undergone some changes over time. For more information on this and other Theosophy terms, see online Theosophical Wiki.

Isis Unveiled: A Master-Key to the Mysteries of Ancient and Modern Science and Theology by Helena Petrovna Blavatsky was published in 2 volumes in 1877 in New York and ran to over 1300 pages. It sold remarkably well at the time and also thereafter.

Leadbeater, Charles Webster (Bishop) (1854 – 1954): writer on occult and Theosophical topics and co-initiator of the Liberal Catholic Church (with J.I. Wedgwood). After starting out as a curate with the Anglican church, Leadbeater's interests aligned themselves more closely with Theosophy and he became a member of the Theosophical Society. In 1884 he met Madame Blavatsky and followed her to India, remaining in India and Ceylon for five years. On his return to England he met Annie Besant and the two became close associates. In 1906, rumours concerning adolescent boys caused Leadbeater to resign from the TS, although he was readmitted soon after Besant became President. He spent some years living in Sydney, becoming Presiding Bishop of the Liberal Catholic Church.

During his lifetime, a number of complaints were made to the police about his sexual proclivities, and several inquities held. Results of these were inconclusive, however, and no charges were ever laid.

Voice recording, **1925**

To access an audio recording of a sermon by Bishop Leadbeater at the Liberal Catholic Church on 'To Those Who Mourn; about the certainty of life after death,' 1925, visit:

http://www.cwlworld.info/html/liberal_catholic_church.
html

Note: this talk is incorrectly captioned: to access the sermon, open the interview with Oscar (Kollestrom interview and that of C.W.Leadbeater are transposed)

Correspondence:

Pedro Oliveira's 'CWL Speaks', 2018 (see bibliography) is a compilation of C.W. Leadbeater's correspondence concerning the 1906 crisis in the Theosophical Society, providing insights into a time of social change and a man who challenged conventions.

Order of the Star of the East: *Declaration of Principles:* The Declaration runs as follows:

I believe that a Great Teacher will soon appear in the world, and I wish so to live now that I may be worthy to know Him when He comes.

I shall try, therefore, to keep Him in my mind always, and to do in His name, and therefore to the best of my ability, all the work which comes to me in my daily occupations.

As far as my ordinary duties allow, I shall endeavour to devote a portion of my time each day to some definite work which may help to prepare for His coming.

I shall seek to make Devotion, Stead-fastness and Gentleness prominent characteristics of my daily life.

I shall try to begin and end each day with a short period devoted to the asking of His blessing upon all that I try to do for Him and in His name.

I regard it as my special duty to try to recognise and reverence greatness in whomsoever shown, and to strive to co-operate, as far as I can, with those whom I feel to be spiritually my superiors.

Note: The International Star Organisation levies no fixed subscriptions from the members but carries on its work with the financial aid given voluntarily by them. Certain National Sections, however, have found it convenient to fix a regular subscription but this practice is not in any way **binding** on the Order as a whole.

Liberal Catholic Church in Australia: The Liberal Catholic Church, with its Cathedral in Regent St Redfern ,Sydney grew out of the Old Catholic Church in England which rejected the idea of papal infallibility and had a number of dissident perspectives on things liturgical. The church had the ability to create its own bishops, and one of these, Bishop James Wedgwood came to Sydney in 1916 and consecrated Charles Wallace Leadbeater as a bishop. The church developed its own Mass, conducted in English, and other rituals as part of its service. In the 1920s, women were not able to participate in church procedures. The Liberal Catholic church does not require celibacy of its priests.

As the *Statement of Principles* of The Liberal Catholic Church, 8th ed., 1986, explains: 'The Liberal Catholic Church aims at combining Catholic forms of worship, stately ritual, deep mysticism and witness to the reality of sacramental grace with the widest measure of intellectual liberty and respect for the individual conscience...'

For more information on the Liberal Catholic Church:
https://www.liberalcatholicchurch.org.au/dbpage.php?pg=history
See also St Albans Liberal Catholic Cathedral, Sydney.

Manor, The, Clifton Gardens, Mosman: This 54-room, Queen Anne-style mansion was built in 1913 by William Bakewell, a tile merchant who initially planned it for his extended family to live in together. The building consists of three storeys, with multiple chimneys, a commanding view over Sydney Harbour and extensive gardens and tennis court. Bakewell's family rejected the idea of living together and in 1922 the Theosophical Society leased The

Manor and soon after bought it. A communal living project and over the years it has been a focal point of Theosophical life in Sydney, and the site of the inaugural transmission of radio station 2GB in 1923.

Masters, The: in Theosophy, these are lordly personages who could change themselves according to different situations, imparted wisdom to 'initiated' Theosophists and other highly evolved people. The Masters dwelt in the foothills of the Himalayas and could be contacted via astral travel or telepathic communication. They could also take on human form.

Radio station 2GB: Following experiments in transmission from The Manor site in Mosman, Sydney, radio station 2GB commenced broadcasting in 1926. The station was owned and managed by the Theosophical Society until 1936 when controlling interest passed to Denison Estates Ltd. The station's call-sign, 'GB', was selected in honour of Giordano Bruno, a sixteenth-century martyr to 'true science'.

Rocke, Dr Mary Eleanor (1865 – 1927): a Welsh-born medical practitioner who worked tirelessly for the cause of Theosophy from 1910 until her death in 1927 at the age of 62. Working variously as secretary to Dr Annie Besant and later as personal physician to Bishop C.W. Leadbeater, she also held senior positions in the Order of the Star (formerly the Order of the Star in the East).

She first visited Australia in 1918 and in 1922 was appointed Australian representative of the Order of the Star.

Dr Rocke was committed to the cause of building an amphitheatre for the Order of the Star (world -wide, it was ienvisaged that there be seven such edifices) and in 1923 purchased from her own funds, five blocks of land at Edwards Beach, Balmoral, Sydney. Two of these blocks were later resold, the Amphitheatre was built on two other blocks and one block was left vacant.

Dr Rocke resided at The Manor, Clifton Gardens, for a number of years and was also active in Co-Masonry.

She died after a ship-board fall while travelling with a party of Theosophists including Dr Annie Besant and Krishnamurti bound for India and Australia.

Sannyasa: In the Hindu philosophy of four life-based stages, *sannyasa* (in which worldly and materialistic pursuits are renounced and lives are dedicated to spiritual pursuits) is the fourth stage, coming after bachelor student, householder and forest dweller (retired). Some of these stages may be bypassed to reach *sannyasa* more directly." An individual in sannyasa is known as a sannyasi (male) or a sannyasini (female).

Sobranie: one of the world's oldest brands of luxury cigarettes. Sobranie of London was established in 1879 to cater for an increasing demand for cigarettes in Europe.

Spiritual Pathway: In Theosophy, this involves a number of stages, aspects of which have undergone certain changes in perspective over time. Information on Initiation, Probation, Disciplehood and Adepthood can be found online at *Theosophical Wikipedia*

St Albans Liberal Catholic Cathedral, Sydney: Located in Regent Sreet Redfern, this church, in the neo-Gothic style was built in 1866 for the Methodist Church. It was bought by the Liberal Catholic Church in 1918 and consecrated in 1918 by the Bishops Wedgwood, Leadbeater and Mazel. The building was eventually sold and demolished.

Star Amphitheatre, Balmoral, Sydney: an open air building with meeting rooms beneath it, was designed by the architectural firm, J.E. Justelius and Son in the Grecian Doric style, was built in 1923 – 4 to seat 2,500 people with another 1,000 standing. It included meeting rooms, and tea rooms and was an ideal space for dramatic presentations, choral performances and so on. Its acoustics were reported as 'excellent' and the view straight out the Sydney Harbour heads 'stunning'. A foundation stone inscribed 'This stone was laid by the Right Reverend C.W.Leadbeater Protector of the Order of the Star in the East on the 28th July, 1923,' was placed at the Star Amphitheatre site. The Amphitheatre was demolished in 1951 and the foundation stone is now in the Mosman Library Historical Collection. During the Great Depression in 1931, the Amphitheatre was sold and used by the new owner for vaudeville and other live theatre and the roof was used as a mini-golf course. In 1936 the Catholic Church purchased the building and in 195, after falling into disrepair, the Amphitheatre was replaced with a red-brick block of flats.

Steiner, Rudolph (1861–1925) was an Austrian social reformer, philosopher and educationist. He was strongly influenced by the works of Goethe, and in 1902 became head of the German section of the Theosophical Society (TS), although he was never a formal member. In 1904 Mrs Annie Besant made him leader of the TS's Esoteric Section (ES) for Austria and Germany. Within the TS, Steiner followed his own path to a certain extent and in 1912/13 led a majority of the German section to split from the TS and form the Anthroposophical Society. Steiner has had an immense impact in a number of different disciplines and his educational philosophy finds expression in the Steiner schools that continue to flourish in many countries of the world.

Sydney Harbour Bridge: The NSW Government passed the Sydney Harbour Bridge Act No.28 in November 1922. It provided for the construction of a high level cantilevered or arch bridge across the Harbour including the approaches, and electric railway lines. Tenders were called and an arched design was chosen. Construction of the Bridge took eight years and it was opened on 19 January 1932.

Wedgwood, James Ingall (1883 – 1951) was the founder and first Presiding Bishop of the Liberal Catholic Church. In 1915 he visited Australia and met with C.W. Leadbeater, returning in 1916 to ordain him as a bishop within the Liberal Catholic Church. Later, Leadbeater succeeded Wedgwood as Presiding Bishop of the LCC. The two men had enduring theological and liturgical interests in common.

SELECT BIBLIOGRAPHY

Cooper, John. Theosophical Crisis in Australia: the story of the breakup of the Theosophical Society in Sydney from 1913 until 1923. Masters Thesis. Sydney, University of Sydney, 1986. Department of Studies in Religion. Sydney.

James, William. The Varieties of Religious Experience: a study in human experience. London, Longmans Green, 1902.

Lutyens, Mary. Krishnamurti: the years of awakening. London, Rider, 1984.

Oliveira, Pedro (compiler). CWL Speaks: C.W. Leadbeater's correspondence concerning the 1906 crisis in the Theosophical Society. Woy Woy, NSW, 2018.

Roe, Jill. Beyond Belief: Theosophy in Australia 1879-1939. Kensington, New South Wales University Press, 1986.

Roe, Jill (ed). Twentieth Century Sydney: Studies in urban and social history. Sydney, Hale& Iremonger in assoc. with Sydney History Group, 1980.

Souter, Gavin. The Star in the East, in Mosman: a history. Melbourne, Melbourne University Press, 1994.

Van Gelder, Kirsten and Frank Chesley. A Most Unusual Life: Dora Van Gelder Kunz: clairvoyant, Theosophist, healer. IL, Quest Books, 2015.

Note: A trove of online material exists on Theosophy and its unique identities.

Printed in Australia
AUHW011556161019
318677AU00005B/21